Namibia Way Beyond the Comfort Zone: Doing Safari the Hard Way

Lucy Webb and Teri Ford

Namibia: Way Beyond the Comfort Zone

© 2018 Lucy Webb & Teri Ford
All rights reserved.
ISBN-10:1719472777
ISBN-13:978-1719472777
Library of Congress Control Number: **XXXXX (If applicable)**
LCCN Imprint Name: **City and State (If applicable)**

Namibia: Way Beyond the Comfort Zone

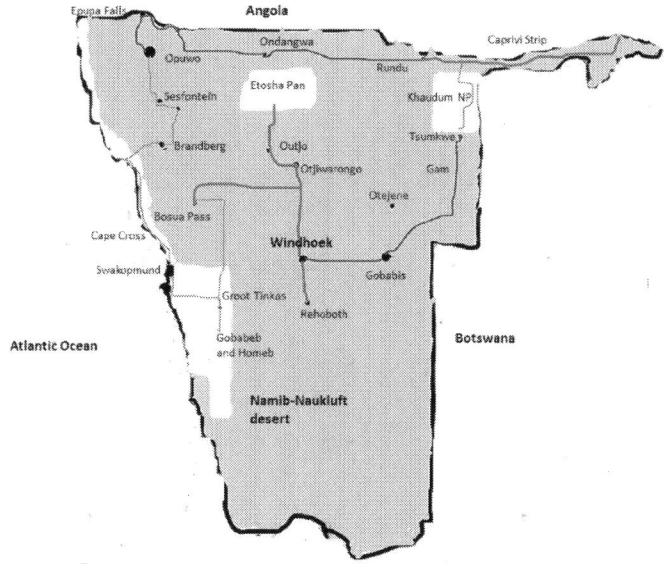

Map of Namibia: Key routes and camp settings.

Namibia Way Beyond the Comfort Zone

Chapter 1

Let's Go Exploring!

There are some things you just have to do. The problem is, life is full of times when you don't do it—that thing you just have to do. Sometimes it is because the crucial moment is not seen for what it is. That moment when you have to make a decision: jump, pull back; shall I, shan't I; go for it, check it out first. We are all guilty of missing the boat because we look before we leap. We weigh up the pros and cons instead of just doing it. We get stuck in "to do, or not to do." The hesitation is fatal. Falter, and the decision will always be "maybe later."

Somehow, Teri and I had made a lot of decisions to "do" stuff that had brought us to the back of beyond. No, actually the *back* of the back of beyond. I was just thinking these thoughts while I stood on a wobbly rock in the middle of Epupa Falls, a narrow river gorge somewhere hard to get to between Namibia and Angola. The water fell away beneath me down a sheer ravine on its way to the Atlantic Ocean. With Namibia to my right, Angola to my left, I felt as precarious as the baobab trees that clung to the vertical walls of the canyon.

Staring into the falling water was dangerously hypnotic. I pulled back and shook myself alert. Teri was also midstream on a rock, straddling nation-states. Deep in Kaokoland, we'd arrived at the most inaccessible tract of land in Namibia. This was home to fish eagles, paradise flycatchers, louries, bulbuls, rose-faced lovebirds, and, er, crocodiles. But we had made it here, on our own, the hard way, and survived. Now was not the time to spoil it by falling in.

There were only three other people at the falls: two elderly European visitors and their Namibian guide. The Europeans had been escorted to this place that few have heard of and fewer have seen. And they had come the easy way. There is now a tarmac-and-gravel road to the falls. It's a bit long and tedious and crosses the wilderness with shiny tarmac. But Teri and I, two English ladies of mature years, had done it the hard way. We'd come cross-country, in a 4x4 we'd had to fix, on a dirt track that frequently disappeared into the river, and through territory inhabited only by the nomadic Himba people.

The Namibian guide struck up conversation once I was safely on the riverbank. He was touting for business; did we want to explore the country, meet the Himba, see the wildlife? I explained how we'd pretty much done all that on the way here, and some. Our hazardous route included impossible tracks and wild camping. We'd been lost countless times, navigated riverbeds, climbed mountains, broken down, and shared our camp with nomads. I expected a telling off about the risks, but he just gave me a big, toothy smile. He was no longer talking to a tourist but a fellow adventurer. We were his kind of people. We swapped notes on tracks, hippos, and sleeping under the stars. He wished us luck and more adventures. His respect made me feel somehow proud. I'd achieved what I'd gone to Namibia for: I'd become an explorer.

Teri and I are fifty-something ladies who are not getting any younger, fitter, or healthier. We were one day faced with one of those "shall we, shan't we" decisions, and we said yes. It might have been because we were quite tipsy (to say the least). It might have been something that was there all the time, like a seed lying dormant. Whatever it was, one evening we decided to go on a trip. Not just any trip. Not like tourists who fly in, take pictures, and buzz off without scratching the surface. We wanted an expedition. We wanted to be David Livingstone, Margaret Mead, Pitt-Rivers. Well, I did, anyway. Maybe Teri had other ideas, but whatever we envisaged, we certainly went exploring. And not just in the places we went to and with the people we met.

For me, I was scratching an itch that had been with me since I was ten. My mother remarried at that time, and I gained a stepfather. But not a typical father. He was like no father I had ever met; not my own, not my friends', my uncles, grandfathers. They were great and fatherly. They were serious, responsible, and authoritative. Sometimes authoritarian. Fathers were people who stopped you doing naughty things. They stopped you making mistakes and steered you onto "sensible" paths in life, like doing schooling, choosing a career, not getting into trouble. My stepfather was nothing like these people. He let me help him dismantle a Morris Minor engine and clean the bits in petrol and get all oily. He took me fishing and let me wade into the river and get all wet. He took me sailing in a dinghy, and we ran aground in the middle of the harbor. Later he taught me how to place a bet at the races, score a darts match, and do a handbrake turn. Useful things.

My stepfather was brought up in an age when being "free, white, and over twenty-one" was a mantra for aspirational young English men. So, after National Service, he took off across Europe and Southern Africa in a Daimler. He told me stories of traveling through Africa, meeting elephants on mountain passes, being locked up in a Zambian prison during a coup, flying on dodgy airlines, and how take it all in your stride.

He lived fast and died at the too-young age of fifty and left behind a wallet full of photographs. They were of Mont Blanc, Lisbon docks, Luanda street scenes, desert vistas, bougainvillea, and baboons. I wore them out with viewing until life intervened and I went to college, university, and worked on a career. But those pictures were imprinted on my memory; cataloged, filed and…waiting.

Teri and I have known each other ever since the induction day on a master's psychology course. We were both "mature" students, with other careers under our belts, and we made "for heaven's sake, we're grown-ups!" faces at each other while being shown how to use a library. Our fellow students, meanwhile, were taking bright-eyed-and-bushy-tailed interest in the workings of the library catalog system. That look between us suggested that our levels of patience and personal expectations were compatible.

That was sixteen years ago. Armed with our qualifications, we went our separate ways, got PhDs, jobs, and long in the tooth. Teri eventually went to prison, and I got into drugs—like you do when you have a career in psychology.

We thought it would be different; doing our own safari in a place very few people could place on the globe. We also knew we'd be testing ourselves. I had been solo camping in South Dakota, in the Colorado Rockies, and South Australia. Teri had lived and worked in the West Indies, traveled throughout Europe, Asia, South Africa. We had it covered. Teri is sophisticated. She can intimidate a hotel manager at a hundred paces. She can pick up the correct fork on a dining table laid for eight courses. She leaves bellboys begging to carry her bags. I prefer to enter buildings through the trade entrance and am frequently mistaken for a cleaner. It's that air of confidence and belonging that says Teri = VIP, Lucy = staff.

I was brought up in the woods of West Sussex in England, where tenant serfs in the still-feudal English countryside know their place. You are expected to lurk in the hedgerows looking bucolic with pheasants and tug your forelock when a Range Rover drives past. However, that upbringing makes me very good at lurking and being self-sufficient in the outdoors but acutely all at sea in posh restaurants. Add Teri and her sophisticated skills and, like I said, safari in Namibia. We thought we had it covered.

Namibia is, according to the guidebook, one of the most sparsely populated countries in the world. A 2012 survey counted 2.1 million people in eight hundred thousand square miles. That's two and a half people per mile. London, according to *Wikipedia*, has a population of nearly eight million and covers an area of 620 square miles. That's twelve thousand people per square mile. Double that per square mile for New York. So, if London had the population density of Namibia, it would have just under fourteen hundred people. That wouldn't be enough to run the buses.

My point is, Namibia is pretty empty, especially since 42 percent of those 2.1 million are clustered around the few areas with streetlamps. It is also one of the safest places in Africa. On a map, it sits northwest of South Africa and used to be called South West Africa. Before that it was called German South West Africa. It still has a few old German forts, some of which were used for prisoners during the Great War (the 1914–18 one).

I put it on my "places to visit before I die" list after watching explorer Benedict Allen on TV ride a bad-tempered camel along the Skeleton Coast. It was the desert sands, abandoned mining towns, and shipwrecks that drew my attention. Later, in mountains patrolled by desert elephants, emerging from my archived memories, another explanation for my attraction presented itself. Along with it came a whole new perspective on how much we really are our own histories.

Teri and I are nearer to thinking about retiring than a new career move. But we discovered during this trip that comfort zones are bad for you. At any age. At any stage of life. Much cod psychology stuff is written about life-changing experiences, so hopefully this book is not like that. We thought we'd simply write about what we did and how we experienced it and explore what happens when you change your environment, jump with both feet into the dark, and spend a lot of time in the middle of nowhere with only each other and the mosquitoes for company. Perhaps it will inspire our readers. If there's something that's been nagging away at you, an itch you need to scratch, just do it!

Our first foray into adventure holidaying was canoeing in Algonquin Provincial Park in Ontario. My idea, I'm afraid. I saw survival specialist Ray Mears canoeing down the Ontario River on TV, going all native in a birch bark canoe. I wanted to have a go. The Canada trip was "challenging" for Teri. The weather was, well, Canada in September: raining, cold at night, and out of season for moose. We'd had to carry the canoe as much as paddle it. *Portage*, they call it, where you have to lug the thing round rapids and rocks, sometimes for several kilometers. Ours was one of the lighter canoes, but we collectively weigh less than twenty stone (280 pounds) and had to carry all our goods and chattels in backpacks as well. So the next trip had to be somewhere warm. "How about a desert?" I said. "Great," Teri said. "Somewhere safe," Teri's husband said. So Namibia it was.

Most people go on safari in organized groups. The more adventurous do self-drive and stop in lodges or hotels. The even more adventurous do self-drive with tents on the roof and call in at designated campsites with loos, showers, and fences to keep the wildlife out. The more adventurous still do the driving-camping bit with a guide and go off piste into the wilds of Namibia. The rich fly in to a remote five-star camp, get escorted everywhere, then fly out, skipping all the uncomfortable bits.

Teri and I did none of these things. Our combination of camping, driving, and adventuring is only for experienced 4x4ers, with maps, GPS, and years of African bush experience. And they usually go in groups with more than one vehicle. We went armed with an old guidebook, a tourist map, and blind enthusiasm.

I grew up on Laurens van der Post books. The African ones are about Bushmen who can hear a leaf fall in the next valley and walk invisibly through a pride of lions. I read *Flamingo Feather* when I was twelve, about trekking into unknown lands. I'd read Rider Haggard's *She*. I'd watched Stewart Granger in a safari hat falling in love with some woman who could find lipstick and a hairdresser in the middle of the African plains. I'd never been to an African country and desperately wanted to have a go at the trekking-in-the-bush bit, preferably before it disappeared or became controlled with "do this, don't do that" rules. So why not hire a 4x4, pack up the camping gear, and head off for who knows where and see what happens?

So that's what Teri and I did.

Lucy's idea of a holiday is completely different from mine. Before a career in psychology, I worked in the hotel industry. When I was about to leave school, a rather jaded career adviser told me that I should consider being a policeman "because you're tall" or perhaps a hotel manager "because people will always take holidays." I liked the idea of holidays, hotels, exciting places, and being able to travel for my work, so I chose the latter.

Over the years I was lucky enough to work in some spectacular places, and I loved the luxury of hotels. Clean sheets every night, someone to make my bed, fluffy white towels. Exotic foods cooked by experts and served with finesse. What's not to like? So when Lucy suggested the trip to Canada, I was a bit bemused and not entirely sure it was "my thing."

Not my thing at all. I'd never been in a canoe. I am a rubbish swimmer, so if we overturned in the rapids, I would drown. I'm a nervous driver in my own car in my own country, so the thought of maneuvering some big jalopy in Canada didn't appeal. I lasted three months at a gym, as I hate any form of exercise. I'd only ever camped for one night in North Wales, and woke up with severe backache.

So, when Lucy suggested driving off into the wilds, canoeing across lakes and down rivers, hauling all my luggage and a canoe for miles, sleeping on the ground in a Canadian winter, only eating what could be cooked in one pot over an open fire? Well, of course I said yes. I'd had more than one glass of wine at the time.

The Canadian adventure established that we could be together in fairly grim conditions and not want to rip each other's heads off. Being cold and wet with no dry clothes and no hope of lighting a fire for a hot drink is a good test. I'd got used to Lucy talking to herself and stopped saying "What? What? And Lucy got used to me keeling over if I didn't get enough water to drink. So we discovered we made tolerable, and tolerant, traveling companions.

After another late night of drinking and philosophizing, Lucy suggested we head off to Namibia. Like a lot of people, I wasn't entirely sure where it was. Africa somewhere. Again, the wine made the decision for me and I found myself agreeing to a month of cultural awakening.

We did our reconnoitering by getting a guidebook. The "where to stay" and "what to see and do" sections provided a rough itinerary. I looked up vehicle hire online and found a cheap provider with the right-sounding name—Value Car Rental—and booked a large 4x4. They also hired out camping gear, but I have my own tried-and-tested tents. I didn't fancy using someone else's sleeping bag, so we took our own gear.

This meant that we'd be sleeping on the ground, not on the roof of the vehicle, where a lot of the self-drive camping outfits rig their tents. We didn't think through the advantages and disadvantages of this at the time. I just thought, as expedition leader, I should know the kit personally and all its foibles. Basically, I needed to know I could put the tents up when we got there.

Not having the tents on the roof meant we could set up camp and then go for a safari drive at dusk. A tent on the roof, however, means lions can't get at you while you sleep. We might also have hired a fridge, and we found out later what could have happened if we had. More of that later.

I booked some extra equipment in the form of a toolkit. This does not mean we would know what to do with it. I just thought it would look really cool if we met other 4x4ers who'd broken down and could be rescued with a simple "Will this spanner do?" In the same vein, we also booked a towrope. Thankfully.

We chose late September because that is the end of the dry season. The waterholes would be busy with thirsty animals. Also, most tourists would be gone home, children back at school, and we'd have the place to ourselves.

We were determined to avoid being like tourists. Teri had done the East African safari bit and enjoyed it of course. Who wouldn't? But we both had a desire to experience sub-Saharan Africa without being blinded by the tourist polish. We wanted to know what the ordinary countryside was like, who lived here and how? Are rural people really distanced from the technology of the modern world? What are the problems with living in a place with minimal infrastructure?

We could, of course, really find out if we did some volunteering when we retired. Teaching perhaps. But that comes under the "maybe later" category of putting off the chance to do something extraordinary.

We flew in on a circuitous route because we're not made of money and airport hopping brings the costs down. To avoid high airport taxes, from England the trick is to hop over to a hub airport in Europe and fly from there. We chose London City airport, to Zurich, to Joburg, to Windhoek via an assortment of airlines. This added to the fun, but that was not what Teri called sleeping on the floor at Joburg airport. But it was cheaper. We found out later that we could have flown direct from Frankfurt and saved ourselves a lot of trouble. But where's the fun in that?

It is worth in mentioning at this point why we thought of writing this book. We are not explorers in the usual sense of the word. We are never going to be sponsored by National Geographic, venturing into the unknown to report back with samples and a Latin name for a newly discovered frog. We are not daredevil adventurers. We are not used to engaging in white water rafting, bungee jumping, nor, indeed, climbing Everest. People do these things, we know. We are a couple of middle-aged English ladies, one married, one career minded, with no kids between us. Just a cat, a dog, one husband (Teri's), an elderly mother (mine), two houses with gardens, one mortgage (mine again), two different careers, and an increasing reliance on pills and reading glasses. But everything is relative. What is an adventure to us and our kind is commonplace to some, impossible to others.

When we returned with our stories, there were so many people, people like us, who were touched by some inner excitement. You could see them thinking, "Wow, that's just what I've always wanted to do!" Some people actually said so. Some, we could tell, were inspired to have a go at whatever they'd always secretly wished. I don't mean go trekking across Namibia or even Outer Mongolia. Perhaps it's something more personal, like get a divorce or get married! Change jobs, move house, emigrate. Who knows? For us, the enterprise was about doing something scary, something beyond our normal boundaries of safety, identity, expectations. Something nonconformist, outside what others would expect of us or regard as "normal" for the sort of people we are: two mature ladies who have settled on their personal and social identities.

We know who we are. We didn't *need* to go on an adventure. We weren't having a midlife crisis. We weren't feeling trapped in the same old same old. We weren't needing to escape from social roles imposed on us by others. I think we simply found ourselves with the opportunity to do something extraordinary, and, for once, no barriers in the way. We could afford it, we had the time, we are both healthy, we have no dependents. Teri had cared for her ailing mother in the last few years, and I had cared for my older brother recently. My mother is as fit as a flea and is perfectly capable of fending for herself. Teri's husband might be less than happy at his wife's adventures, but what the hell; he'll cope. I think the cyclones of our busy lives had suddenly opened into a window of calm and opportunity—the eye of the storm of the ridiculous busyness of life.

So we arrived in Windhoek with two backpacks, a holdall full of camping gear, clumpy boots, bush hats, antimalarials, and a desire to get out of town as soon as we could.

Epupa Falls, Kaokaland, Namibia

Chapter 2

Up It Yo—Windhoek and Beyond

Windhoek airport is not up to much. It is small and hard baked, and disembarking passengers have a long walk across hot tarmac to reach the air conditioning. Inside, however, it is quite civilized and efficient. And miles away from Windhoek. The ride into town was our first introduction to African wildlife. Teri and I amused our poor driver with frequent squeals of delight at seeing baboons and even warthogs by the side of the road, not to mention the baby baboons! Cute! Aww! He quickly took the lead by trying to spot them before we did, so being a "guide." On the return trip, we remembered our excitement on that journey; after getting up close and personal to some much less endearing creatures. What tourists we were!

Windhoek itself betrayed its revolutionary influences in street names such as Fidel Castro, Mugabe, and Mandela (is there a city in the world without a Mandela Road/Street/Avenue/Place?). Unfortunately, everything we required in Windhoek was on a street we could not pronounce, such as Mandume Ndomufayo Avenue. Why couldn't it be on Independence Drive? We had fun with the taxi drivers with that one. Windhoek was also surprisingly orderly and, well, Germanic. Colonial architecture reared up from well-trimmed grassy traffic islands, statues of suitably Germanic heroes overlooked the daily chaos from proud horses and waved their swords as if to command the busy traffic. The Hilton Hotel gleamed modernistically over central upmarket businesses. Like Munich on a hot day. A very hot day. Oh, and of course we didn't stay at the Hilton.

The alarm bell should probably have rung in our heads while Lucy and I were at the customs desk and the customs lady insisted she'd never heard of the Motown Inn. Never in all her twenty years of processing tourists' paperwork had anyone ever stayed at the Motown Inn. We'd made our selection of accommodation based on the middle-of-the-range principle. It had two stars, it was close to the center of town, and it was described as "clean and comfortable." It also, we found on arrival, had two larger-than-life-sized American Indian statues standing sentry on either side of the entrance, resplendent in gargantuan moccasins and each carrying a giant tomahawk.

Our room was sadly neither clean nor comfortable. It was instead a dark cell with two narrow beds and bars at the grimy windows, which overlooked a railway yard. We later discovered that the railway had a siren that went off every time a train went past the yard. There were freight trains throughout the night.

Lucy went through her usual hotel room ritual of unpacking every item of her luggage and doing a stock-take of her belongings. It was only when she had decanted everything into piles all over her bed that we spotted the little flecks crawling over the sheets.

After invigorating showers, shared with a couple of mosquitoes, a small swarm of ants, and a torn shower curtain, we headed off into town to sample the culinary specialties on offer. Namibia owes its gastronomical style to its mixed cultural heritage, so the food is an unusual blend of German and African. Bratwurst served with maize-meal porridge was unusual but not unpleasant, as was the roast springbok with sauerkraut. Lucy quickly developed a taste for the Windhoek beer, while I was delighted to find that the local white wine came in five-liter containers.

Teri and I were due to escape town the next day, with our transport and supplies all sorted. So we had to pick up our four-wheeled companion from Value Rentals. Also on Mandume Ndomufayo Avenue. Taxi drivers again. The taxi system in Windhoek is like London, only upside down. The more official a taxi cab looks, the less efficient it is. If it has numbers on it, don't get in. They pick up anyone else they spot on the way, and if that person wants to go somewhere more lucrative, they dump you off wherever the routes diverge. We only suffered this twice.

Value Car Rentals is next to a more glamorous outfit that has shiny floors and offices. Bizarrely, they seem to share the same vehicles. They also share the outstanding feature, a completely wrecked Toyota HiLux on display that appears to have lost an argument with a herd of elephants. At least, that's what we first thought. There are notices on each door with ClipArt pictures: "Passenger one: died on the operating table: Passenger two, disabled: Driver, killed outright: Passenger three, survived after surgery." Is this supposed to get customers queuing up to rent their vehicles? It's supposed to warn us about driving too fast on dodgy roads. The chance would be a fine thing.

We were shown our shiny white vehicle, which we called "Up It Yo" because that's what it said on the number plate. It seemed to share our attitude, so we took to it immediately. Except that it was ginormous! Up It Yo was a double-cab Toyota HiLux three-liter with chunky tires, double fuel tanks, and two spare tires. It also had bull bars on the front big enough for running over a rhino. Teri and I both shuffled to the rear at the thought that one of us would have to drive it out of the depot through a narrow alley—with everyone watching.

Lucy lost the debate about who would drive first. She drove Up It Yo on our inaugural drive through downtown Windhoek to purchase our supplies before heading out of town. Lucy manhandled the great brute with only a few mild expletives, while I navigated using a surprisingly accurate street map. It even had the gas station locations marked out. It was only much later, when we'd been driving for hundreds of kilometers through the bush, that we realized the significance of being acutely aware of where to find the nearest gas station.

Halfway down Mandume Ndomufayo Avenue, we found a car park accessed through an extremely narrow alleyway. By now Lucy was accustomed to the sheer bulk of Up It Yo, and she swung through to the multilevel car park with confidence. We paid the entrance fee (equivalent to thirteen pence) and headed upward. There were no spaces on the first four levels, and we were starting to worry, but then we arrived on the roof level. Plenty of spaces, lovely awnings to protect the cars from the sun, and even a smartly uniformed young chap to look after the surprisingly stylish cars. We parked and decided that it was the best value we'd ever had. The uniformed young man approached and explained that we had parked our scruffy vehicle in a private, members-only section. The particular space we'd commandeered was usually home to a Porsche belonging to a wealthy Windhoek businessman. However, since the businessman was away for a few days, we could have the space for an additional sum. We were more than happy to pay an extra twenty pence for the privilege of giving Up It Yo an awning and a personal bodyguard.

Our first visit to a Namibian supermarket was enlightening. The fruit and vegetable selection was plentiful and appetizing. The same couldn't be said of the meat counters: all manner of strange-looking cuts roughly butchered, presumably with a blunt machete, slivers of bones, and an alarming range of colors, from pale pink to an unnerving greenish brown. We resolved to convert to a low-protein diet for the duration.

Namibians clearly love their cereals, as there was an aisle devoted to grains in sacks and boxes of all sorts of sizes. We'd been advised that we'd need plenty of maize meal in order to ingratiate ourselves with the Himba people out in the wilds, so we filled half our trolley with paper sacks of the stuff. With that and various "campfire-friendly" food items, we were pretty much done. We headed toward the drinks aisle for a case or two of lager and one of the mammoth wine containers, only to discover that alcohol is off limits on Saturday afternoons and all day on Sundays. There were no cordons, no barriers, just a small, polite notice informing us that we couldn't purchase any of the many bottles and cans spread out so invitingly in front of us.

Our first destination was Etosha National Park; start with an easy one, we thought. The main road out of Windhoek heads directly north and unswervingly ends up at the national park, so we could hardly go wrong.

Teri wanted to see wildlife "as soon as," and I was secretly worried that we could drive around Namibia forever without seeing anything. So, we'd start somewhere with a nailed-on guarantee to encounter animals: an elephant, a giraffe, *lions*? Would that be asking too much? At least we'd go home with photos of one of the "big five" to prove our expedition was not all a mission to nowhere.

It is surprising now to think that we were so anxious to do the "Africa thing" that we started somewhere we would later do our best to avoid. However, Etosha was a good place to test out our camping skills and wildlife spotting. We needed the practice! There were about thirteen hundred kilometers to drive first, so we'd take it in turns and probably stop overnight somewhere on the way.

The roads in Namibia come in various sizes and senses of humor. The straight-laced B roads are often tarred, straight and, by European standards, devoid of traffic. Driving on these is great for the first half an hour. The scenery out of town is uniform bush, high fenced, usually, but occasionally sporting a warthog family by the roadside. We got stupidly excited on spotting a zebra on the other side of a fence, then passed the entrance to a "game reserve" with advertising boards suggesting luxurious lodges, swimming pool, bar, and game drives. There was quite a rash of these places on the road to Etosha. One even promised to taxidermy your kill for you. Umm…

The only people we saw on foot were poor-looking locals bundling up wood to sell by the roadside. I thought we ought to stop and stock up but felt intimidated bartering without yet understanding the money system, and I was unsure if they were really selling it or waiting for some mates to come and pick it up. It could all get embarrassing and make me feel like a patronizing Westerner. Colonialism has a lot to answer for, not least in making me feel too uncomfortable to give them my custom.

This B road, like all the ones we experienced, was interspersed every ten kilometers or so with a picnic area: a pull-in with a fixed concrete table and seats under a tree and a convenient rubbish bin, often overflowing. Some even had metal awnings for shade. We saw one sorry-for-itself saloon car pulled in at one with about ten people having their lunch. It explained why many Namibian cars look like their suspension has collapsed.

We later experienced C roads; untarred but well-maintained gravel that kicked up quite a bit of dust and taught us to wind up the windows when approached by oncoming vehicles. The pickup trucks often carried cargoes of people, all standing jammed together in the back. Obviously they got covered in dust, which was a shame for the Herero women who wore amazing Victorian-style dresses in bright colors with headdresses that emulated the horns of a bull. How did they stay clean?

While the B roads tend to have bridges over river courses, the C roads go through them. This is fine most of the time, as Namibia is very dry. However, when it rains, it rains. Flash floods are the norm, and the rivers and gullies flow across the roads. This means C roads are frequently interrupted by steep-sided fords, announced sometimes by a road sign, sometimes not. In England such a feature is called a ha-ha. They are large gullies dug out around stately homes to prevent the deer from getting into the garden, but hidden so they don't spoil the panoramic view from the house. When attempting to walk in the garden, on reaching the gully, you find you have to scramble down and up its steep sides; hence ha-ha. It's a bit like a castle moat but more cunning. So when we approached one of these gullies, whoever was driving had to shout a warning to the map-studying navigator, otherwise the lurch, bump, crash, pitch of the unexpected gully spoiled the passenger's day.

The tricky bit on these roads, however, is going round a corner. Corners don't happen very often, so you get lulled into a false sense of security, doing about ninety kilometers per hour. The corners are where the loose gravel accumulates and, hey presto, that's where the wrecked Toyota back at Value Car Rentals got its dents.

There are no A roads in Namibia. Fortunately, the B and C roads accommodate two-wheel-drive vehicles. The D roads are the jokers. You have no idea what they will be like until you are on them, and even the kindest can suddenly turn nasty. D roads can be anything from single carriageway gravel to deep sand, rocks, or basically, nonexistent. Our guidebook says, "Don't be fooled into thinking that a 4x4 will get you everywhere and solve all your problems." This is a bit of the guidebook we failed to notice until about week three. It was buried among other helpful tips like getting used to 4x4 driving at home first. Ho-hum.

I'm not a petrol head. I drive because I have to and not because I love to. So I was happy to let Lucy take the wheel for the drive through downtown Windhoek. With four-lane main roads, taxis ignoring the usual rules and making left turns, right turns, and U-turns at will, and street vendors and pedestrians treating the road as a pavement, it was certainly challenging enough to hold her attention. Mine was focused on the map, and soon we left Windhoek behind. The road north to Etosha was long and straight, and this is when Lucy started to get a bit fidgety. Not enough excitement—no hills, no potholes, no one to overtake or undertake, just a straight road. The car had a built-in speed alarm and bleeped at us if we went over 120 kilometers per hour. Unfortunately, on the long, quiet, monotonous roads, you can lose perspective of speed and distance, and when Lucy had been bleeped at for the umpteenth time, I felt I had no option but to volunteer to take my first turn behind the wheel of Up It Yo.

Lucy drives hunched close over the steering wheel and with the sun visor down, regardless of where the sun is. She likes her water bottle in the cup holder on the dashboard and surrounds herself with tissues, bits of paper, receipts, guidebooks, and various food items. She creates a nest from which to drive. I am the opposite: I like to sit farther away from the wheel, and I like full visibility, so the sun visor stays up at all times (that's what sunglasses are for, isn't it?). I have my water bottle in the recess between the seats, but other than that, I like the driver's side to be clear and uncluttered of detritus. So changing drivers wasn't a simple question of each hopping out, running around the car, and hopping back in the opposite side. No, it demanded pulling over and doing some serious redistributing and adjusting. But eventually I was on the road in command of a huge truck with no rearview mirror and a snorkel for driving under water that I hoped we would never actually need to use.

The road was flanked on both sides by high game fences, through which goats and warthogs made easy access, but which were effective at keeping other wildlife off the road. We saw a lot of cattle, and at one point I glimpsed a giraffe's head towering over the scrubland, but as we were driving at the speed limit, by the time I'd alerted Lucy, the giraffe was way behind us.

We were very curious about a lot of zigzagging tracks evident in the gravel parts of the road. We eventually identified them when we saw donkey carts being driven along the verges.

The tracks definitely matched the wheels on the carts, but why on earth were they so shambolic? We postulated that, because the roads were so interminably long, the distances between towns and homesteads so great, and journeys by donkey at around five kilometers per hour would take hours and hours, people would just fall asleep at the reins and leave the donkeys to meander their way home as they saw fit.

At the start of our adventure, we were very excited by road signs with pictures of elephants, lions, gemsbok, and various other game animals. Naively, we thought that if there was a picture of an elephant, then an elephant wouldn't be far away. After all, it worked with the warthog signs—there were families of warthogs virtually posing for pictures under their signs. But we searched and scanned the area surrounding the elephant signs, keeping our hopes up for miles, but never saw an elephant in the vicinity of its sign. In the logical light of day, this of course makes perfect sense. Elephants roam for hundreds of kilometers, so why would they hang around obligingly next to their personalized road signage just to keep the tourists happy? We wondered who decided which signs to erect where—and really, what is the purpose of such signage? We're in Namibia. Namibia has lots of different animals. Lions roam the plains with the wildebeest and hyenas and vultures— we know this, so a random picture of a hyena, for example, isn't particularly insightful or helpful.

Having said that, the signage was beautifully executed. It must be quite an art to produce easily identifiable pictures in black-on-white silhouette. I first became fascinated by the pictorial road signage. As well as the animals, there were detailed pictures of dumper trucks, tractors, and road-clearing vehicles. I particularly liked the picture of lots of dots followed by a dense black line, indicating that the road would be changing from gravel to tarmac.

Then I started to take more interest in the symbolic road signs: the exclamation mark that meant any sort of dangers might lie ahead—or nothing remarkable at all. The arrow bending to the right on the top of a blind brow, placed just before the road took an abrupt left turn, and vice versa.

Sometimes the arrows indicated the correct direction, so every arrow was a cause for speculation instead of certainty.

There were road works going on throughout the country, and when they were laying tarmac, there were signs advising us that there were no lines. But the people charged with carrying out the road works were obviously from a different department from the guys that were in charge of erecting the No Lines signs. They were quite often out of sync, so we'd be cruising along a lovely flat tar road with perfectly marked white lines down the middle, and every few kilometers there would be a sign telling us that the lines weren't there.

Of the written signage, probably my favorite was the one we encountered when we'd been driving through the desert for most of the day. It simply advised, "SAND."

We managed to have an uneventful ride on our B road with nothing more than a broken windscreen wiper. I rather thought that the wipers would be redundant in a dry country, but they are essential for cleaning the dust off the windscreen at regular intervals. Even on this nice tarmacked B road, the dust soon accumulated. A quick flick of the washers, and the wipers went into action and a bit flew off. Teri was driving, so I blamed her for breaking the wipers. I would contribute to a lot more breakages later. We stopped in a vain attempt to find the missing bit of plastic that held the wiper to the arm. This is easily done in Namibia because you can just pull over and wander around the main road with no other traffic to worry about for long periods of time. That doesn't make finding a small piece of plastic any easier though, so we soon gave up and improvised. We needed a bit of string to tie the wiper on. Teri wears various bits of bangles on her wrists, so a thin strip of leather was soon put to good use. From then on, every time we used the wipers, one would swish across the windscreen trailing a bit of leather to remind us that we had broken our nice, shiny vehicle on day one.

We broke our journey to Etosha at Otjiwarongo, a small town that fortunately had a great store that sold sandals with car-tire soles; I had by then decided that Namibia's heat was too much for my walking boots. I was keen to test out the tents but couldn't resist a night of comfort, so we booked in at Otjibamba Lodge. Just out of town, this was not promising safari drives or stuffed game, just African-style bungalows with wire mesh for windows, ceiling fan, decent beds, and a bath to please Teri. We were still clearly novices, because this seemed like a real safari lodge, even with its own pet springbok roaming around in the bar. We soon grew to like springbok cocktails (Amarula layered on crème de menthe) and even laughed to find our al fresco evening meal being bombarded by ridiculously large flying insects. Sitting outside at night under floodlights is a great way to get to know the local critters. Earlier, we'd happily watched weaver birds making hanging baskets in the trees. In the early morning, we were thrilled to see a shy female ostrich drinking from the pond near our bungalow. We crept to the windows, cameras at the ready, whispering. She looked up. We froze. She bent again to drink. We crept some more and got as far as the veranda before we realized that she was another tame pet.

These early days were so exciting. And we were so naive. On our return journey back to Windhoek, our attitude to game reserves and the artificial keeping of wildlife was to be much more informed, and much more critical.

Typical road sign in Namibia, with donkey cart tracks.

Chapter 3

Etosha and the Pink Bus

Etosha National Park is described in one of our guidebooks as one of Africa's greatest parks for game viewing, with some 114 mammal species, 110 reptile species, over 340 bird species, and over one hundred daily visitors. So it seemed a good idea to go when it was quiet.

Most of the area is a huge salt pan that from space (courtesy of Google Maps) looks like a white snow field and takes up more area on the planet than the whole of the Alps. Viewed through the heat haze from the horizontal, it looks like the sea—very deceptive for any nineteenth-century explorer trekking across the plains and hoping for a quick dip. I've often scoffed at the idea that zebra could actually be camouflaged, but now I know how those stripes work! The dark wildebeest looked like they were floating on the sea; the zebra disappeared.

As a psychologist, I am aware of Francis Galton, the "father" of intelligence testing, among other things. He coined the phrase "nature versus nurture" to debate the influence of genes over upbringing. His other interests included exploring Southern Africa and studying genetics and inheritance. He also started the craze for eugenics, the notion that humans could/should breed for improvement. This type of thinking obviously leads to the notion that there are those who should not breed and jumps unerringly to Hitler, the master race, and gas chambers. These things are not directly Galton's fault, I hasten to add. He was a cousin of Charles Darwin, so perhaps he shared some genes that led to exploring strange places. Galton apparently trekked to the Etosha Pan in the 1850s, having been told it was a vast lake—only to be disappointed. Though I am sure he was as impressed as we were by this bone-dry salt crust that seemed to stretch northward from the Etosha veldt to infinity.

The plains skirting the pan are open bush. We both anticipated that spotting elephant on this vast expanse would be simple. There are few trees, no rocks, nowhere for an elephant to hide. Nope. We didn't realize that elephants wear invisibility cloaks. As do herds of springbok, wildebeest, and rhino. The only things we could identify on our first day were ostriches, which look like topiary bushes from a distance. We spotted loads of them once we got our eye in; or perhaps we saw lots of bushes. In fact, we proved quite useless at spotting things at first, to the point that Teri nearly elbowed a lioness.

So, Etosha was a good place for us to practice safari—getting the feel of Africa, putting safety measures in place (checking our shoes for scorpions like it said in the guidebook), and testing our camping gear and cooking arrangements. We'd done well in Canada to protect our gear from bears. In Algonquin Provincial Park (arguably the size of Texas), we'd hung our bags on zip wires that ran between trees like washing lines. The trick is to throw a line over the zip wire and haul your baggage up so that it sways suspended, bear proof, while you get some kip. Apparently the bears are cottoning on and can travel commando-style along the wires. We'd read up on the safety tips for being near game in Namibia: do not feed the animals. Later on, we were to be in uncomfortable proximity to things that might eat us, so I for one was going to follow this tip.

All the campsites I've experienced in different countries have their own little ways. Cultural differences are obvious: In the US Rockies and Black Hills of South Dakota, a round metal fire pit is standard issue, but no grille. In Canada, you make your own fire pit lined with stones. In southern Australia, fires are not a good idea and are actively discouraged. In the Scottish Highlands, you need to take your own gas Primus and cooker, as there's no dry wood, and the hurricane-force wind will test the patience of a Navajo just to light it. In Namibia, the organized campsites we used all had fantastic raised concrete braais, some with built-in grilles. Our Estosha campsite even had a concrete table and seats. Teri thought this was civilized. I was disappointed. Where's the challenge in this? Why I find it necessary to make life challenging, I have no idea, but I was going to find my challenges very soon, so I was happy to indulge in a spot of soft camping. Apparently, my notion of "proper" camping soon rubbed off on Teri.

Etosha is a lovely game park. A bit tame by our adventurous standards now, but a good introduction to sleeping on the ground with various animal noises to keep you awake, while still having the use of a fresh water tap, a basic toilet/shower facility, and a fire pit. The price of these luxuries is in the region of nine pounds per night and includes watering holes within walking distance. Ours had a reasonably comfortable rock to sit on while we watched a rhino perform its ablutions (much scratching of back against fallen trees, a lot of satisfied grunting, and some farting on a spectacular scale). Lucy and I decided to base ourselves at a camp in Etosha for three nights and explore the entire park while we got used to the whole living-rough thing.

We picked a camping space as far away from everyone else as possible— not difficult, as there were only two other tents— and set off at around six in the morning for a day of wildlife spotting.

We had the windows open, elbows out, trying to accommodate the tiniest of breezes as we navigated our way slowly past a group of three inexplicably parked cars. Seeing three cars in a day was unusual, seeing three all together was unheard of.

As we edged past, I glanced down to my right, out of the driver's window, and encountered three sets of amber eyes, about four feet away from my own. A pride of lions and lionesses and a few cubs! Some were already strolling away, while the final three were lying on their sides gazing up at me languidly, so close that if I'd stretched out my arm, I could very nearly have touched the muzzle of the nearest. Hmm—that explains the impromptu car parking arrangements then.

A little farther along, we found a rhino chewing on a sturdy little sapling in some stark scrubland about thirty feet away. We stopped the car, wound down the windows, and switched off to watch at a distance of about thirty feet. The rhino paused and lowered its head, looking directly at us. It pawed the ground when Lucy clicked on her video recorder.

What was quite remarkable, when we viewed the footage later from the safety of a sofa in Shropshire, was the matter-of-fact tone of our conversation as we watched this huge beast at close quarters.

Lucy: I wonder if rhinos are like bulls and paw the ground when they're angry.
Me: Ooh—I don't know. Perhaps I should turn the engine back on in case it starts coming towards us?
Lucy: Not yet—let's not disturb it!
Me: Fair enough. I don't know how fast rhinos can run, but hopefully we can drive fast enough to escape if we have to. If not, it'll probably do a bit of damage to Up It Yo. Maybe the car people will use it as an example of what happens if you get hooked up on a rhino horn. Up It Ro!
Lucy: More clip art? Not sure they have a suitable image for "hoisted by a rhino horn." Ah. Better start the engine—it's heading this way…

Before we left for our trip to Africa, we had been given all sorts of advice ranging from the incredibly useful to the bizarrely unhelpful.

Useful:

- Take plenty of costume jewelry for trading with the Bushmen and plenty of maize flour and cooking oil for trading with the Himba.

- Drink lots of water.

- Wear a hat.

- Always check that you have enough fuel before setting off into the desert/bush.

Unhelpful:

- If a bull elephant is flapping its ears, he's just cross.

- If an elephant's ears are flat to his head, he's going to charge.

- All animals except bears kill their prey before eating it, so you can't get eaten alive.

- Take a gun in case of attack. Shoot your friend in the knee to give yourself a chance to escape while she's writhing around distracting the predator.

This last was advice from one of the more inventive prisoners that I worked with. He also suggested rigging up traps to catch smaller animals for our larder. I don't think he really understood the principles of ecotourism.

As it happens, we were close to finding out about elephants' ear movements and their link to elephant behaviors.

We were crawling through the park at our customary ten kilometers an hour, searching the undergrowth for movements and shapes. We had fallen into a bit of a pattern: Lucy peering through her binoculars out of the passenger window, me scanning the landscape on the driver's side, casting an occasional eye on the empty road ahead. Up It Yo had no central rearview mirror, but as there was rarely any traffic, I'd got out of the habit of checking the road situation to the rear.

I drove round a sharp bend just as a large elephant decided the coast was clear enough to make a ponderous crossing of the road. Luckily I hit the brakes and not the accelerator in my panic. The elephant was also a bit surprised. He stopped, stumbled a bit, and swung around to face the car. His ears were definitely flapping.

"I can't remember!" I screeched. "Is it when the ears flap it's going to charge? Or is it when the ears are back?!"

"Who cares?!" shouted Lucy. "Stick it in reverse, and put your foot down! Now!"

So that's what we did—we drove backward until we were out of sight of the raging vehicle crusher. Thank heavens there were no cars on the road behind us, or we'd have had road rage to contend with as well.

That evening, after a delicious fire-smoked plaas sausage,[1] we went to a different watering hole and sat quietly for several hours with our drinks, waiting for something, anything, to make an entrance. Unfortunately, two young South African tourists were also there that night, and whether due to excitement or ignorance, were very noisy companions. We threw them a few dirty looks and tutted a bit, but with great British reserve, failed to turn around and tell them, "For heaven's sake, shut up!" Instead we returned to our little camp.

We were a bit fazed to see that the South African watering-hole couple had pitched camp quite close to us. Well, no, that's not strictly true. Their jeep was parked up at a pitch quite close by, and their camp was indeed being set up. But not by them. They had brought a servant with them **to do all the** hard work while they caroused at the watering hole frightening off any wildlife in the vicinity.

Sitting in our humble little site, with our smoky-washed socks and towels hanging from the nearest tree, drinking beer from the bottle and wine from a plastic cup, we felt smugly that we were far more attuned with nature than these imposters. And then we were rendered almost speechless. We watched firstly covertly, and then brazenly with complete incredulity, as the manservant prepared their evening meal. A table was unloaded, and it was covered with a tablecloth and laid with silverware and wine glasses, napkins, and a cruet set. Two chairs were placed just so, and a cushion was plumped onto each. The manservant used a gas Primus to produce, no doubt, a sumptuous meal. No campfire required.

I'm sure the young couple felt that they had been at one with nature and probably regaled their friends back home with how they had "roughed it" in a campsite. But I'm equally sure

---

[1] We had no idea what plaaswurst was. The sausage looked like a bratwurst, was easy to cook on a campfire with minimal implements and tasted great. We decided not to ask what plaas was until we were on the way back to England. Just in case it was donkey. It isn't. We think. Plaas just means "farm," so I suppose technically it could be donkey.

that they probably saw very few wild animals and probably have few fond memories of their night in the jungle.

At that moment we both agreed that we were experiencing Namibia in exactly the way we wanted to. We were a bit grubby, our clothes were sand washed, and our hair smelt of smoke. Our tents were small, our bedding minimal, and we had almost constant rictus in our neck (Lucy) and back (me). But we were loving every minute!

The following morning the intrepid travelers and their manservant packed up and left. We had our privacy back, and the only creature to share our campsite was a honey badger. He came slinking in at dusk, sniffed all of our bags and my ankles, then bustled off into the night. Honey badgers are about the same size as our British badgers or American racoons but have markings that make them look as if they are wearing a barrister's wig. We thought he was comical and were hoping that we might entice him to return by leaving a couple of biscuits by the tent.

A couple of weeks later, we were shocked to be told by a conservationist that honey badgers are extremely vicious and have been known to kill leopards. Wow.

Our second attempt at game viewing was a great improvement. So much so that we started to look down on other tourists who clearly took less care and attention to experience this place. In Etosha it is hardly challenging to spot game; animals are everywhere. Herds of zebra, wildebeest, and springbok grazed beside the game tracks, a sleepy lion snoozed under a tree by the road, and we were even overtaken by a twenty-strong herd of giraffe that moved like cranes across the skyline and gently sidestepped our hastily parked Up It Yo. Our main success, though, came on the return journey. The land was open plains of rolling hills, and we cruised at around thirty kilometers an hour, eyes peeled. Teri thought she spotted something on the skyline. Or was it a tree stump? We stopped, and I scrambled out of the window to sit on the sill with the binoculars trained across the roof on the hillside. There was the unmistakable shape of a cheetah sitting up. Hard to spot, and would have been impossible if she hadn't been on the skyline. Yes, it was a she, and we knew because, when she stood up and slinked along the hillcrest, she was followed by a smaller shape. A cub. We were about sixty yards away but had a full view as they both followed the line of the hill. The mother would walk, stop, and look round, waiting for the cub to catch up. Then she would walk on again, shoulders rising and falling, tail training behind. Two vehicles came up to us and paused. We noticed the occupants gaze vaguely in the direction we were focusing, but in no time at all they drove on. They were either disinterested or couldn't see the cheetahs. After our earlier faux pas with the pride of lions, we were starting to feel like old hands.

Lucy and I had got up early that morning and driven the length of the park for as long as the daylight allowed. We'd seen a springbok giving birth at the roadside and a lion sleeping under a tree. The same lion was still slumbering under the same tree at three in the afternoon. We returned at dusk to our tents, weary and hungry. Lucy lit the fire, and we were sipping our drinks quietly while planning what to eat for dinner. Maybe the tin of chakalaka. We'd never had it before, but the picture on the tin looked nice—various beans in a tomatoey chili sauce. I could make some sort of herby bread depending on what vegetation I could find. Probably watercress or parsley. And then the peace was shattered. A large, shocking-pink bus pulled up less than twenty feet from our tents. Around forty teenagers and half a dozen adults swarmed out of the bus. Within minutes they'd rigged up portable barbeques, a sound system to blast out pop music into the dark, starlit African night, and dustbins filled with psychedelic cans of fizzy drinks.

We watched in horror as our peaceful evening was subsumed under the sheer volume of noise and activity. The final straw came when they started walking across our pitch, ducking under our makeshift washing line, and filling their various pots and pans from OUR TAP! Lucy was incensed and muttered darkly about camp etiquette and ignorant youths. We decided there was no other option than to remove ourselves and our tents to a far corner of the site away from the invasion.

The following morning, we were even more furious as the children from the pink bus had been singing and creating general mayhem until late. We made small retribution by making as much noise as we could while packing up at sunrise, and then we drove to the site manager's office.

I had slept for most of the night, but that says little for our new neighbors being considerate, as I can sleep next to a brass band. Well, nearly. I once chose a place to put my tent at a lovely campsite in Cheyenne, Wyoming, to attend the World Championship Rodeo. The campsite was packed, but there was quite a bit of space up by a large hedge that ran the length of the ground. All the tents, RVs and lesser motorhomes were as far away from the hedge as they could get. So I pitched camp next to the hedge. That night, I realized why no one else was camping there. On the other side, immediately the other side, was the Union Pacific Railroad. It carried freight all night. The trains must have been miles long, as each one trundled past for at least half an hour until, with a short respite, another soon followed.

So the pink bus only impinged on my consciousness every now and again. Clearly, Teri had not slept well and was not happy. What did upset me, though, was the sheer rudeness of the pink bus group leaders. Teri and I were trying to get away from the razzamatazz of the average tourist, and instead got forty-odd teenagers rampaging like it's Glastonbury Festival. At least we were leaving that day and heading southwest into unknown regions away from tourists. This was exactly the sort of experience I wanted to get away from and put distance between us and Etosha.

Teri, however, was not going to go quietly. We parked outside the manager's office, and I watched her disappear into the building. My confidence in Teri dealing with hotel managers was high; I had witnessed her arch disgust at minor infringements of hotel star ratings; Teri could spot a fault that wouldn't register on my radar, so what she was going to do to this manager I couldn't imagine. But I was going to keep well out of the way.

I'd worked as a hotel manager for many years in my earlier career. There were three pieces of advice I learned at college that have stayed with me over the years:

- When serving hot food, make sure it is really hot, and when serving cold drinks, make sure they are really cold; the quality is second to the temperature.

This is unfailingly true—even the best filet mignon or beef Wellington loses its appeal if served lukewarm. And the best gin and tonic served warm is inferior to a lesser brand served iced with a slice.

- When removing the elastic bands from lobsters' claws, it's better to use some sort of implement and keep your fingers at the tail end. This was learned by practical experience rather than in a lecture. The live lobsters were to be cooked for the evening restaurant service. I and a friend decided that we couldn't bear the thought of boiling them alive, or even stabbing them in the head, so we waited until everyone had gone off to change into their chef's whites, grabbed the box of lobsters, and legged it down to the seafront (luckily our catering college's restaurant annex was in Clacton-on-Sea) to release them. Getting the fiddly bands off was somewhat painful. But we didn't feel at all sorry for the customers who had ordered lobster bisque and instead were given a hastily constructed pea soup.

- Compensation for a bad experience is a pointless exercise. If a customer has had a horrible night in your hotel, offering a monetary refund won't alter something that has already happened. I tested this theory a few times in the hotel I managed in Knightsbridge in London. When customers made idiotic complaints about traffic noise or being kept awake by too-bright streetlights— we were in the middle of London, for heaven's sake!—I found a grudging offer of ten pounds in front of other guests usually made them feel a bit small.

The difference between good hospitality management and poor management is recognizing what customers want and expect, and delivering exactly that. "The customer is always right" is a ridiculous and illogical axiom. Customers are not a homogeneous mass. They are individuals, and as individuals, they will as often be wrong as hotel clients as they are wrong in other areas of their lives. But it is this individuality that needs to be addressed if hotels and myriad other lodging facilities are to offer customers what they want. This necessitates properties deciding on an identity and delivering on that identity.

The Gatwick Hilton is an airport hotel. Its customers require reliable early-morning calls, twenty-four-hour transport links to the terminals, plenty of in-house baggage trolleys, and access to screens providing flight information. And this is what it delivers.

The Motown was a cheap and cheerful, centrally located, short-term stopping spot for travelers who need an economical place to regroup before onward travel. Again, this is exactly what it delivered, despite being a bit grubby for our tastes.

The chap at Etosha hadn't considered the expectations of his guests but had taken bookings from groups with vastly different expectations of his hospitality. Lucy and I had paid for solitude and animals. The pink bus had booked in for a boisterous teenage party. Clearly the two were incompatible. I hoped to explain to him that it would be useful if he could decide whether his establishment was a party venue for hire or a wildlife camping lodge for guests to see, er, wildlife, and then to ensure putative guests were aware of the lodge identity.

I strode into the camp office and asked to speak with the manager. The receptionist tried to put me off by saying that he was busy. Unfortunately for her, his office was behind the desk, separated from the reception area by a large glass window, through which he could be seen drinking coffee and reading the paper. I explained that I intended to speak to the boss and if necessary would address my concerns to him from where I stood, at volume, from a distance, and in public if he persisted in his refusal to invite me in. Unsurprisingly, I was ushered in and even offered coffee.

I knew that I didn't want any financial recompense for the disastrous night we'd just had (see above!). I just wanted an apology and an assurance that no one else would experience such disturbance.

"Are you aware that there is a pink bus full of noisy children on your campsite?"

"Yes, that's right. They booked to come here last month."

"They parked about twenty feet from our tents! Do you think that is acceptable?"

"Er...no?"

"They played music at extremely high volume! Do you think that is acceptable?"

"Um...no?"

"They sang and danced until gone midnight! Do you think that is acceptable?"

"No, no, definitely not!"

"They used our water tap! Do you think that is acceptable?"

"Er, no, again definitely not!"

"You took our booking, and you took our money, but you didn't warn us that we would be sharing our space with a pink bus full of children who would crowd our space, play loud music, use our facilities, scare away the animals, and keep us awake most of the night! DO YOU THINK THAT IS ACCEPTABLE?"

The manager had now picked up on my incandescence and thought he should possibly attempt some sort of conciliation. He offered to refund us the cost of our disturbed night. I pointed out that he couldn't refund us the peaceful night we had lost, and that was worth much more than the nine pounds the night had cost us. I told him that as a recompense, I wanted him to make sure that if any buses, pink or otherwise, ever book to stay with him in the future, he must be sure to let any independent travelers know before accepting their bookings. I sincerely hope that he does so.

Chapter 4

Waterberg, the Tame Zoo, and Why We Thought It Bad

Our rough plan after Etosha was to head cross-country on the C39 road to what is known as the Triangle, a fairly civilized area of rich agricultural and mineral land, towns, and interesting things to see. There's the great Hoba Meteorite for a start: a huge lump of iron weighing in at about fifty tons, which crash-landed goodness knows when and is claimed to have been discovered in 1920. I suspect the locals knew all about it long before some European "discovered" the thing. Naturally people soon started chipping bits off it, so it had to be declared a national monument and is now protected by an entrance fee and even has a picnic area and kiosk, apparently. We never found out because we didn't get there. Our itinerary was blown at the gates of Etosha as we were leaving.

We left our campsite at Etosha with Teri indignant and with a touch of "and that told HIM!" about her and me quietly admiring her ability to complain, a skill middle-class English ladies normally have removed during infancy. Up It Yo got us as far as the gates, and there was some bit of paperwork we didn't have. So we turned round and went back to the HQ in Etosha to get stamped out. Then back to the gate. This journey is several kilometers long. We had had to do this when we arrived: get to HQ, don't have the right paperwork from the gate, go back to the gate, get paperwork, go back to HQ. I think the guys on the gate and at HQ deliberately fail to tell you what paperwork you need, then fall about laughing as you trek up and down the road between them.

On our second arrival at the exit gate, there was a gentleman waiting with two boys. He was a worker at the park and looking for a lift.

Of course he asked us; of course "we" said yes. I can't imagine anyone saying no. Apparently Teri can.

He wanted to go to Outjo, and we didn't. But it was, kind of, on our way. OK, not "kind of" at all. We wanted to go east; he wanted to go south. We went south. Just this once. We could turn northeast from Outjo when we'd dropped him off. So we set off with this chap and his two sons on their way home for the weekend. It was our good turn.

We managed to collect some friends of his from somewhere, so when we arrived at a police checkpoint, we had two adults and three children in the back. Apparently that is illegal. We had seen plenty of open-topped trucks going past with hordes of people jammed in the back, but five passengers was "overcrowded." It's unnerving, approaching a police roadblock in a foreign country. You always think you've done something wrong, especially if you haven't. In Canada we were stopped by a rather handsome Mountie. There are times when doing something wrong is a bonus. Though we hadn't done anything wrong on that occasion. They were looking for some suspicious chap on the run. Very exciting! Luckily, we weren't in the habit of picking up hitchhikers in Canada. In Namibia though, it's kind of an obligation.

Fortunately, this time Teri was driving. I say that because I look suspicious. Teri looks like Goldie Hawn. Everyone has heard of Goldie Hawn. Even Namibian traffic police. One beaming, disarming smile, a cheery "good morning," and an air of innocence always seems to work. I rue my dark-haired genes. So the police officer mutters, "Are you overcrowded in there?," glances at the adults with several children on their laps in the back, receives another charming smile from Teri, and waves us on. Still going in the wrong direction.

After the hassle of getting out of Etosha, going on the round trip to Outjo, negotiating police roadblocks, Teri being a bit miffed, and me feeling guilty about the hitchhikers, we decided to abandon the plan and kept on going south and east. A quick look at the map identified Waterberg Plateau, and we needed to find a campsite for the night.

The Waterberg Plateau looks like the eponymous feature in the film *The Land That Time Forgot*. It is a high lump of earth rising sheer from the plains around it. It has its own cloud system that looms over it like a cartoon depression. Apparently (consulting the guidebooks again), it is about fifty kilometers long by twenty wide and is home to many rare species of flora and fauna. That'll be the dinosaurs then. We may also find black rhino, roan antelope, Cape vultures, leopards, and brown hyena. Reading this list out to Teri, hoping to impress, I got the retort, "And we're *camping* there?" Fair enough. Now was the time to be mentioning a bath, bar, swimming pool, air conditioning. One thing we couldn't fathom, looking at its vertical sandstone cliffs, was, how do we get up there?

Following the guidebook instructions, we found ourselves at the bottom of a steep, sandy, single track that headed upward. We swapped seats, and I put Up It Yo into four-wheel drive, which dutifully ground its way up and round a twisting, turning ribbon through the bush and up the mountain. One sharp bend announced a German cemetery, perhaps for the visitors who didn't make it. I had a strange feeling we were not entering this park in the conventional manner. This is a popular game park with a fancy resort somewhere up there, with bungalows, a swimming pool, and people! How do they get there?

Eventually, however, we "arrived" somewhere; a reed-roofed building appeared, and a friendly lady greeted us when we wound down the window. Yes, there was a campsite just there, and the fancy resort was farther up. Teri had moved into "go with the flow" mode, so we found the site and set up camp. Teri even found a fridge at the reed hut in which to stash the beer and wine. It was already stocked with drinks, with an honesty book to sign, but we decided just to use it for our own gear; carefully labeled as ours. Cold drinks later. Marvelous!

Wherever we went, there were very few people. We'd seen a few in Etosha, as expected. But Waterberg was quiet. There was one other occupied site, which had been claimed by a young couple who had hiking gear. Fortunately they were not the same couple we'd encountered at Etosha. With a toilet block, warm showers, and the amazing fridge, we were happy campers.

We found out that we'd come up a service road. Typical. The main entrance route was farther along the main road. Looking at the map when stationary is much easier than when being bounced around in Up It Yo as it tackles the lumps and bumps of Namibian tracks. The guidebook, when stationary, also reveals interesting facts about Waterberg. There are organized game drives from the resort that cost about N$280 per person (I think that's about four poundish), but visitors can't go on their own drives as they can in Etosha. Hiking is popular though, and there are many routes. Since we weren't equipped for hiking, and Teri is no fan of physical effort, the main attraction for us was a good place to camp among wildlife. The cemetery, we found out, was because there was a large-scale battle in 1904 between the Germans and the Herero people who were defending what they regarded as their territory. As the Germans were armed with machine guns and Herero with ancient rifles, the outcome was a foregone conclusion. I'm surprised there is anyone interred in the German cemetery.

We stumbled across a swimming pool of sorts, which I then shared with various floating insects, including the largest wasp I have ever seen. Teri found a similar-sized arachnid in the toilet block. We went on a short hiking trail near the campsite but simply scared away any wildlife. All we heard was a crashing of undergrowth somewhere ahead in the dense bush. This was not going to be our sort of place. The braai was equipped with a levered grill system that took me half an hour to work out but functioned brilliantly, and we pinched a couple of wicker chairs from the reed building after the reception lady went home, had a great meal and drank cold alcohol in diverse forms till the moon came up. Our next stop was going to prove very different and infinitely more bizarre.

Both Lucy and I are sensible enough to know that nature is red in tooth and claw. We'd seen the remains of road kill. We'd seen lions gnawing at unidentifiable bloodied carcasses surrounded by a circle of patient vultures. We'd worried for the sweet little baby boks born by the side of the road, and we'd been forced off the road a few times to avoid hitting cattle that randomly darted out from the scrubland. We'd even noted how all of the flocks of guinea fowl had a "village idiot" in their midst. Guinea fowl have a penchant for scuttling along the road in front of the car before breaking rank, with some heading to the left verge, some to the right, but there's always one who invariably would turn and run back straight toward the car wheels. We'd so far avoided these kamikaze birds.

So we accepted that in nature, unfortunate things happen. The weak, slow, maimed, or elderly get killed and eaten. This is why our next stop, the Wildlife Camp, was such an anathema to us. We'd headed southeast, aiming for Gobabis with a plan to head directly north from there across uncharted territory. On the way was the Wildlife Camp, which promised some comfort before more rough camping. And it would be interesting to see how the conservationists made medical interventions while preserving the "wild" nature of the animals.

We drove over a cattle grid and were a bit taken aback to see a group of young Americans playing football on a manicured lawn with twee little footpaths marked out in symmetrical stones. Also cavorting on the grass was a motley selection of warthogs, springboks, ducks, and geese. The springboks and impala were sporting rubber tubes on their horns. Clearly the dignity of the animals took second place to the comfort of the footballers. A lorry load of donkeys and horses waiting for unloading or transporting seemed bizarre. Stumbling about like a very ungainly ballet dancer in an ill-fitting tutu was an ostrich with a club foot.

We'd chosen this particular camp because the guidebook said there were lions in the area. We planned to drive out at dusk and surround ourselves with the incredible sight and sound of several lions announcing their territorial boundaries with earth-shattering roars.

Unfortunately, we weren't able to sneak off alone in Up It Yo. Instead we had to take a scheduled trip out with a very charming guide who drove us down a bumpy track in a bouncy Mini Moke. We stopped at a small enclosure with two or three wooden benches. We were in the cage while the lions were roaming free in a reserve on the other side of the fence—an unusual juxtaposition of the usual arrangement.

Our guide called to the lions and threw lumps of donkey meat over the fence in all directions to encourage their presence. They duly obliged but more like conditioned circus performers than kings and queens of the jungle. The lions did indeed roar at sunset, and it was indeed stirring, spine tingling, and exhilarating. However, we still felt that we had been party to a somewhat demeaning spectacle.

Back at the camp, we stared out glumly over the smart lawns. The lodge was fairly expensive by Namibian standards. The furnishings were "stylized African," which teetered between being a chic cultural touch and a bit twee. The printed fabrics of the curtains and bedcovers were in beautiful rich earth shades, and the floaty muslin at the windows was practical in keeping the mosquitoes at bay, and gave an "olde worlde" colonial feel to the room. The various ornaments honed from animal parts—skins, horns, fur, and the like—seemed inappropriate in an establishment that purported to protect wild animals. Interior décor was another way to get entertainment out of the wildlife. We wondered where the truckload of horses and donkeys fitted in. Remembering the chunks of meat thrown to the lions, I think we could guess.

The bathroom was rather lovely, with a monstrosity of a bath molded from fiberglass about four feet deep and painted an exotic dark blue-green. When camping, we had no washing facilities except a bowl of tepid, slightly rank water from the reservoir in the back of Up It Yo, or occasionally a swift dip in a river that may or may not have crocodiles in it, so this bathroom was a hit with both of us.

We tried to view everything as favorably as possible to make up for the disappointment of the lion-roaring experience, but it was frustrating to find petty annoyances in our accommodation. The promised hairdryer was nonexistent, the fan didn't work, and neither did the air conditioning. There was no torch and no outside light, so when we tried to get out to the truck in the evening to get some provisions, we had to battle greedy ostriches in the dark, which was scary and funny in equal measure.

And then I saw the cattle prod. Expect that it wasn't called a cattle prod. No, far more charmingly, it was called a "pokey sticky," and there was a terrible notice above it explaining to guests that the pokey sticky was to enable them to prod animals in a "kindly way" if they got too close. I think this was when our efforts to view everything favorably crumbled, and we indulged in a long bout of grumpiness and fury on behalf of the animals.

From here, our next destination would be the wilds of East Namibia, which was omitted in both guidebooks and had no roads marked on the maps. I'd become quite good at playing down the itinerary and felt it wasn't a good idea to explain to Teri just yet why we were going to attempt traveling north to Bushmanland from Gobabis. The reason was simple, however. While researching our trip, I had seen a 4x4 blog/website that had an unanswered question from a South African: Did anyone know of a route directly north from Gobabis to Bushmanland? I went to trusty Google Maps, satellite version, and saw rather vague signs of tracks heading approximately due north, intersecting from time to time, but, encouragingly, mostly arrow straight. All we had to do was get on one, and it would take us up to Bushmanland where we planned to camp. The problem was, there was unlikely to be any diesel available to buy for several hundred kilometers, and then we'd need a lot of cash to top up when we got to the central "town" in Bushmanland, Tsumkwe. One thing we didn't need was to part with the cash we'd reserved for fuel. We needed to pay our lodge bill here by card and had checked beforehand that this would be OK.

The following morning we packed up at sunrise ready for an early getaway and went up to the main office to pay the bill. Our financial arrangements for the trip may seem a bit chaotic, but they worked for us. Lucy had a Namibian dollar credit card and held the cash kitty, and we each had our own personal cash fund. I should point out here that Lucy was the proud owner and wearer of a pair of British Army surplus shorts with many pockets. She liked to stuff cash, hankies, coins, the Swiss Army knife, the credit card, receipts, matches and countless other "essentials" into these pockets with no particular reason or logic I could fathom. Thus, when the time came to pay a bill from the kitty, she would plunge her hand into one of the pockets and pull out a bunch of creased banknotes wrapped round whatever else was lurking in there.

We'd tried to pay our bill the previous evening because we wanted to get away from the tame zoo as quickly as possible. Unfortunately the ATM machine was down, as was the credit line. In the morning there was also a crisis in the park that was causing the office staff some distraction. A porcupine had been mauled by a leopard. We weren't sure if the leopard and porcupine were fellow inmates, in which case it was quite remarkable that the leopard hadn't picked off a few lame geese or rubber-sheathed springboks in the past, or if the leopard was an intruder from over the fence. Either way, the lodge manager was out of the office and tending to the injured porcupine, and there was no one else available to help us pay up and leave. We were asked to wait and return to the office in an hour, when hopefully the various cash and credit systems would be up and running again. We spent the hour trying not to look at the invalid ducks that swam in circles on the quaint little pond with dainty shells arranged in a charming fashion.

I had a sudden thought and asked Lucy to remove the cash contents from all of her pockets and put all of the money we needed for fuel in her rucksack, leaving a random amount of less than twenty pounds. It went against the grain a bit for Lucy to sort out all the cash into one cohesive place, but she did so obligingly. We returned to the manager's office, to be told that nothing was working (except him—he had apparently performed surgery on the stricken porcupine in between his receptionist duties). Expressing sympathy for the poorly porcupine, we had to explain that we couldn't possibly wait any longer as we were planning a three-hundred-kilometer drive (true) and we'd already had to waste an additional hour. He agreed and suggested that perhaps we could pay by cash? I pointed out that the bill was in the region of one hundred pounds, and we weren't in the habit of carrying vast amounts of cash in the bush—maize meal, cooking oil, and necklaces in large quantities, but not cash. I dug into my purse and extracted all my money—approximately £60. Lucy also brought out "all" of her cash—the £19.27 that was left in her shorts. With a mixture of imperiousness and pathetic pleading, I proffered the £80 in payment. The manager must have been eager to go back to check on the progress of his latest patient; he accepted the cash, and we were on our way. We vowed to spend the money we had saved at the tame zoo on a worthy cause as soon as we could find one.

We had topped up the fuel tanks at Gobabis and only driven about eighty kilometers since then, but the maps and guidebooks all indicated that we'd be lucky to find fuel at Tsumkwe, three hundred kilometers as the crow flies from our starting point. There would be another two hundred kilometers to the next reliable source of fuel to the north. Crows fly straight. Namibia's D roads do not know the meaning of the word "straight." Neither are they easy on fuel. Four-wheel drive was thirsty work for Up It Yo, and the tracks on the map wandered and crisscrossed each other, making it easy to go the wrong way and have to backtrack. Our options were to go via Otijene to our west, where there was a gas station marked on the map at Otijene. This would take us on a two-hundred-kilometer dogleg detour. We decided to head straight north and hope Tsumkwe had diesel. At least the cash we had for fuel was still safe.

The district we were about to cross was called Omaheke, which we immediately changed to "Oh My Heck." It seemed more fitting. The maps both showed the D3031 going arrow straight three hundred kilometers across virgin territory. This was the road I had seen on the satellite from the comfort of my home in England. The challenge would be making sure we hit this road from the maze of other D roads we were setting off from, and we'd already found that maps were unreliable. We left the tame zoo, turned immediately left, and got confused. The roads were not as marked on either map, the distances on the maps were having a laugh, and other roads had obviously been constructed since the maps were made. We saw a sign to Gam, which was at least to the north of us, so we turned right and found ourselves on a passable road that needed only two-wheel drive and seemed to be heading north. A result.

We weren't on the straight road I'd seen on the satellite, but we were on a road that was insistently signposted to Gam, and the maps indicated the C44 heading out of Gam north and then west to Tsumkwe.

We were in cattle country. The landscape had changed from fenced-off bush and private game reserves to open countryside, villages, kraals with goats and, often, large herds of well-fed cattle. We picked up one hitcher, a young man on his way to work at an environmental research establishment. He told us that the farms in this area are big and rich, and most local people work on them. The villages we'd seen were workers' houses, and they owned the goats for their own subsistence rearing. We saw no tourist rentals, no pink buses (thankfully), no wood collectors, loafers, or craft sellers. We saw smart school buildings, donkey carts, folk riding donkeys while on their mobile phones, shop shacks, roadworks, and general self-absorbed busyness. It was refreshing to be away from the tourist routes and seeing the everyday life of many rural Namibians embracing what economic development provides. We were off the tourist routes and becoming explorers.

CHAPTER 5

THE ROAD TO GAM: TAXI SERVICE, CLINICS, AND A PLACE CALLED JACOBS

By now Lucy and I had three maps. Unfortunately, although they were definitely purporting to be of Namibia, they all told very different stories. The road numbers varied according to which map we used. The first map showed us a B2050, but this became the D5006 on the second map, and the entire road disappeared altogether on map three. Equally perturbing, the distances between marked points varied by up to as much as one hundred kilometers. So were we 26 kilometers or 117 kilometers from Gam? We learned to get used to crossroads that existed on the map but not in reality, and we got used to the three maps telling us simultaneously to go left, go right, and go straight on, when none of those options was available to us. We even got used to the maps (one, two, or all three) telling us that the road ahead was so dangerous that we needed at least two vehicles in convoy to traverse safely, and then finding that the road was in fact a nice new stretch of tarmac. It took a while, but we even coped with the opposite—our maps showing us a lovely, straight, wide road, only for the reality to be getting bogged down in sand with wheels spinning and nothing on which to gain purchase.

There is no public transport worth the name throughout the country, and cars are very scarce. We could drive for a day and only see two or three cars throughout the three hundred or so kilometers that we'd covered. The people who lived in the more remote areas may only see one car in a month, so our progress often caused much excitement. We got into the habit of stopping for hitchhikers and were constantly amazed by the incredible distances these people had to walk to get to work, the clinic, the school, or the shop.

Our first taxi service that day was for a child of about eight years old, her mother, and her aunt. They had been waiting for two days for a car to pass, as the child was unwell and needed to get to the clinic, but she was too ill to walk and too big to carry. We weren't sure what was wrong with the child—we think it was some sort of Namibian flu, hopefully not contagious—but we had no moral choice but to take the little group twenty-five kilometers on to the clinic.

We indulged in a spot of "tag-taxiing" whereby we stopped to pick up an elderly gentleman and a student. After several kilometers, the student saw an old friend waving us down, so we squeezed him in. The student then hopped out at the entrance to his school, and we drove on to the elderly gentleman's clinic. When we arrived at the clinic, the elderly chap asked us to wait, and within a few minutes a different old chap came out of the clinic, climbed in, and off we took again. We must have covered over one hundred kilometers over three hours with at least one and up to four passengers in the back.

There were two problems with this arrangement for me. Firstly, my propensity for dehydrating to the point of migraine meant that I had to drink five liters of water during the day to stay upright. But what goes in comes out, and Namibia isn't big on Portaloos. A lot of the time it's not big on handy trees and bushes, so comfort breaks during our travels often amounted to me leaping out of the truck, running to a tussock of spindly grass about a foot high, and just getting on with it. Lucy used these breaks to wander to the boot and extract one of her favorite crunchy cereal rusks to chew on. We became quite coordinated in timing my need for the loo and her need for a rusk.

Having said this, we did find an unexpected Portaloo in the Etosha game park. We'd been driving through the bush for ages, turned off the track to explore some interesting noises over to our left, and came across a bright white, three-sided metal cabin, complete with a toilet—unplumbed, obviously, but rather splendidly majestic in its location—and sporting a loo roll. Lucy stayed in the truck, but as I'm never one to refuse the offer of a loo, I grabbed the wet wipes and hopped out. It was one of the strangest experiences of my life: sitting on a loo in the bush, shielded on three sides, listening to animal noises, and not knowing if the dung beetles working at my feet and the moths flapping around my head might soon be joined by something larger—a rhino or a lion, maybe.

Anyway, while my toilet arrangements were manageable in the isolation of the bush, I wasn't prepared to take my comfort breaks under the interested eyes of up to four passengers, so taxiing on several occasions became an uncomfortable feat of endurance for me. Especially if we were driving on one of the bouncier roads.

The other problem was food. We had a limited supply of food—particularly as we had been a bit overgenerous to the smiling, waving children we came across and had handed out all of our oranges and apples. So we didn't really have enough food to share our lunches with hitchhikers. I offered a bag of mango-flavored sweets to the passengers on one occasion. The lady in the back took the whole bag and divided them between herself and her fellow hitchhikers. So we had an unspoken rule that we wouldn't eat if we had people with us, which meant that we got very hungry at times.

We arrived in Gam—at least we think we did; it was hard to tell. There was no sign announcing the name of this collection of shacks. This appeared to be typical in Namibia and a bit of a challenge for the navigator to tell whether this village/town/homestead was the required landmark or not. "Take the left-hand road after Gam" is a useless direction if you don't know if you've been in Gam or not. By process of elimination, we decided this was Gam because we'd seen nothing else that had more than five people in one spot. Gam was a kink in the road around which had gathered several shacks, kraaled homesteads, and a watering hole for livestock. People turned to stare at us as we slowed through the winding shacks. One tin construction advertised vehicle repairs but offered no sign of life. Another shack appeared to be the village's ubiquitous bottle store, but there was no evidence of a grocery store. There probably was one, but why would such a store need to advertise? Everybody who lived there knew where it was. The road wound round and back through the village, and it was difficult to tell if we were on the main road or navigating someone's driveway. We were both a bit nervous because the staring people seemed rather hostile. Shall we stop and ask for the shop? We decided to keep going or we'd get mobbed. Just as we cleared the main village, we were flagged down.

This next person on the list of our passengers was on her way to work. She asked us to take her to Jacobs, where she worked in the shop. We looked on all the maps. Nope—no Jacobs. We didn't know if it was someone's farm or a bottle shop. She said it had fuel and was not far away, just up the road and turn right for a bit, but she was unable to quantify the distance from the main road. So we tried asking how long it takes to get to Jacobs. Again she was unable to quantify the length of time the journey took. Discussing this together later, we realized that for her, the journey took an unspecified amount of time to make, because there were so many variables in her life that affected it.

It really is hard for us to imagine such a precarious way of carrying out one's social duties. Take the children's schooling, for example. You could make the decision to expect that there would be no lift, and set off on foot, allowing adequate time to walk the (let's say) fifteen kilometers. As walking speed is approximately five kilometers an hour, this would take around three hours. But if, after you've walked only a kilometer, a car stops and offers a lift to school, the trip will only take twenty minutes. So now you've arrived far too early and have to wait with the children until the teacher turns up.

The arrival time of the teacher is no more fixed than that of the children, as he/she has the exact same transport issues.

Then the mother sets off for work. If she gets a lift, will it be from a car or a truck or a donkey cart? The length of time the journey takes will be defined by the mode of transport and the speed of the driver. How can her boss in the shop have any sort of staff rota system when the employees have no means of guaranteeing their arrival time? Given the vast distances people have to travel between home and work, their arrival could vary by several hours. Does the shopkeeper close the shop if the employer hasn't arrived for work? But if he does so, what about all the customers who are making their own arduous journey to purchase their supplies?

Basic social functions such as work, shopping, schooling, and getting medical attention for yourself and your family are clearly beset with logistical problems. What was remarkable was how all the travelers we encountered were unfailingly cheerful and resilient. We also noticed the nonchalant attitude they all displayed in accepting the lifts, being grateful, but not overly so, and thanking us, but not profusely so.

Jacobs was named after a South African chap called…well, called Jacob. We pulled up at the gas station, which was well populated with people sitting on makeshift seats—logs, sacks of maize, etc.—leaning on any available surface, and generally standing about with an air of silent nonexpectation. The only real activity was a small, disheveled, and dirty white child who was running about barefoot in the dust with a puppy. The atmosphere was very odd. We didn't feel uncomfortable exactly, but we were disappointingly underwhelmed by Jacobs. With so few towns in Namibia, one always wants to find something interesting or distinctive—preferably in a good way.

While Lucy was topping up the gas tank, I went into the shop to top up our water and beer supplies. There was a South African lady (whom we later discovered to be Mrs. Jacob) doing a bit of shelf stacking with a random selection of goods in a rather random order. Tins of sardines were on a shelf next to a pile of baseball caps, while bags of maize meal were propped up against washing-up bowls, and baked beans were located alongside toothbrushes. This disorganized shelf stacking seemed to be a feature of a lot of the shops we visited. On the one hand, it made finding what you were looking for difficult, but on the other, the enforced scouring of the whole shop meant that we made some spontaneous and unexpected purchases. This shop had no beer and no water, but Mrs. Jacob directed me back out to the forecourt and pointed out a caged window, through which I was able to buy beer and even a bottle of wine.

Mrs. Jacob was delighted to see tourists, as Jacobs is not on the usual route for travelers. She was interested to hear that we were traveling independently and was surprised when we told her that Jacobs didn't even feature on our maps.

Our purchases were made and the tank filled, and we were ready to retrace our route back to the road to Gam after our lengthy detour. A young woman came hurrying over and asking if please, could I spare a minute to go to see the garage owner, as he wanted to talk about the fact that the garage wasn't on the map. This made sense, as we could see that such an omission would have a major impact on his business. Lucy stayed in the car planning the next stage of our journey under the incurious gaze of the inhabitants of Jacobs, while I crossed the forecourt with an offending map and went into a small, dusty office. Seated behind the large desk was the owner of an even larger paunch—Mr. Jacob. He urged me to sit down so that we could "have a chat." I said that we were eager to get going again, but I would be happy to give him the details of the map that had the temerity to airbrush his garage. He again insisted that I sit. So I did, while still proffering the map. He made no move to take it and instead started to tell me about his life journey which had brought him from a city in South Africa to a sandy outpost in Namibia. Inspired by his birthplace, he had decided to create Jacobs. He nattered on and on, telling me he owned the town shop, the garage, a cement works, and (surreally) a photography business. He was the most successful businessman in the region; he employed many local people (he gestured his huge bling-ringed hand at the two young typists in the corner in a lordly manner). By now I'd spared more than the original minute he'd demanded and had listened to his personal promotion for nearly twenty. I stood up and edged for the door, trying unsuccessfully to say my polite good-byes. He continued to verbally pin me to the wall with an endless flow of egotistical autobiographical anecdotes, until eventually I made my impolite good-byes. I left him midsentence, dashed across to the car, and told Lucy to get moving sharpish. She looked a bit surprised but didn't argue, and we left the garage with a skittering of gravel.

I can appreciate that investors from South Africa, or indeed any other country, can bring pockets of prosperity and employment to Namibia, and that is great news. However, the implication that such investors operate from a purely altruistic perspective is wrong. Mr. Jacob is an example of how a small investment in a poor country can result in wealth, status, and a sort of paternalistic sense of entitlement.

While Teri was chatting with people in the office, I filled the tanks, amazed myself by actually getting cash from a dispenser, and paid for the fuel. Then I waited for Teri and read the maps. Then I moved on to the guidebooks, then started on the rusks. There was no point wondering what was taking so long. It was becoming clear that nothing happens fast in Namibia. There were no screams coming from the office, no frantic waving from the window, so I presumed all was well. Teri can look after herself when it comes to people; it's usually me who needs rescuing from social situations.

The guidebooks explained a little about where we were heading. Bushmanland lay ahead, part of the Kalahari Desert but actually quite verdant in the rainy season. We were about to enter a conservancy, but not for animals so much as people and environment. This is where the Bushmen live in a more traditional way, as hunter-gatherers. We were planning on finding a community campsite; some of the villages have established their own rudimentary campsites in order to gain something from tourism and reduce the negative effect of people "wild" camping in what is their hunting grounds. This sounded reasonable to me. However, it would still be challenging, as trying to negotiate to camp with people with very different cultural norms from us, who don't speak English (while we don't speak German, Africaans, or Bushman) and may want to join us round the campfire (quite common, according to the guidebook), was daunting. And I wasn't sure what Teri would make of it. I could imagine she'd end up cooking for a whole village, and I'd be minding a campfire while being watched by experts.

By the time Teri emerged, a bit ruffled, from the office, dived into the passenger seat and said, "Just drive!" or words to that effect, I'd sorted out the next leg of the journey. First we had to get back to where we'd turned off on an interminable sand track between Jacob's and the C44. We sincerely hoped that no one would demand a lift, but we were now in a hurry and, thankfully, no one popped out of the shade to wave us down. The mood Teri was in, I think we'd have simply covered them in dust.

It was curious how different Teri and I were in our view of local culture and how to relate to it. I think I'm more open to different experiences because I have traveled to strange places purely for that very reason. Teri has worked with different cultures and had to draw her own boundaries with more definition and was more at ease with that. I tended to feel uncomfortable if not abiding by the local ways of doing things. I guess that's why I was quite happy, most of the time, to pick up strange waifs and strays, because that's the "done thing," but less comfortable with staying within the role of the visitor and tourist. I have a fear of being viewed as the "white colonial," and I see that identity as far too close a bedfellow to the European tourist in Africa. I am afraid of being patronizing, of asserting the power that Teri and I clearly had in monetary terms in relation to the people we were encountering. I suspected Teri was used to it, having worked in Jamaica, had got over it, and was much more comfortable in keeping a boundary between her comfort zone and the unquenchable need all around us. I realized that I had a lot to learn, but at the same time, I was exposing Teri to experiences that she may not have had otherwise. We were both, a lot of the time, out of our comfort zones, and it was doing us good!

Our next destination was the Kalahari and the Panveld. The Kalahari is not a true desert. It is mostly semiarid savannah, very sandy and dry, but has rainfall enough to produce vegetation and provide habitat for everything from elephants to leopards to giraffe. While much of the Namibian side (as in "not Botswana") is farmed, the Panveld is part of a conservancy that restricts the heavy cattle grazing we'd seen since Gobabis. As the name suggests, the area is characterized by large "pans" that fill in the rainy season and provide at least some form of waterhole the rest of the time. This is also where the Bushmen live. The guidebook describes the area as remote and the roads impassable in the rainy season. The scattered communities of Bushmen can hunt and live traditionally in this area, so infrastructure such as signposts, drainage, roadworks, and the like is nonexistent.

Our several maps all had two landmarks that we thought might help. One was "Big Tree," and the other was "Hollow Tree." Since there were quite a few trees about, this didn't seem all that promising. Big Tree was named Giant Baobab on one map, so we guessed that was the same landmark, and it was on our route north, so we tested our navigation skills to find Big Tree. If the maps had been accurate, or we had started where we'd thought we were, Big Tree should have been on our right. Obviously that was never going to happen. I suppose we'd done quite well to find it at all, but find it we did. At least we presumed it was Big Tree, because it was enormous. It stood out among the scrub bushes not just in height but by its huge, gray girth and outsized branches. Seeing how it looked like someone had pulled the tree out of the ground and upended it, leaving its roots in the air, I understood then why baobabs are also called "upside down trees." Without much around it to get its scale, we thought at first it was just the size of a good English oak, which would be large in comparison to the camelthorn around it. We had to get up close and stand by it to really appreciate why these trees are landmarks. Teri went over to stand under it while I took a picture, and she seemed to shrink the nearer she got to the tree. As a psychologist, I can appreciate errors of perception and illusions. The Müller-Lyer test sprung to mind:

The left-hand line looks longer than the right-hand line because of the perceptual "depth" illusion (they are the same length, honest!). Strangely, this illusion doesn't work with people who are not brought up in a structured environment—like the Bushmen. If you've never seen a square room and lived all your life in a round hut in the natural environment, why would you learn about corners and cornices? I loved learning about the cultural biases in Western science like this when I was an undergraduate. I've always harbored a secret wish that one day Western hubris would get its comeuppance.

I had read about the Bushmen when I was a child. They seemed to me to be a remnant of our early human culture, hunter-gatherers. They have attracted attention for the wrong reasons recently because of their threatened lifestyle. But there is something mystical about them, perhaps because they live an existence that many of us have become so removed from and yet still harbor in our genes. I was brought up in rural West Sussex, one of the most wooded areas of England. It is also still a very feudal area, or at least it was when I was a child. The aristocracy own much of the land and still appear to exercise feudal rights and customs in rural areas. Yes, this is the same Sussex which now claims Prince Harry and

Megan Windsor as Duke and Duchess. Lord Cowdray was the local "lord" who owned most of the land and villages around and "ruled" in quite a benevolent manner. As a local child, I had free rein over the estates, free entry to watch the polo, even to roam around the areas immediately about the main house. As a member of the Girl Guides, I swam in the house swimming pool, sat on the wooden polo horse(for practicing one's swing), walked the golf course, climbed all over the Cowdray Ruins (there was an entry fee for "visitors"), and watched professional Argentinian polo players practicing on the training grounds. Cowdray's neighbors were the Earl of Egremont (Petworth Park), the Duke of Norfolk (Arundel Castle), and Lord March (Goodwood House and large tracts of land to the sea). It was open country for a "peasant" local like myself. When I moved to the Midlands, I came across another landowner, non-aristocracy, who put fences up everywhere and "Private" notices to keep people out. Different values, I guess.

Anyway, I felt I had an affinity with the Bushmen—on a very different level. The land belongs to everyone and no one, and barriers feel like an infringement of human rights. Woodie Guthrie got it right: "This land is your land, this land is my land." Woodie Guthrie would have liked the Bushmen.

But I was under no illusion that my childhood image of them was going to match the reality. Perhaps that's why we were heading their way, to test out the myth and discover for ourselves how people like them were adapting to twenty-first-century Namibia. Were we, as tourists, just part of the problem, encroaching on their hunting grounds, or part of the twenty-first century that was an inevitable process of change? And was that change being managed to their benefit, or were they, again, the people who would suffer?

Apart from some general knowledge about the Bushmen and some swatting up before and during our trip, we both knew very little. One thing we did know, that communication was going to be a challenge. The Bushmen are also renowned for their strange clicking language that only those brought up with it can manage fluently. When written down the clicks are represented by the symbols !, /, //, and ≠. Which meant, according to one of our guidebooks, we needed to seek out the head man, or *n!lore kxao*, or something. This was going to be tricky.

Unlike Lucy, I have never really heard about the Bushmen, but I was fascinated by the strange Bushman communications and loved to eavesdrop on their conversations. The men added a bass guttural quality to the dialect, and the ladies accompanied their clicks with expressive hand gestures. It's a great language for chastising people!

I found myself on the receiving end of a clicky tirade from one of the tiny bush ladies who attended to the toilets at the entrance to Etosha. I'd been delighted to find proper loos and went off for a wee. I tried several times to flush, but unfortunately the flush didn't work. I went to wash my hands and resolved to mention the malfunction to the chap at reception.

As I went toward the towel, a mini whirling dervish ushered me back to the cubicle, uttering admonishments using clicks and tuts and hand gestures. I actually wanted to giggle because the clicky-tutty lady was so incensed about something so minor. She rattled on the flush, pushed it up, pulled it down, wiggled it about a bit, repeated the performance a few times, and turned to me triumphantly when it finally flushed. I left the toilets duly admonished.

'Big Tree', Nyae Nyae Conservancy, Bushmanland.

Chapter 6

Bushwomen—and the Rhino in the Night

"Jewelry? What sort of jewelry?"

"Well, I don't know," replied Lucy. "I'm not an expert on beads and bangles!"

This is true. Lucy is the least girly girl I know. I've only ever seen her wearing a skirt once, and I doubt she possesses a single necklace or bracelet. Her wardrobe consists mainly of jeans and T-shirts with writing on. Any half marathons, conferences, cross-country races, beer festivals, or political rallies Lucy had ever participated in would be emblazoned across her chest at a later date in the form of a freebie T-shirt.

I'm not averse to accessories, but I tend toward Rasta beads and leather bracelets bought from local shops and shacks on my travels. So when Lucy said that we had to take with us lots of jewelry to exchange with the Bushmen, we were both a bit stumped.

I decided that quantity would be more important than quality, and headed off to the charity shops. I thought that the bush ladies would probably like bright, shiny things, so I purchased the gaudiest and sparkliest jewelry that I could find. In one shop, the lady behind the counter was someone I knew, and to save my embarrassment at buying so much shiny tat, I explained that I was buying them for "bush ladies in Africa." Judging by the look she gave me, I don't think she believed me.

When we arrived in Bushman territory, I reminded Lucy that I had a bagful of jewelry in the back. We decided that we should probably wear a few items, as it would be more casual to proffer something from around our neck than to rummage in a bag in the boot. We drove through the Nyae Nyae Conservancy incongruously attired in dusty shorts and T-shirts and blinged up to the eyeballs with rings and necklaces.

As we progressed to the center of the conservancy, we met few bush people, but those that we came across were full of smiles and curiosity, coming to the car and peering in to see what goods we were carrying. We handed out oranges to their delighted smiles and hoped that we weren't acting like benevolent colonials. Although dressed as we were, we couldn't really take ourselves seriously, so I guess the bush people didn't either.

We eventually arrived at the little Gamsa village where we'd been told we would be able to camp at a spot close by if we made payment to the people in the village. The village was a little huddle of straw-and-mud huts, with a few goats grazing on the dry ground. There were one or two young men in evidence, but mostly, the population seemed to comprise women and girls. A tiny old lady appeared to be the matriarch, and she and Lucy negotiated a camping area with much gesturing and nodding, pointing and smiling. Then she remembered something and indicated that we should wait by the car. She went into one of the huts, and a few minutes later returned with a grubby sheet of A4 paper. It had been folded and unfolded so many times that the creases were virtually disintegrating. We were dismayed to read the fading typeface. It was a "menu" of activities and spectacles that we could observe, with a price against each one. We could watch bush people dance, we could listen to them singing, we could visit their village or share their food, all at a price.

Lucy and I were in Bushmanland because we wanted to avoid organized entertainment and a conventional tourist itinerary. Why would we travel so far only to be presented with a false and structured tourist attraction? The drive to Gamsa had already given us a small insight into the lives of the Bushmen, and if we were to have any sort of interaction with them, we wanted it to be spontaneous and not preplanned, preordered, and prepaid.

We made it clear, with more expressive gesticulating, that we were only interested in the campsite, paid the appropriate fee for camping, and drove slowly in the direction she'd indicated, followed by a small procession of curious villagers.

Our "campsite" was a small patch of scrub alongside a big, dilapidated stone well. There were a few rocks scattered about, a single-file dirt track to the front, and a handy tree to park under. That was it! We were definitely "going bush" now—that lack of any basic facility was exactly what Lucy had been planning when she took me on a sliding scale from a five-star hotel at Heathrow to the flea-ridden Motown Inn, then a lodge with a pokey stick and boisterous ostriches, followed by a campsite with a firepit, shower block, and a tap. And now here I was, standing in the middle of Bushmanland, surveying a patch of scrub and trying to decide if the single-file path was a rhino run or a Bushman track. Rhino runs are quite easy to spot, as the vegetation along the sides of the run grows in a sort of barrel-shaped tunnel, joining together above rhino height. Generally, people tracks are narrower, and the vegetation doesn't grow together until about a height of six foot. However, as the bush people are so small, it was difficult to decide if this was a path used by them, by rhinos, or both.

As we were admiring our pitch for the night, the procession of ladies came to observe us. The tiny, wrinkled matriarch approached Lucy with a tribal necklace (a plastic red, blue, and white beaded choker) which Lucy had no choice but to accept, offering her shiny purple necklace in return. The other ladies shyly accepted the rest of the jewels we were wearing.

We started to pitch our tents, and the ladies returned to their village. Lucy went searching for firewood, and I delved through the luggage in the boot trying to find the rest of the jewelry. I then laid it out on the tailgate of Up It Yo. We wanted to give it all away, but it would take forever if we could only hand out the beads we were wearing, so I thought a little display might be in order.

Later, the ladies came back to our camp, as they needed to draw water from the well adjacent to our tents. They came for a curious look to see how we were faring. When they caught sight of the "jewelry counter," their eyes lit up. Again, the matriarch was at the head of the group, and she selected the pink pearlized necklace with gobstopper-sized beads. The rest of the ladies gathered around, trying on rings and bracelets. They showed an inherent sense of fairness and respect for each other, and no one took more than one item, so that there was enough for everyone to have something. They stood posing, admiring each other's choices, turning their hands this way and that to make the rings and bangles sparkle in the sun. Staff in the jewelry department in Harrods have never witnessed such delight in the most expensive diamonds and pearls as we witnessed at the jewelry counter in the bush.

This was our first proper safari-style camp. It was just a clearing in the bush, well away from the village, behind Gamsa's makeshift well, which had been put in place by Raleigh International—or so was carved on a wooden plaque. The only amenities were those we'd brought with us. Now we were proper explorers!

It was my job to put up the tents and make the fire, and Teri was in charge of food and housekeeping such as storage of utensils, loo roll, and the like. Teri performed her duties from cardboard boxes stuffed full of goodness knew what in the back of Up It Yo, and woe was me if I tried to find something among the compartmentalized storage system. My kit was simpler; there was one big blue holdall for the camping gear. As the trek went on, and the tracks got worse, the cardboard boxes slowly disintegrated, and the blue holdall collected increasing amounts of sand, twigs, stones, goat poo, and creepy-crawlies.

Firewood was easier. We had a roof rack and bungees galore. Anytime we passed likely looking piles of dead trees, we'd stop and forage for suitable lengths of dry logs. These were easy to break up because they were tinder dry, and all I had to do was jump on them. Then we'd load them onto the roof, strapped down with bungee ropes and cargo netting. This did not stop some branches working their way down between Up It Yo's cab and the fiberglass cover over the back, one of which we could not get out and is probably still there. We wondered several times on our trek what the guys back at Value Car Rental would make of the various additions we'd made to Up It Yo. Frankly, a piece of wood jammed behind the cab was the least of them. One thing that was starting to irritate, though, was Up It Yo's alarm. Sometime in our travels, we had managed to set the alarm to go off if anyone unlocked a door. This was amusing when in Gobabis and Jacob's garage. It was not so fun when it went off in the middle of the peaceful Kalahari next door to a Bushman village. A car alarm is loud in a city. In the desert, people over in Botswana must have heard it. This was not doing our bush credibility any good. I had taken to creeping up on Up It Yo and testing the key in the lock in fear of waking the dead.

The first rule of setting up camp in sub-Saharan Africa has got to be "don't pitch a tent in the middle of an animal track." We had fallen foul of this rule in Canada and learned the lesson. Having found a lovely, isolated island in a lake, we paddled there to spend the night. Throwing the tents up quickly, we happily fed and watered ourselves and listened for beaver coming out to play in the moonlight. Nothing happened. So we went to bed, and instantly there were beavers dive-bombing into the water and scurrying around the tents, churring and chuffing loudly when they crashed into the guy ropes. In the morning, there were tracks everywhere, with a clear, well-used run across the island we hadn't spotted earlier. I guess we could be grateful it wasn't a bear run.

This time we'd found no track across the camp area, checked under relevant stones for scorpions, and I put the tents up, both on fairly flat surfaces cleared of sticks and stones, and upwind of where our fire would be. And of course the wind changed direction as soon as I lit the fire. This was an uncanny phenomenon in Namibia. I think it is because, once the sun goes down, the land cools and breezes spring up to fill the low-pressure areas of existing warmth. So, every time I checked the wind direction before sunset, put up the tents, and started the fire in daylight, the setting sun sparked off the swirling breezes and filled the tents with smoke. We got used to it.

Another important part of the camp to arrange is the seating. We could have hired fold-up camp chairs from Value Car Rental, along with a fridge, Primus stove, table, Tilley lamp, blankets, and probably a cook. But we were going "bush," so we used whatever was to hand. The toolbox proved very useful—a big oblong box of robust, rigid plastic about one foot high by two feet across. There was also usually a thick tree branch lying around, or a large stone. Up It Yo's tailgate was our kitchen surface. Teri would prepare our meals there, load up the barbeque grille we'd bought specially, and rustle up something surprisingly edible and tasty. We also had a collapsible water carrier that served as the washing-up bowl, and Up It Yo was equipped with a ten-gallon water tank for nondrinking purposes. What more did we need? Oh, yes, I had brought a well-stocked first aid kit that would serve as a mini dressing station if war broke out and an air compressor with tire attachments that plugged into the cigarette lighter, and we'd hired extra tools, a spade, and a tow rope. We only lacked an elephant gun and bearers.

Later that evening, in the twilight after dusk, we sat by the fire listening to the night noises. There were no roars, sadly, but at one point, there was a tremendous crashing about in the direction of the track ahead of us. Well, that answered that question: it was definitely a rhino track. Not even an entire tribe of Bushmen would be able to make quite such a racket. We doused the fire and crawled into our tents. We needed an early night, as we would be on a rhino-stalking mission at the crack of dawn.

We were up before the sun, and it was very cold. We wanted to get going with our rhino hunt, so didn't waste time on the half-hour ritual that a cup of tea would entail: lay fire, light fire, find last night's dirty saucepan and clean it with cold water from Up It Yo's tank, find the tea bags and sugar—somewhere on the back seat, but it's dark—fill saucepan with water and wait interminably for it to boil, make tea, drink tea that tastes of twigs and smoke.

Lucy grabbed her stick—she always had a long stick available for fire poking and other emergencies—and we set off into the bush down the rhino track.

If we were bush women, we would starve, as we'd never be able to creep up on an unsuspecting impala with a spear. We tried to walk as quietly as possible in our big boots, but with every step there was a crackle of leaf litter underfoot, a snap of small twigs, a rustle of leaves, or a muttered expletive as a thorn bush dug its barbs into our bare legs. Then we heard a stumbling, crashing noise ahead—rhino! It seems strange now, but as we stopped still, holding our breath, we were disappointed that the crashing seemed to be heading away from us instead of toward us.

I first encountered the idea of Bushmen, or San people, reading Laurens van der Post books when I was a teenager. These books describe the veld of Southern Africa and some of its amazing indigenous people, especially the Bushmen. A hunter-gatherer people who live in some of the most barren parts of Southern Africa, the Bushmen are believed to have been around for forty thousand years, give or take a few millennia. By all accounts, that puts their direct ancestors squarely in the middle stone age. The Bushmen have also been persecuted by every neighbor they've had the misfortune to rub up against, and have been pushed into the inhospitable Kalahari Desert. Lesser folk would have given up, but the San, as they are more respectfully known, simply became experts at living in a dirt-poor, dry environment. Their tracking skills are thought to be second to none, they know every edible and medicinal plant in their land, and can stalk and hunt game with nothing but flimsy spears and bows and arrows. They appear to be able to live off nothing, which is a good job because, even today, starvation is still one of their main natural threats. In several of the areas they live around the Kalahari, they have been banned from hunting, prosecuted for "poaching," and forced to rely on handouts. Their hard-won skills and knowledge are under threat.

Perhaps they are more famous for their use of plants to stave off hunger, such as *Hoodia gordonii*, which has, unsurprisingly, become attractive to the obese West. Apparently there is no scientific evidence for its effectiveness as an appetite suppressant. Perhaps it only works on the San. But of course lack of evidence is no barrier to industries keen to exploit the Western world's fear of food, and companies soon marketed Hoodia supplements. This brought some hope that the San could gain from the centuries of starvation and marginalization they have suffered by trading the plant. Not to be.

Hoodia was soon declared an endangered species and had a CITES (the Convention on International Trade in Endangered Species) export ban imposed on it. Some might argue that the San could do with the same concern, as they and their way of life are endangered. At our next stop, we would find out a little of what was happening in Bushmanland and other areas of Namibia to protect ways of life, and manage the pressures of agriculture, tourism and economic development.

Teri and I left our Gamsa village folk behind, waving cheerfully and a bit reluctantly, as we thought we could have spent more time with them. We were aiming for the "town" that is the center of Bushmanland: Tsumkwe. This is described as not much more than a crossroads, a couple of shops, a petrol station, and a school. This petrol station was an essential stop for us; our carefully saved cash from the Wildlife Camp was destined for this out-of-the-way place, which was unlikely to take plastic. Discovering Jacob's had been an unexpected bonus in fuel terms, but we still needed to top up both tanks for the next leg of our journey. To get to Tsumkwe, the traveler is advised to be completely self-sufficient, as it is "remote." We were not expecting much.

To reach Tsumkwe, we would be traversing the Nyae Nyae Conservancy from the "wrong" direction. Our trusty guidebook said that an experienced driver would get to Tsumkwe from the northwest along the main road in a two-wheel drive, but other roads in Bushmanland require a sturdy 4x4 and a good guide, or a GPS, or both. We seemed to have ignored the instructions again. Most visitors take the main road to Tsumkwe from Windhoek and then plan which areas of the conservancy to visit. This might entail a guided visit to a village to watch how rural crafts and skills are performed and perhaps a guided "hunt" with the San. We had arrived from the south and already managed to meet the locals without the assistance of a guide/interpreter and managed to trek through the bush with wild rhino and exchange goods and services with the nearest village. So we were doing quite well in sidestepping the tourist routes.

The journey there took us past giant baobab trees and lots of scrubland. Never quite sure whether we were on the right track, we stopped by a San couple we encountered walking toward us. He was armed with a pick and clearly on a mission. She carried supplies in a small bag. Both wore Western clothes that were, by anyone's standards, rags. We were at least glad they were going the other way, as we envisaged more taxi service duties. As usual, they were incredibly smiley and cheerful, a little in awe of our truck and us being two women on our own, I suspect.

Of course, they spoke no English except, "Cigarette?" We smiled cheerfully back, hellos all round, and said "Tsumkwe," and pointed up the road. This worked after a period of them repeating what we were saying, pointing in a diagonal direction from the road and looking at each other quizzically. Finally we got confirmation that Tsumkwe was up the road, not down the road, and decided to distribute some oranges. They were pathetically grateful and only made me feel guilty about all the food we had in the back. We set off again and reasoned that they pointed diagonally from the road because, being always on foot, they would walk in a straight line to Tsumkwe through the bush, not along the track as we were forced to do. Simple really. How we get fixed in a Western way of thinking.

True to form, Tsumkwe announced itself as do most small towns in Namibia, with the out-of-town cuca bars: shanty huts that sell nothing but alcohol and announce themselves as the Try Again Bar, Anytime Bar, and Good Will Bar. We only realized we'd actually arrived when we came to the crossroads. Yes, Tsumkwe was just a crossroads—with goats. At least there was some activity. Someone was herding cattle down the main street, people were milling around a shack that, on second look, turned out to be the petrol station—with a shop—and there was a small crowd gathered at the church. Tsumkwe was buzzing!

We'd driven up and down the main road to check out the facilities and to get a feel for the place. A previous paternalistic benefactor, a reverend, had built a school from which tiny children were heading home, presumably after Sunday school. The teacher made a most incongruous sight—an elegantly dressed lady with beautifully coiffed hair and full makeup riding a quad bike along the chalky road. The good reverend had also built a church, which was very well attended; there were many people in their best dresses and suits, ladies in extravagant hats, and children in lacy confections, all spilling out onto the grass verges outside the church.

We pulled up at the "supermarket," which was a small, dark tunnel, not really super, but it had a few dusty tins and packets. While Lucy locked the car and wrestled with the car alarm, I went into the shop on my never-ending quest to purchase enough water, wine, and beer to keep us both adequately and happily hydrated. As I walked in, there was upbeat piped music playing. Except that it wasn't piped, as almost immediately the radio station changed from what I assumed was a Namibian pop music station to a religious station, and the volume was turned up. The strains of communal hymn singing, not so much Negro spiritual but more songs of praise African-style, poured down the aisles. I found a young woman at the back of the shop sitting next to the radio and almost obscured by a pile of blankets and cushions. I was unsure as to whether these were for sale or if this was her home. Lucy had followed me into the shop by this time. Our eyes met across the sardines and soup packets, hers narrowed in puzzlement and mine widened in a mute warning as I tried to tell her telepathically, "Don't say anything disparaging about the music. There's a young girl over there that put it on especially for us!"

Discussing it afterward, we couldn't make our minds up whether the woman in the shop had been listening to illicit pop music on a Sunday or thought we were unbelieving heathens who needed a bit of musical persuasion to convert and cleanse our souls. Either way, the supermarket couldn't provide us with anything to drink except a rather alarming milky protein liquid that came in rusty, dented tins, in chocolate or vanilla flavor. We definitely didn't want that, so we headed off to the garage, which also had a shop. The Herero ladies behind the counter were friendly and polite, and the other customers stared a bit, but no more than one would expect people to stare at two white ladies in the bush, one wearing army surplus shorts and a red, blue, and white bead choker and spilling out handfuls of cash, the other wearing baggy brown shorts and bright pink Doc Martens. Clearly Tsumkwe, despite its religious proclivity, didn't have the same reservations about selling alcohol on Sundays as the shops in Windhoek, and we made our purchases and were ready to move on.

On returning to the car, we found some bush ladies waiting for us. We thought they might want to barter with beads of the type that Lucy was still wearing. Or maybe they had fruit or vegetables or porcupine quills or anything that we could buy and give them money in exchange. But they didn't—they just held their hands out and begged for money. We felt awful, but we couldn't just give them money—it would be demeaning for us and degrading for them. We would be diminished by being cast into the role of rich white tourists giving out handouts to the poor black people, and the bush ladies would be diminished by considering their skills, abilities, and humble crafts as being unworthy of sale, offering us only their palms for cash.

We couldn't help but compare the begging bush ladies to the employed Herero shop assistants and felt saddened by what seemed to be a hierarchical class structure between the tribes. We also thought of the proud, shy, and happy bush people in Gamsa, who were true to their heritage and engaged with tourists with some self-respect, offering services for remuneration. In contrast, by leaving their natural habitat and gravitating to civilization, where there was retail and tourism and so-called progress, these beggars had lost far more in dignity than they could gain in charity. We like to think that tourism and tourists are a force for good in poorer countries, but this episode served to illustrate to me how delicate the anthropological infrastructure of a country is and how industry can unbalance centuries of cultural adaptation.

Tsumkwe felt odd to both Teri and me. The disparity between the modern school buildings, the church, and the rural African shacks, goats, and general hanging about didn't add up. There also seemed to be a class difference between Herero residents who were at the church, operating the garage and the stores, and the San, who were clearly destitute and begging outside the store. One of the guidebooks described the Reverend Hendriks who aided the San by distributing food in exchange for crafts to sell on their behalf. After meeting the ladies at Gamsa, the women begging outside the store felt all wrong. There was clearly an issue here. Something about a clash of cultures and attempts to try to forge something positive out of inevitable tourism and the preservation of a way of life. I decided on return to England to investigate what we were witnessing. What I found was enlightening and confirmed that our gut instincts about the begging women were on the money.

The Nyae Nyae Conservancy is an area in Bushmanland (around nine thousand square kilometers, being 0.43 times the size of Wales) that is protected by law and given over to the community to manage. The population living in the conservancy is mostly from the Ju/'hoansi ethnic group of the San, so this conservancy enables them to live in their traditional way as hunter-gatherers, but they are also encouraged to benefit from the wildlife and other resources, tourists, and infrastructure development. The historical persecution of the San appears, arguably, driven by other populations (pastoralists) seeking grazing for their cattle and goats, resulting in overgrazing and so reducing the flora and fauna on which the San depend. They also suffered during the 27-year-long border war with Angola from the 1970s when South Africa governed Namibia. The San were often used as trackers to seek out SWAPO forces, making them doubly unpopular with their SWAPO-sympathizing neighbors. Also, the army presence overpopulated the area and exploited the very poor and naive San in ways in which armies throughout history have exploited civilian underclasses. The cuca bars are perhaps the least harmful remnant of those days.

Attempts at recompense were made, firstly, to help the San develop as pastoralists and so farm the area. Well, it would have been easier to stop baboons raiding rubbish bins. People who have been hunting for forty thousand years aren't going to take to farming in a hurry, and the San proved resistant to the planning needed to become agrarian. So that idea was abandoned. The current assistance being offered is to provide education for children and adults. A village schools project was set up; hence the lovely school Teri and I saw. Apparently, however, getting the San to bring their children to school, and getting the children to stay in school, is proving difficult. The San are described in a recent report as "the most difficult" to work with for educational initiatives, with little increase in school attendance since the project started, and very high dropout rates. Sounds even worse than inner-city London, though I guess San children are not bunking off to smoke dope, indulge in a spot of shoplifting, or generally hang around making a nuisance of themselves. These children are probably working in their villages, engaged in the acquisition and preparation of food, and other general survival activities.

The Nyae Nyae Conservancy idea seems to take a more holistic approach to the San and their way of life, as Teri and I discovered from the Gamsa ladies. At least it means that the San benefit from utilizing their skills and knowledge to manage wildlife, and it recognizes their value to Namibia, the tourist industry, and environment management. The conservancy is zoned so that grazing and wildlife are managed apart, and hunting by the San is allowed and incorporates an audit of wildlife, as everyone reports their catch to community leaders. We certainly noticed the absence of cattle and goats before we reached Tsumkwe. Each community is charged with managing its territory and is encouraged to exploit the tourist industry by trading crafts, offering campsites, and demonstrating their skills to visitors. They are also allowed to harvest a plant known as the devil's claw, a prickly ground-spreading thing that does actually have scientific evidence supporting its use as an anti-inflammatory.

Teri and I had been concerned that the San appeared to be driven to beg from tourists, and we worried that tourism will destroy their communities. We worried that we were as much a threat to them as smallpox had been in the nineteenth century. Perhaps, though, tourists might be their saviors. Without the attraction of wildlife, native culture, and the wilderness environment, the San's world will get increasingly smaller, the wildlife poached and outgrazed, the environment denuded of rich flora, and the San will find themselves in a world they are not adapted to, either by nature or by nurture.

Back in England, while researching literature on global health, I came across an anthropological report of research in the Pyrenees. The team were investigating fossilized footprints in caves, dating back about seventeen thousand years. Researchers before them had interpreted circles of footprints as people dancing. This current team, however, had an edge. In an inspired moment, they had brought Ju/'hoansi San trackers with them. The researchers were stunned by what the trackers could tell from seventeen-thousand-year-old tracks. The San trackers used laser pointers to show what they were discussing and explaining to the interpreter. They identified people by age and gender: they could tell a three-year-old boy from a three-year-old girl. The dancing circle was just one person, a fourteen-year-old female, circling and pressing her feet into the ground while carrying a babe on her hip, as a mother would when reassuring a crying infant. The researchers were stunned at the richness of the information the San provided. As one of the researchers put it, "We were blind before." Reading this report, I thought of our Gamsa ladies and the couple on the road with their oranges and clear sense of direction. I hope they can keep their skills and culture and have it recognized and valued and rewarded, as their land opens up to the twenty-first century.

Bushmanland: no amenities here

Chapter 7

Norma and Gottfried and the Elephants Who Wouldn't Share

Khaudum National Park is described by the Republic of Namibia Ministry of Environment (NMET) and Tourism as "not to be taken lightly." They describe it as rarely visited, very large, and extremely wild: Namibia's "forgotten wilderness." Bordering Botswana, it's unfenced, so migrating animals can cross between Botswana's Okavango Delta and Angola. It's part of the Northern Kalahari but not a desert. The dense bush all grows from stable Kalahari sand dunes, cut with *omiramba*, an Herero word meaning "vague riverbeds." *Vague* is a good word for things in Namibia. Apparently, large herds of elephant wander through the park constantly, and it is home to lion, cheetah, leopard, wild dog, and rare antelope. It's game heaven.

The guidebook's recommendations for accessing this area were that you be completely self-sufficient with provisions for at least three days, have a minimum of 120 liters of fuel and 100 liters of water, and be prepared to use four-wheel drive constantly. The tracks were described as deep sand, and, in the wet season, wheel chains might be useful, but you should avoid the black-cotton soil, which will be totally impassable.

Obviously, when planning our expedition, as soon I discovered this part of Namibia, I realized that this was definitely in the itinerary. I'd worry about what Teri would say about it later. It was also closed, according to the NMET website. Apparently the elephants always wreck the two bush camps, so they had been abandoned to the animals. This was all music to my ears. One snag, however, was that entry was limited to parties with two or more 4x4 vehicles. Bugger. However, if it was closed, did that mean that there would be nobody to check who was going into the park? If it was unfenced, who was to know? I checked it out on Google Earth to see if there were any tracks visible, and yes, there were. Clear, distinct lines could be seen from satellite running vaguely (there's that word again) north-south, eventually linking up with a major B road in the north and a D road to the south. So, navigating should be a breeze, just drive north from Tsumkwe, and eventually we'd end up hitting the B road to civilization. Simple.

A little voice was nagging away in my head while we were in Tsumkwe stocking up on fuel and provisions. Were we being too gung ho? Was this madness? Was I leading Teri into unreasonable danger? What if we broke down, got stuck in the sand, lost? No one would find us for days or weeks, no one would know where we were. We had no phone signal, and no one knew we were going into Khaudum. I tried to problem solve rationally. We had a great truck, we wouldn't drive through anything that looked too ridiculous, we had enough provisions to last for a fortnight and could boil up our spare washing water if need be, and if stranded, we'd follow the advice of TV wilderness expert Ray Mears: stay with the vehicle! A big white Toyota is easier to spot than two people legging it through the African bush.

There is a "cultural center" in Tsumkwe that I thought might be interesting to visit. My Bushman necklace was fine, but maybe checking out other crafts would be good too. Much to Teri's incredulity, I like to take all manner of curios home with me. But no. The cultural center was a shack with several San women loafing around, and it looked about as inviting as a Glaswegian betting shop. We had pulled into their yard, which always seems to attract attention, but more so when Up It Yo's alarm went off again, and a large Herero gentleman wearing a game warden pullover and a large smile strolled over to us from a hidden office. He was a godsend. Not only did he fix Up It Yo's door alarm, he was *sooooo* relaxed when we confessed fancying trying out Khaudum. What was it like, was it closed, can we get through, et cetera, et cetera.

"Two sensible ladies like yourselves will have no problem," he said, clearly mistaken. "This vehicle will get you through. The park is all open now." He went on with instructions of how to get there, said we'd find a park warden, no problem, lots of elephants. Phew!

Bolstered by his validation, I relaxed, a bit. Teri seemed encouraged too, and I realized I was getting anxious because she was quiet. Or was it the other way around? Anyway, anxiety is catching, whoever starts it, but we both felt more confident in taking the Khaudum route north. And Up It Yo was now behaving.

I wasn't going to rely entirely on our game warden friend's confidence, however. Perhaps he says that sort of thing to everyone. Had he mistaken us for hardened safari experts? No, maybe not. We didn't even know how to manage Up It Yo's alarm system. He just pressed the key fob a couple of times, and hey presto! No, I was still doubtful of getting through the southern gate without a second vehicle. Both guidebooks were clear on that rule. If the park is open, there will be someone on the gate. If it's shut, our game warden friend was making it all up. Still, what was the worst that could happen? We could get there and get turned away. Off we went on the north road from the Tsumkwe crossroads, round the obligatory goat, and promptly ran out of tarmac.

The road (I use that term advisedly) to the southern gate is about fifty kilometers of deep sand after the first hundred meters of tarmac. The only thing going for it is that it is wide enough to pass for a European dual carriageway. There the resemblance ends abruptly. There is no drive-on-the-left rule. It is a case of drive in the tracks of the last vehicle, regardless of whether it was going north or south. We made steady progress in four-wheel drive, considering. Teri got bounced a few times when I switched tracks to something more promising, with Up It Yo rearing over the humps of sand between tracks and our gear crashing about in the back. As the sand deepened, the engine moaned with the extra effort, and I slowed to prevent losing traction. As the sand hardened, Up It Yo would surge forward, engine whining in relief. I learned to spot the deeper bits because the sand color changed to a darker red, though this didn't help to avoid ploughing into it. The deep tracks we were following would "steer" Up It Yo, and a sudden turn would yank the wheel violently round, so I soon learned to keep my hands soft and my thumbs well away from the inside of the steering wheel. I didn't want to break my wrists! Teri said this self-steering was what unnerved her about driving in sand. I guess it makes you think of driving in ice, when self-steering is a sign of being out of control and about to collide with a tree. I wonder what hardened safari drivers would make of a bad winter in the English Pennine mountains? Pah! Softies!

My growing confidence soon evaporated when we realized we were catching up with another vehicle. We had seen dust in the distance, but it was clearly getting closer. Then we caught sight of it on a long stretch of "road," through the sand plume it was kicking up. We got nearer and more choked. We backed off and got bored. So we approached again and took a wider track from theirs, hoping they'd see us and let us pass. It was a Toyota Land Cruiser with camping gear on the roof. Arguably a better vehicle for this sand than ours, but going more slowly. Probably more sensibly. But we didn't come all this way to get stuck in a traffic jam, and I had an idea, so we drew up alongside and waved them down.

"Hi. You going to Khaudum?" Start with a stupid question, why don't I?

"Ja, Khaudum," the male driver said. German. His passenger, a woman, eyed us up.

"We need two vehicles," I said, "to get through the gate," hoping the inference was obvious.

"Ach, ja." He nodded and smiled. "We are two vehicles!" He indicated our trucks and laughed. OK, a German with a sense of humor I understand. Brilliant.

"We'll wait for you at the gate," I shouted. "If we need each other."

"OK," he said, waving and smiling. His passenger smiled and waved too.

Great! My last obstacle was overcome. I was happy. Teri thought I was mad, I am sure. But, bemused, she simply said, "They'll have our dust now."

And so we drove on.

And on. Endless sand, ruts, bucking Up It Yo, engine whining. Fifty kilometers is a long way when you have to concentrate hard and can only make about twenty kilometers per hour. I had a headache.

When Lucy and I were discussing the forthcoming trip from the safety of steamer chairs in the garden, I laid down a few non-negotiable driving ground rules. As I've said, I'm not the most confident driver, having managed over the years to steer my cars into a ditch (deep snow and traveling at five miles an hour), a tree (sheet ice and trying to travel at five miles an hour down a slope, gathering speed alarmingly), and a field of cows (that deep snow again). On one memorable occasion, I hit an unexpected pool of water and pirouetted three or four times into oncoming traffic before coming to a halt facing back the way I'd come. I recall at the time two emotions:

fear, certainly, but also anger at all the drivers sounding their horns at me. Did they think I was spinning on purpose and would stop if they tooted their horns?

So I put my foot down (metaphorically) and said that I would not be driving in sand. Or through water. Or up mountains. I would happily drive the long, straight Namibian roads that you could see stretching for up to fifty kilometers ahead, chalk white in the sun. Lucy agreed readily: she would do the exciting driving, and I could do the dull stuff. Both of us were happy with this arrangement, and it was yet another example of how differently we view the world despite being so similar in temperament in other ways. What was exciting for Lucy provoked moderate to severe anxiety in me, while knowing exactly what to expect road wise for the next fifty kilometers was a soothing comfort to me and a source of frustrated boredom for Lucy. I think my temerity had a polarizing effect on Lucy's bravado, too. If she knew I was mildly panicked, any doubts she might have about a situation had to be suppressed—otherwise we'd both lose the plot—so she would wear a mantle of confidence in times of adversity and only later admit that she'd been a bit unnerved herself.

When we were approaching the prospect of driving fifty kilometers of deep, sandy road to get to Khaudum, I reminded Lucy that she would be taking the wheel, and she agreed that she was looking forward to some serious, hard-core 4x4 driving. When we actually drove out of Tsumkwe onto the sandy stretch that would be our path for the next several hours, Lucy was in exhilarated mood and greeted Up It Yo's bounces and lurches with whoops and hollers. I, on the other hand, spent a lot of time grimly hanging on to Up It Yo's roof with both hands. One particularly vicious lurch bounced me right out of my seat, cracking my head on the helpfully placed compartment on the windscreen where the rearview mirror should have been. I drank some more water. Lucy ate a few more rusks. We couldn't have stopped to changed drivers even if I'd been willing to—if we stopped, the sand would swallow our wheels and we'd never start again.

I had another look at the maps and noted that some of the route into, and the entire route out of, Khaudum was marked with exclamation marks. The maps showed the road as a thin green line, and along the middle of it, like the white lines in the middle of the road, were all these exclamation marks. Generally, an exclamation mark is a friendly sign, denoting something funny. This is not the case on Namibian maps—nor on Namibian road signs. On a map, an exclamation mark means that the road is so treacherous that you must travel in a convoy of at least two, just in case one car gets bogged down in sand, trampled by an elephant, or punctures more than two tires (they only carry two spares each) or any other of the myriad disasters that can befall one in a desert.

On Namibian road signs, an exclamation mark can mean anything at all. Sometimes, it means there's a big dip ahead, or there are workmen in the road, or there's deep sand, large rocks, a steep slope. We particularly liked the exclamation mark signs that were situated on the blind brows of hills. The excitement and anticipation we built up: Would we be turning sharp left? Were there rocks in the road? Would the road be so narrow we could barely squeeze through the trees? It often ended in anticlimax. "What?" we would complain to each other. "What was that exclamation mark about? There's nothing exclamation marky here—just more road."

I was pleased to see Norma and Gottfried's car. They were clearly independent adventurers like us, and their company might be useful when we got to the ! bit of the road, although Gottfried seemed a tentative driver, and his wife was an elegant, petite blonde who didn't look as though she'd be much help in a crisis.

Lucy had been hunched over the wheel for hours, and I felt that the excitement of 4x4 adventuring was wearing a bit thin. I tried to encourage her to drink her water and fed her cereal rusks and mango sweets. Lucy's water bottle was a metal affair, given to her by a friend for use on our adventure, and Lucy was determined to use it. It sat in the cup holder on the dashboard in the sun. The metal container got hotter and hotter, and the water was virtually at boiling point most of the time. It was quite unpalatable, and Lucy didn't drink much. I wasn't worried though, as Lucy didn't have my mad metabolism that required me to constantly guzzle from a one-and-a-half-liter bottle of Namibia's finest spring water.

We finally reached the entrance to Khaudum. No gates, just a sign and a stonking great elephant skull propping up the erstwhile gate pillar. No one about either. We paused. Experience so far told us that there is often someone lurking in the undergrowth somewhere who pops out when a vehicle arrives. Nope. Not a sausage. So we shrugged, didn't need to wait for our German friends—now nicknamed Norma and Gottfried—and drove on. More deep sand, but at least we were in Khaudum National Park now, the most out-of-the-way, game-filled, unpopularized, and best-kept secret in Namibia. Cool!

The southern campsite, Sikerete, was only about ten kilometers into the reserve. I'm not calling it a park anymore because that suggests something civilized, with flower beds, benches, and ducks in a pond. This is a park like Yellowstone is a park, or the Amazon jungle is a park (OK, it isn't, but you get the picture). The track to the campsite was just the same deep sand as the road, but we'd got used to it by now. The road then forked. A hand-painted plyboard sign said Camp Office one way, Bungalow the other way. Bungalow? A bit odd. We took the office route.

The office turned out to be a shack, a bit like my falling-down garden shed, but boarded up and heavily defended against attack with wire mesh over all the glassless windows. There was no one about, no other vehicles, no sign of life anywhere. There was a work store of some sort, with stacks of piping, timber, and barrels. There were clearings under the trees, which I took to be campsites. We parked up, and I did the routine unpacking of tents and put one up because I like to get organized as quickly as possible.

It was then that I realized that I was overheating. It was just after noon, the hottest part of the day, and my skin was starting to feel chilly. A clear sign of hyperthermia. I'd been drinking water but not enough, as I had been concentrating on the driving. The windows had been closed because of the dust we'd thrown up. I had a headache, so it was time to sit in the shade of the work store, drink, and eat.

One thing about Teri, she always seems to relax. She got the food out onto plates and lounged on a rock with her book. In the sun! Perhaps it's the Jamaica living that's made Teri impervious to heat. In Canada, in a chilly autumn, I was as happy as a polar bear. Rain, wind, and freezing nights. Teri…well, not a happy bunny. So the tables were turned now. The revenge of the canoe trip! I did not feel well.

After a bit of a siesta and refueling on water and rehydration powder (always blackcurrant flavor!?), I realized I was being eaten alive by mozzies so decided to put the other tent up. It was a good job I didn't bother earlier. It hadn't occurred to us to wonder why Norma and Gottfried had not settled for this campsite. We'd had neither sight nor sound of them. The vehicle that did arrive in the camp was the warden's. An open-topped jeep in olive-green and khaki safari colors and sporting an official-looking logo on the doors swept into the camp to park by the office. A cheerful local (Herero?) chap in a smart, dark-green game warden uniform jumped out and strolled over, and sporting the usual cheery smile, commenced with the Namibian niceties we were learning to perform.

"Good afternoon. How are you today?" he said.

"Good afternoon to you too. We're very well, thank you. How are you?" Teri replied. I smiled and nodded.

"I am very good, thank you. My name is Philip. I am one of the wardens," he replied, smiling and holding out his hand. "I am very pleased to meet you." Teri took the hand.

"Hello, Philip. I'm Teri. This is Lucy."

There followed a thorough round of "Hello. Pleased to meet you," accompanied by handshakes.

This performance, we'd observed so far, is carried out by everyone regardless of relationship. We'd performed the ritual with the car park attendant in Windhoek. We'd done the same with the taxi drivers, the Motown Hotel receptionist, the man on the Windhoek street when we stopped to ask the way, even the San couple we'd met earlier and given oranges in exchange for directions. It was impossible to shorten it, circumvent it, or improve upon it. I am not sure what would happen in an emergency. What if there's a fire in the hotel? What happens if you get arrested? What if you are desperate for the loo, and there's an attendant present? We were to find out about at least two of these.

He proceeded to give us lots of information about Khaudum and supplied us with a sort of map, marking which waterholes were dry so not to bother with, which tracks were "deep sand" (?), and where the elephants were—of which, he said, there were hundreds. Wow. He also explained, before he disappeared again, that we could camp there if we wanted, but the bungalows were a bit safer, if a bit wrecked, and there were washrooms by them. Bugger. I had to take the tent down again, pack it in Up It Yo, and feel an idiot. We drove down the track signposted Bungalow.

Some eight hundred meters down this track was the official campsite, or what was left of it. Opening up before us was a war zone. Like the Vietnamese villages in *Apocalypse Now* after the helicopters had bombed the hell out of them. They had been wooden huts with reed roofs, meshed windows, and even plumbed, but the elephants had rearranged the furniture, big time. Apparently they try to get to the water within the plumbing and destroy everything in their efforts. The huts were dotted about singly among the trees, quite apart from each other, making lovely secluded spots for each company of campers to enjoy some solitude. There were only two habitable huts left. The rest had stripped roofs, caved-in walls, or were just foundations and rubble. Teri and I found one fairly intact shack with mesh windows and most of the roof left in situ. At least I wouldn't have to put the tents up. Unfortunately, no tents meant no mozzie protection. We had mozzie nets with us—just in case—so we arranged these in the bungalow to cover our sleeping mats. I had to screw them into one of the roof beams and hang them down over the mats, spread out on the floor and weighted down with various tins of beans, beer, and handy rocks. Seemed to work OK.

It was late afternoon, and there was a waterhole called Tsoanna only six kilometers away where Philip had said there were elephants. So a quick drive down before the sun disappeared was in order. We had only seen one elephant, and that was in Etosha, which felt rather tame and controlled. Khaudum was different. The area was unfenced, and completely wild animals migrated across it at will. It was their territory. So when we crested a small hill and saw the pan and waterhole below us, *heaving* with forty to fifty elephants, we were blown away! From the small hide we crept into, we watched families from several different herds sharing the water and shepherding very small infants among the mass of tree-trunk legs and backsides to the water. They splashed themselves, wallowed, flapped their dripping ears, caressed each other with their trunks, and, group by group, moved away or entered to take their share. We watched in awe. We were the interlopers, being privileged to observe them.

A sudden stirring from a sentinel elephant on lookout announced a group of lions. Three lionesses appeared to our right, hovering on the edge of the muddy side of the waterhole. There, it was churned-up mud with no clear water. The elephants were hogging the drinkable stuff. We watched as the matriarch lion made her way round the hole and crept closer to the water. The sentinel flapped its ears and trumpeted at her. She persisted, creeping, belly low, toward the water. The other two lions, possibly her fully grown cubs, watched from a safe distance. The sentinel elephant moved. He came round our side and stood defiantly, blocking her way to the water. She backed off and slowly made her way round the elephants back to her brood. Was she in a bad mood! As soon as she reached them, there was an almighty scrap. She laid into one of them with no messing, dust flying, roars and growls of fury! She gave them what for!

We just got back to our falling-down hut before sunset—a sudden change from light to dark with little twilight to warn you. My rusks had gone. I'd left them by my sleeping bag in the hut. A full packet had been raided through a meshed and secured "safe" hut, and not a hint as to the culprit. This was where we would spend the night.

Tsoanna waterhole, Khaudum.

CHAPTER 8

THE ART OF FIRE MAKING AND THE CASE OF THE STRANGE WHITE POWDER

So, this was real safari! We were on our own in the middle of nowhere. Lions free ranging, elephants wrecking camps, and nature going on around us with all its teeth and claws. No help on the end of a phone (no signal); no shops, safety gear, guides, or rule books. We were living out of the back of Up It Yo, thanks to Teri's head chef skills, and living off the land thanks to my fire foraging and tending. Even the wardens had long gone, and we never saw them again. Our fellow campers were ensconced in one of the bungalows and kept themselves to themselves. So far, when we had encountered anyone, they seemed to have gas cookers and lights, comfy fold-up chairs, and hot water. Pah! Although, Norma and Gottfried did seem awfully comfortable.

We slept on the floor of our bungalow inside jury-rigged mozzie nets. I say "slept"; I, for one, had an ear tuned to the rustlings somewhere above my head, the basso profundo roars in the distance, and the incessant, high-pitched whine of a highly motivated mozzie.

Breakfast was becoming a well-oiled machine: get the fire going, kettle on, nose about for lions, rhino, or any other what have you that might be lurking, drink tea, ablute, eat porridge, pack up tents. Teri is more domesticated than me. She washes up diligently, neatly stows away, and tries not to tut while I forget where I put the tent bags.

Our next challenge was to drive through Khaudum to the northern gate and find the official camp area to spend the night. As Teri rightly pointed out to me (several times), the track was marked with exclamation marks on the map. This meant, basically, "Don't go there." However, we were forewarned by Philip that the western route was deep sand and dry waterholes, but we could take the eastern route, taking in the waterholes at Dussi and Leeupan. Note to self: always follow the advice of knowledgeable locals.

The track was by now no surprise, perhaps even better than we had grown to expect. Up It Yo coped ably in four-wheel drive at about twenty miles an hour, which gives plenty of time to not spot the antelope and bushbucks that spring through the undergrowth in a blur. The first waterhole was a rather too well man-made reservoir that was devoid of animals. We paused awhile, waiting in Up It Yo to see if anything would happen. Nothing did, so we drove on to the next. As we rounded a hillock, the waterhole opened out in front of us, and even we managed to spot the roan antelope gathered on its edge. Diverting round the area, we approached the hide on stilts from behind. No other vehicles, nobody about. Great. We parked and crept up to the hide to climb the steps, and suddenly a voice said, "Hello." Jeez! It might just as well have said "Boo!" A guy in camouflage fatigues lay underneath the hide, reading a magazine and cradling an AK-47 in his lap. Teri quickly resumed normality through years of customer service training and exchanged pleasantries while I got over the fright. It's not every day you chat about the weather with someone sporting the world's most ubiquitous killing tool. Being English, Teri and I are not used to weapons of any kind. The UK government even frowns on my pruning knife if it strays beyond my garden. I tried not to see any resemblance between our new best friend and newsreel footage of participants of guerrilla warfare, and to be fair, his indolence was reassuring. From a slightly strained and limited interchange, we gathered he was there to turn the water on and off. Clearly a taxing job; however, he mentioned keeping an eye out for rhino poachers, which probably explained the AK-47. He also pointed to a small tent in the distance with signs of domestication, so he clearly lived on site for the duration. We had got used to the idea that workers in remote places (most of Namibia, obviously) often lived on site, be that at roadworks or, in this case, guarding duties. This evidence of legitimacy at least meant he wasn't actually a poacher and had some governance over his behavior to us. I wondered if he'd ever actually fired his AK-47 at ne'er-do-wells. Quite possibly.

Rhino horn. Hmm. In England, stately homes have been burgled not for the duchess's jewels but for the rhino trophies on the walls, sporting their magnificent horns. Since rhino horn is highly prized in China as a cure for cancer (which it totally isn't), the price of a rare commodity clearly goes up. It is even worth raiding museums for antiquated rhino heads. We had of course known about the poaching threat to rhinos before setting foot on African soil, but seeing Namibia's antipoacher tactics brought it home. Ensuring the more remote areas are guarded is only one approach. Co-opting locals as governmental eyes and ears, as we found in Tsumkwe, was another. But Namibia has gone one step further. There is now a program to surgically dehorn every rhino in Namibian national parks. This is no mean feat, considering the horn grows back every four to five years, so repeated operations are in store for these patients. And there are estimated to be about 1,750 Namibian rhinos, so someone is going to be busy. This program is not without critics, of course. There is the argument that it makes rhino horn even more rare and so more valuable; the stockpile of removed horn could sustain or encourage a commercial supply if it is released for sale; the surgery is a threat to the rhinos and, apparently, it might not even work. Poachers are reported to still shoot dehorned rhino either because they can't tell it's dehorned before shooting, or they simply want to take out dehorned rhino to save them tracking the wrong animals. Also, the stump that is left is still valuable. Some people will stop at nothing—literally. There is also a plan to use drones to monitor poachers. It is not clear how this will work in the parks with all the visitors' vehicles driving around. Perhaps Up It Yo will soon have an identifying number on its bonnet to show it is an innocent tourist. Perhaps the chap with the AK-47 is not such a bad idea.

We drove to the next waterhole and found a rather dramatic hide. A set of rustic wooden steps led up to a wooden platform, which had a low rush wall around it and plank benches. We sat on the benches and waited. Within minutes a group of elephants with a baby approached from behind our hide and headed toward the water. Then another group of elephants approached from the far side of the waterhole. They drank and swam and wallowed a bit. We spent an hour or so admiring the lumbering great beasts and watching how they interacted with each other.

Then we decided to return to the car, only to find ourselves separated from our vehicle by another group of elephants. We turned back to the hide and saw that the original group were on their way home, a route that was bringing them directly toward us. Knowing that elephants can run faster than humans, and not wanting to draw attention to ourselves with an unseemly sprint to the hide, we just walked very, very fast, and thankfully scrambled up the wooden steps before they got too near. We watched as they ambled off behind us from whence they came. After allowing them a reasonable length of time to be on their way, we again headed for the truck. This time we made it and started the slow drive off back to camp.

Except that after only a few minutes, we found ourselves on a narrow track with an elephant ahead, another two off to our left, and one more on our right. We had no option but to stop the car and wait. We were pleased to see that the baby appeared to be with its mother; it would have been a disaster if we'd unwittingly put ourselves between those two. It was bad enough being in the thick of them as it was. After a tense hour or so, they eventually got on the move again, so that we could too.

Khaudum campsite is at the northerly end of the park, about seventy or eighty kilometers from Sikereti. The route between the two campsites opens out into wide plains in places so we were able to see how well populated the park is for many species of kudu, wildebeest, hartebeest, and oryx, as well as steenbok and duiker, which we had learned to distinguish. We'd even seen a troop of vervet monkeys, about twenty to thirty in all, hanging around one much-depleted tree beside a waterhole. We had seen baboons from day one—alongside the road from the airport—but I was gratified to see the monkeys. Apart from the Big Five, surely monkeys should be ticked off the safari spotter's list? In the park there are reportedly also leopard, wild dog, and spotted hyena, but they are hard to see, as they stay in the dense bush.

The farther north we went, the wetter it became as we approached the Khaudum Omuramba—clearly a green, wide river valley more reminiscent of natural English lowland. There were more trees and fords to negotiate, and the usual deep-rutted tracks, which were now wet mud. We found the campsite on climbing out of the omuramba and cresting a hilltop that gave a wide view of the land we had just traversed. A good spot for a camp!

There was no one around as usual, but we quickly identified the wrecked shacks that amounted to a toilet/shower block after the elephants had visited. We drove round in a few circles inspecting each one, but there was only one still standing, so deciding where to pitch the tents was easy. As we did our reconnoiter, we noticed a strange white trail along the track. This was odd. It ran in a thin line in the middle of the track, running almost continuously, with the odd lump here and there. It went round the whole campsite. We parked up, and I went to investigate. Tracking back, like the Great White Hunter following spoor, I followed the trail round the circle we had just driven, arriving, inevitably, at the tailgate of Up It Yo. Ah. Our neatly packed foodstuffs included three large bags of maize flour we wanted to use to exchange with likely locals. The bags were well mashed, and flour was everywhere. We wondered if we had left a trail all the way back to Sikereti. Probably.

When we were halfway through putting up tents, a strange fellow came walking slowly down the track to our camp. He seemed quite bemused by the white trail. He stood and stared. Not the great conversationalist, this one. I left the socially awkward moment to Teri, who worked some charm on him, enough to send him whence he came, though he made us both nervous. It was the only time I felt uncomfortable about us being two lone females in the wilderness. I think, without saying so, we both became a little more watchful over each other and ensured we didn't leave the other alone.

I love making the campfire. In Namibia the challenge is not to burn down the whole shebang: fire, brush, tents, and trees. We would see fires out of control later—not caused by us! In Canada, the challenge was getting it to light with wet wood. I'd found the perfect fire starter in the Canadian boreal forest: birch bark. Its resin keeps the wood dry and burns like phosphorus. Another Canadian trick was collecting the shavings left by the beavers. These made great kindling to put on top of the bark. There are neither of these commodities in Namibia, but kindling can still be a challenge. Small sticks and twigs are so dry that they burn up before the bigger logs can catch. Medium-sized logs were now often in short supply, whereas earlier I'd found myself spurning them as being not big enough to warrant bending down for. Bit of a mistake. I'd already experimented with dry rhino dung as fuel, but it clearly lacked the essential qualities—much to Teri's relief, as I was storing the deposits on the back seat. By now I had learned the difference between the challenges of Canada in autumn and Namibia in the dry season and had made sure we had a good range of thick and medium logs, while smaller kindling was always on hand wherever we were.

That evening I strode into the immediate bush for the small kindling to get the flame going. I was after small tree litter, dry grasses, twiggy branches. The bush floor was speckled with the fallen leaves of aspen-like trees: small, round, golden brown. Just the kind of speckling of, say, a leopard. It may have been because of my heightened sense of danger from our strange visitor, but I became very aware that I would not see a leopard if I tripped over it. I stood and studied the bush around me. The tents and Up It Yo were just over there behind me, Teri rummaging in the food boxes waiting for a fire to cook on. Between us was bush was closing in around me. In front, more bush, leaf litter, camouflage. Camouflage everywhere. Leopards everywhere. I imagined a pair of amber eyes drilling me with their intensity, hunched body tensed, ready to spring, flattened ears, quivering with excitement and the nearness of dinner. Me. Erm, Teri…

I shook myself out of it. Stop it! I think I've got enough kindling. Yes, definitely. Time to make my way back, slowly, backward, back to camp. That was the only time on the entire journey that I had that sense of acute awareness of being prey. Considering we were camping in the wild most of the time, with free-ranging predators and large beasts always a possibility…was it just stupidity, or were we simply become accustomed to the reality of the dangers in the wilderness? They say the most likely cause of death for tourists in Namibia is road accidents, though we had noticed that locals delight in telling you how someone and so-and-so recently was eaten/killed by a lion/crocodile/hippo. Personally, I think the most dangerous, and annoying, animal in Southern Africa is the mosquito.

Our tents both had in-built mosquito nets, which was useful for me because I am a mosquito magnet. The mosquito is, of course, the world's most prolific killer, or at least is the plasmodium parasite it carries. It kills about one million people every year, mostly children, and mostly in African countries; 90 percent of deaths are African, and most victims are under five years old. It is one of the reasons that sub-Saharan Africa was little known by Europeans until the nineteenth century. Any European spending much time there would not get home to talk about it. Teri and I were hardly comparable to the early European explorers because we were equipped with medicine. Yes, Up It Yo and the local supermarkets were contributing big time to our little adventure, but what was really making it possible was antimalarials, yellow fever jabs, and boiled/purified water. Early explorers made the mistake of following the major rivers to enter the inner heart of the great continent rather than attempting the impenetrable bush. Overland treks with horses didn't work because the horses soon sickened. Bearers were attempted, but often they became sick, while the European deaths easily outnumbered the local death rates. So river journeys were attempted. These were even worse because that's where the mosquitoes are most dense and will deliver malaria, yellow fever, or dengue fever. Take your pick. When will the mosquito-borne Zika virus in South America soon spread to Africa and become endemic? Just add another pest to the list.

The thing about malaria is that, even if you survive it, it never leaves you. Once in the body, the parasite invades the cells and hunkers down for a bit while feeding on the hemoglobin and multiplying themselves. At a synchronized time, the infected cells burst, and new parasites swamp the body. The immune response kicks in to fight the "infection," creating high fever while it does so. In Namibia, local people have malaria. With every breeding cycle of the plasmodium parasite within their red blood cells, carriers will become feverish with their own immune response to the debris from the breakdown of their red blood cells. The new parasites invade more red blood cells, and everything dies down again until the next generation explodes from the cells. Hence the cyclical nature of the fevers.

The anemia caused by malaria is chronic. The red blood cells become poor at carrying oxygen; they become sticky and clump together. It makes the infected person permanently tired, lethargic, and prone to cold. Death from a diseased spleen is not uncommon. This is what is thought to have killed England's once lord protector, Oliver Cromwell. No, he didn't go to Africa, but England had malaria once, especially in the wetlands of Norfolk where Oliver Cromwell lived until he decided to start the English Civil War in the 1600s. Most deaths, though, are caused by cerebral malaria; the clumps form in the capillaries of the brain and cause a blockage and swelling, and then death.

Our taxi driver at Windhoek had told us he'd just recovered from a bout of malaria. We were a bit surprised. I don't know why. I now know that most people in rural, malaria-rife environments will be living with it. Perhaps it's no wonder we had found life in Namibia on a go-slow. Everyone is probably anemic. The scary thing is, the plasmodium adapts to the antimalarials faster than the pharmaceutical companies can develop them. Bill and Melinda Gates, plus a lot of governments and mining/oil companies, are pumping loads of dosh into global research to keep up. If they fail, countries blighted with malaria will constantly struggle to gain a robust population to compete with the industrial nations of the world.

Elephants block our escape route in Khaudum.

CHAPTER 9

THE ROAD TO NOWHERE: PYLONS AND "THE RIME OF THE ANCIENT MARINER"

We left Khaudum to the destructive elephants and headed up to the far northeast of Namibia. This is the location of the Caprivi Strip, home to hippos, crocodiles, and water buffalo, as well as the usual wildlife. We also thought we would have a little casual hop over the border into Botswana.

We set off with confidence. The road was fairly unnavigable, so Lucy was at the wheel, and I was reading the maps. We circumnavigated a vast salt pan and drove through dense scrubland dotted with dilapidated kraals and tumbledown mud huts. For quite a long stretch, we followed the course of a bush fire and drove over smoldering embers of twigs with little plumes of white smoke. At one point the fire had encroached onto the track, and we drove over the flames, which was a little bit alarming, but Up It Yo coped, and the tires didn't melt.

This part of our trip was devoid of wildlife, and the scorched landscape was the least attractive scenery so far. There were no people about, and the radio didn't work, so we had nothing to entertain ourselves except each other. We tried a bit of I Spy, but after we'd done *s* for *sky* and *s* for *sun* and *s* for *sand* and *s* for *smoke*, we lacked further inspiration and inclination.

After an hour or so, the right-hand turn promised by two of the maps had failed to materialize. Instead, a little later, we were confronted by a fork in the road. What to do? Lucy looked at me enquiringly, and I stared back with equal blank indecision.

I was reminded of a cognitive course I delivered to a group of young prisoners a few years ago. We were discussing the fact that life comprises a series of decisions. "What would you do if you arrived at a fork in the road?" I asked. Everhard, who wasn't too bright and had a limited grasp of polite language, replied, "I'd f——king pick it up, miss." But when I suggested to Lucy, "F——king pick it up!" she looked at me as if I had completely lost the plot. Which I think I had to some extent—the tedium of the journey had sent me a bit bush crazy.

I think we made the decision based on where the sun was. Inept calculations about where it had risen, what time it was, and the direction we wanted to head told us to keep the sun on our right. So we took the right fork and carried on. For hours. Ploughing through deep sand, bouncing over sporadic rocky outcrops, driving around the occasional tree that had been struck down by the fire, and keeping the sun on our right.

Lucy ate rusks.

I drank water.

Lucy drove on grimly.

There was one highlight amid the tedium: we saw the most amazing electric-blue bird. We first spotted it sitting on a blackened tree branch. It was about the size of a magpie and had a similar two-tone blue-black plumage. And then it took flight, and the bright turquoise-blue of its underwings was just stunning against the burnt black and gray landscape. We saw lots of brightly colored little birds throughout our trip, and indeed entertained many of them at various campsites. Everything except me, it appeared, liked Lucy's rusks, but this bird was truly magnificent and (possibly) made the interminable journey worthwhile.

After another hour or two, we realized we were lost. Not only were our maps rubbish, but clearly the sun had been disobligingly moving in the wrong direction. It was then that we came across a pylon. No, more than that—a row of pylons. We reasoned to each other that you don't see many rows of pylons in the Namibian bush, and if we just followed the pylons, they would eventually lead us to something. If we were lucky, they'd lead us to a town. If we were less lucky, they'd lead us to an electricity substation. Either way, they would lead us, we surmised, off the road to Nowhere and back on a road to Somewhere. By this stage, our expectations of getting where we wanted to go were zero. Anywhere would do. So despite the fact that there wasn't actually a track of any sort, we turned the truck and headed off through the sand in the company of pylons.

The drive through Khaudum had been fun! I loved weaving our way through scrubby bush and round fallen trees. Up It Yo was constantly lashed by whippy branches, which just proved that not a lot of traffic passes this way. Teri would yelp every now and again as a branch came into her open window. At one point the wing mirror her side was flattened by a sturdier-than-expected sapling. It was suggested that I steer a little less vigorously into the bush on her side of the track. I didn't have much choice, as the branches were coming in my side too. Teri just picked thorns out of her elbow. We swapped over for a while as the track was quite hard sand. Teri drove through the trees, and I tried to video a "typical day's drive" from the passenger seat.

The bouncing handheld shots were not supposed to be special effects. Neither were the expletives coming from the driver's seat.

When we left Khaudum National Park, the track was no better. The maps at this point were worse than useless. The track seemed to go in all directions, none of which was the right one for us. We should have been hitting a track heading northeast, so we took one that was vaguely going in a northerly direction. And then it went left, then right, then round. Then there was a crossroads, a fork, and then we were in a village. Slap bang in the middle of someone's backyard. Surrounded by cattle. And a barking dog. There were kraals, round huts, and a big tree where there was clearly a meeting going on, because all the villagers were sat under it. Of course, they all turned to stare at us. I was driving again because the sand had become really deep, and there was no stopping because the last place I wanted to get stuck was in the middle of a village where everyone and all the invited neighbors would come and watch as I dug Up It Yo out of one hole and into the next. The sand was nearly up to the axles. I was driving in preexisting tracks that had caved in, with the clearance under Up It Yo in minus figures. There was no way I was going to stop. If the barking dog persisted in jumping in front of Up It Yo, it would be an ex-dog. Teri waved politely, employing her best diplomatic body language, I gripped the wheel, eyes focused on the track. Bugger the dog. There were two exits to this village. One track diverted left around the village through more sand; one went right and uphill, onto harder ground. I went right.

We had no idea what the etiquette should be for arriving in a village. The polite thing to do, presumably, would be to stop, say hello, ask, "Does anyone want a lift to the nearest town, road, sign of civilization?" Then at least we'd have a navigator. With hindsight, this would have been a good idea. I think what put us off was the interminable greetings that would ensue, the exchange of goods, the inquisitive bodies all trying to get in the back of Up It Yo, and probably the rigmarole of negotiating everything through sign language with the local bigwig. And of course we'd probably end up taking several people on exchange visits between villages. So we drove on. In the wrong direction.

After a while we agreed that the track we were following was not the one on the map. This road was undecided whether it wanted to head north, northwest, or suddenly turn south. We had a compass, which only told us we were going in the wrong direction, and we had the sun, which confirmed that the compass was not lying. This was an important moment in our whole adventure, one of which we should have taken more notice. In Namibia there is no point trying to navigate as you would in Britain, or France, or Canada, or, well, anywhere with tarmac roads that stay put. You have to navigate as though you are at sea: with a chart (our maps), a compass (yep, ticked that one), and dead reckoning (impossible when you can't read the milometer because the sun shines on it, and it's covered in dust anyway). Yes, we could have used a GPS device. But they only tell you where you are. Not how to get to where you want to be.

I was starting to worry about Teri by the fourth or fifth crossroads/fork/180-degree bend. She'd gone quiet, which is usually a bad sign. We'd just been round another three- or four-mile semicircle and arrived at another crossroads. By "crossroads" I mean our track in deep sand was crossed at ninety degrees by another vague set of tire tracks in deep sand. We'd been through a fire, which was alarming, as it grew the closer we got to it, and I don't think it was quite the "controlled burning" we told each other it might have been. We'd passed a few kraals that appeared to be the farthest from the reach of the modern world you could get outside the Amazon jungle, and we were using a lot of fuel.

Our circular track had taken us from heading northeast to heading southwest, so this other track was oriented northwest-southeast. Any direction north would do. Also, it was a service route running alongside arrow-straight electricity pylons. Deep joy! All we had to do was get into its tire tracks and follow wherever it went. This was easier said than done. Our deep-sand track weaved its way through dense bush. The northerly tire tracks did the same, also in deep sand. We had to somehow turn on a narrow track through the virgin sand to get on the other track, while hemmed in by trees. It's a bit like changing direction in a train. But we didn't have any points we could use to swap tracks.

I tried going straight for it at first, attempting to bounce Up It Yo across the bank of sand, but the back wheels just got bogged down. Although I was in low-ratio four-wheel drive, Up It Yo simply couldn't get a grip on the dry sand to climb over the bank, and there was no room between the trees to get a run up and drive straight through, back wheels following the front wheels. Up It Yo was a long-wheelbase vehicle, and the front wheels were cutting their own track, but the back wheels were burying themselves in sand and brush. The last thing I wanted to do was get the spade out and dig a route through to the other tracks, so I had a think. I noticed that the front wheels had made a new track, so I backed up and used the front wheels to make a route through the sand for the back wheels. Teri thought I'd gone a bit potty, as this entailed driving in the wrong direction and then going back and forth a few times. But it worked. Up It Yo bounced across, sand flying, bushes scraping, Teri yelping as her head hit the roof again and her vertebrae took a beating, but we were suddenly pointing northwest and facing down a line of telegraph poles as far as the eye could see.

Which is a long way in Namibia.

I had read somewhere that a useful measure of whether an experience can be considered an uncomfortable trial or a full-on ordeal is how much of "The Rime of the Ancient Mariner" you could read before the experience ended. Neither of us had read the "Rime," but I think we could safely categorize the pylon journey as an ordeal. We could probably have read Nelson Mandela's biography, all eight hundred-plus pages of it, and still had time for a couple of verses from the Ancient Mariner himself.

I have since read the "Rime," and think that, based on this work, Coleridge seems a miserable sort of a poet. Deathfires, drought, rotting corpses, a dead albatross, and inclemency of weather don't make for particularly cheerful reading. I came across a verse that I wish I'd known before our trip, as it would have been perfect repeated ad infinitum as we struggled through the sand:

"There passed a weary time. Each throat

Was parched, and glazed each eye.

A weary time! A weary time!

How glazed each weary eye."

I was also taken with the description of the protagonists: "We were a ghastly crew," but I fear that if I'd told Lucy what I thought of us in our pylon purgatory, she might have hit me between the eyes with a rusk.

The pylon route took us several more hours. We tried to keep positive and assured each other that we'd made the right decision in abandoning a track for a pylon, and we encouraged each other by agreeing that we seemed to be driving in a northerly direction, which had been the original plan, so we weren't doing too badly. But deep down, I think we were both feeling a strange hybrid of boredom and anxiety.

When we eventually reached the end of the line of pylons, it was to emerge onto a lovely tarmac road. Yes, it was the substation option and not a lively town with people and petrol, but it was a road! We were once again on the road to Somewhere.

Lucy pulled in to the next roadside picnic area we came to. Instead of the usual drink of water with lunch, we decided we'd earned a cup of tea. While Lucy got the wherewithal for a fire and a cuppa, I perused the maps and discovered that we were about sixty kilometers farther west than we'd intended, but the lovely road was heading Botswana-ward.

The Botswana-Namibia border on the Namibian side is patrolled by vets in military-style uniforms, as are many of the conservancy borders within the country. The first time Lucy and I were accosted by vets who demanded to check out our cargo, we were a bit perplexed. I was driving, so got out of the truck and went through the polite ritual of hellos and how are yous before opening up the boot.

Unfortunately, this was the day after a regrettable incident with a wine carton. The previous evening, I'd propped the five-liter box of wine on top of the tool box to make an impromptu bar, but had inadvertently left the little tap a bit askew at the end of the evening, and the wine had dripped out slowly throughout the night. The following morning, when going into the back to seek out porridge and teabags, we were assailed by the stench of a warm brewery. And as the rear of Up It Yo was enclosed, with no windows, the heat of the day had only reinforced the pong by the time we got to the checkpoint.

The vets recoiled in amazement when I flung open the tailgate and invited them to search through our belongings looking for illicit foodstuffs. Although why anyone would be transporting raw meats and dairy through the desert in an unrefrigerated truck was a bit beyond me. They took in the smell, the huge (and sadly, nearly empty) wine box, and the crate of beer. They looked from one to the other of us and enquired if this was all for our consumption. We brazened it out by stating that we were on a very long trip and would possibly be sharing with (fictional) friends, so there wasn't really an excessive amount of alcohol in the car. And then I tried my distraction ploy—smiling winningly, admiring the vets' uniforms, and cooing over a little boy with a puppy who was with them. On being given the puppy to hold, I overcame the natural instinct to avoid potential rabies, pinkeye, or kennel cough, and stroked and cuddled enthusiastically.

On that occasion they waved us through, and we incurred no penalties. At another border, we weren't so lucky—the vet decided that our tin of Viennese sausages contravened the regulations, so he offered to take it off our hands and have it for his lunch. Further, he suggested that if we gave him N$10, he'd be able to buy some bread and a beer to go with his (our) sausages. We considered this a fairly modest bribe and obliged him with his luncheon voucher.

At the border with Botswana, we filled in forms in triplicate and spent half an hour or so being questioned in the cramped border offices before getting the necessary stamps in our passports. We returned to the truck, watched by two languid-looking officials who were relaxing on a bench in the sun. They waited until I'd started the engine and was heading off to the Botswana gate before one of them leapt up and shouted at us to wait to be inspected. I felt inexplicably grumpy with them, probably because I was bored with the officialdom and irritated by the rude manner in which we were being addressed. I stopped the truck and told him to help himself and to have a good look in the boot, but made no move to open it up for him. He clearly didn't take his work too seriously, as he just peered into the cab, took in the rusk crumbs, warm water bottles, used wet wipes, and torn maps, and waved us on.

We then went into the offices on the Botswana side of the border and filled in identical forms in triplicate. By the time we'd finished answering questions about our car, our visit, our intentions, and our cargo, we knew not only our own but also each other's passport numbers off by heart, as well as the chassis number of Up It Yo.

Botswana was not radically different from Namibia on first impressions. The main difference was that the houses were small brick-built oblongs as opposed to small mud-built circles. The roads were potholed, and the donkeys grazed by the roadside in much the same way either side of the border. We were hoping to do some shopping in Botswana—fresh fruit and vegetables would be nice, maybe some Botswana wine, a souvenir or two, and most importantly, petrol.

I tried to remember when we'd last filled up with fuel. Up It Yo had a reserve tank that held eighty liters, and this was used first before the main tank kicked in and the fuel gauge started to move. So for the first eighty liters, we were driving blind, the gauge showing a reassuringly full tank. We'd got into the habit of asking each other, "Are we using any fuel yet?" checking the stationary gauge, and saying happily, "Nope! Not yet!" As soon as the needle started to move, we would make filling the reserve tank a priority, thereby ensuring that we were always at the maximum fuel capacity that we could be. We'd filled up in Tsumkwe, but the pylon route had been so lengthy that we were probably at the end of our reserve tank.

We checked the maps and were relieved to see that there were several petrol stations in the nearest big town, Shakawe, and more in Maun, a bit farther south. As we pulled up at the first petrol station, the fuel gauge was indeed moving downward. There were two ladies sitting under the shade of a beautiful tree with bright blue flowers. They were playing cards and made no move to serve us with our fuel. Lucy jumped out and asked them if they'd be so kind as to fill our tank. She was a bit nonplussed to be informed that there was no fuel in the gas station but rallied and asked with an optimistic smile when they were expecting a delivery. Her optimism waned visibly when they explained that they had no idea when there'd be a delivery, and the last one had been three months ago.

Naively, we encouraged each other that, no problem, Shakawe was awash with garages, so we could simply drive to the next one, which was only a few miles away. Except that when we got there, the news was even worse: the pumps there were dry and had been for six months.

I'm afraid I started to feel a bit panicky at this stage. We'd been warned that fuel supplies in Namibia could be a bit hit and miss, and that occasionally gas stations would run out and we might have to await the next weekly delivery in order to fill up. While this would not be ideal, we envisaged that waiting in the vicinity of a gas station for up to a week would be inconvenient but manageable. But the Botswana fuel situation was in a whole other league. Would we really be marooned in Botswana for months with no means of transport? Our entry visas were only for three days, for heaven's sake. And I'd only booked a month off work.

Having established that the fuel situation in Botswana was a bit critical, we decided we should conserve what petrol we had left and find somewhere nearby to stay. Norma and Gottfried had told us about a lodge near the border where you could eat a full English breakfast on a terrace and watch crocodiles in the river that flowed through the grounds. Although crocs with an egg and bacon accompaniment seemed a surreal combination, we decided to give it a go.

The sign for the lodge had the name and a directional arrow but no mileage cited, so we turned off the main road and just hoped that it wasn't too far as we watched the fuel gauge edging down to our last half tank. Several kilometers later we drew up at a splendid wooden chalet-type building on stilts, with a sweeping staircase up to the large, airy reception area. Looking at the shiny floors, the massive sofas with overstuffed cushions, a gleaming bar area, and huge vases of exotic flowers, we felt distinctly underdressed with our shorts, dusty feet, and battered bush hats. In any other situation, we'd have beaten a hasty retreat to somewhere less imposing (and less expensive), but, acutely aware of the petrol situation, we weren't going to push our luck driving any farther.

I left Lucy shuffling from foot to foot uncomfortably by the reception desk and dived into the ladies'. I was even more discomfited when I looked in a mirror for the first time in days. I'd washed my hair a few days ago, but lack of hair dryer and styling products had left me with a haystack on my head. Makeup of any sort was fairly pointless in our style of travel, but I had been determined to "maintain standards" by wearing mascara and occasionally a slick of lipstick if it hadn't melted too much in the heat. But with my sunburnt face, baggy shorts, and bush hat complete with an assortment of feathers and quills collected on my travels, I was hardly a picture of elegance. A lot of people who know me were aghast when I told them of my plans to schlep around Africa without a full complement of toiletries and an extensive wardrobe. So, as a bit of a self-parody, I purchased a full-length black jersey evening dress with jewel-encrusted collar and wore it occasionally with my hiking boots and bush hat. Lucy took a few photos to prove that Teri couldn't rough it in the bush without mascara and a ball gown.

We were almost relieved to hear that there was no accommodation for us in this stylish place, but we really needed somewhere to stay close by, so we asked the proprietor for his recommendation. He was delighted to suggest a property on an island in the Okavango that could only be accessed by boat. It also happened to be owned by his son. The boat would be leaving from his jetty in about half an hour, when a South African family had organized themselves and their luggage for transport.

We fetched our rucksacks and a big coiled plaaswurst we'd purchased earlier and couldn't leave in the hot truck for a night. Then we adjourned to the manicured lawns near the jetty and awaited our boat.

The South Africans appeared to be traveling with their entire worldly goods, and it took most of the lodge staff several trips to get the various suitcases, cardboard boxes, carrier bags, ice boxes, fishing paraphernalia, an oxygen cylinder, and the four travelers to the jetty. The travelers themselves didn't actually carry anything; they just issued directions to the staff about what they wanted carried and where they wanted it carried to. I felt inward indignation on behalf of the Namibian staff who were being treated with casual arrogance.

Eventually, an hour or so later than planned, we set off. The boat driver was a knowledgeable and informative guide. We saw a crocodile draped elegantly over rocks on the river bank almost as soon as we set off, and I was convinced that it was a stunt crocodile, perched there conveniently for the tourists to exclaim excitedly and take photos. I resolved to check if it was still there on our return journey. We saw bee-eaters and cranes, all sorts of river birds of various colors, giant sapphire dragonflies, and the tail end of a few more crocodiles as they slid into the river on our approach. We saw hippo tracks through the rushes, but the hippos were a bit camera shy, and we didn't see any sets of eyes peering at us from water level.

The South African party were quite dismissive of the wildlife. They were here to fish, and that was the extent of their interest in the river. The large older gentleman, who kept his oxygen cylinder to hand, asked if anyone would mind if he smoked. We really wanted to say that yes, we would very much mind if he smoked, but in the interests of civility, Lucy replied that we would cope as long as he stayed downwind of us. He looked a bit startled, as he was clearly expecting to do exactly as he pleased regardless of how it affected others, so Lucy's stipulation came as an extraordinary curtailment. Apart from this, Lucy and I were ignored for the most part, which piqued me, although I was almost relieved that we were treated with the same disdain as the lodge staff.

We arrived at the jetty, and the hotel owner, clearly primed by dad, was waiting with a flotilla of staff ready to transfer the South Africans and their belongings from the boat to the lodge. Lucy and I had been allocated a solitary member of staff to escort us to our accommodation for the night. Given our disheveled state, we were delighted to find that our room (a wooden hut on stilts with copious muslin curtains, a shower, electricity, and a veranda) was at the far end of the estate and located on the river's edge. Perfect hippo-hunting location!

After hot showers and a sundowner on the veranda, we took our plaaswurst to the bar to entrust with the bartender to keep in his fridge and enjoyed our first cold wine for a week.

After Khaudum and the pylons, Teri and I seemed to now be in the lap of luxury. The hotel on the mainland looked like Treetops in

Kenya—famous for being the place Princess Elizabeth was staying in 1953 when told that she was now the queen of England, Scotland, Wales, and Northern Ireland and head of the entire Commonwealth. She would not have been out of place here. The lawns were immaculate, and Makalani palms swayed respectfully in a gentle breeze while garden staff raked already-raked paths just to be on show. And then the illusion was shattered by the party of South Africans who reminded me of everyone's distant relatives who turn up at weddings and embarrass the happy couple. Not only were they were loud, late, and rude, they were also heading for the same island resort in the Okavango as us, and we had to share the boat with them.

Fortunately, Teri and I have grown thick skins, so we ignored them ignoring us. The boat journey was fascinating anyway as it took in the local wildlife. The pilot took us into the banks to see skimmers, scarlet bee-eaters, and the ubiquitous crocodile. The South Africans were unimpressed, as they were only here for fishing. Kingfish are apparently prized for the battle they put up, and are quite edible too. People come a long way to the Okavango to fish here. In fact, everyone we met on the island was there to fish.

Having survived not being blown up on the boat by the too-near juxtaposition of an oxygen cylinder and a cigarette, we found our host was a joy where the unfortunate family were not. The other guests were interesting too. Mostly German, they were wary of Teri and me until Teri turned up for the communal evening meal in her bright pink Doc Martens. One brave soul complimented her on her footwear, and the ice was broken. These communal meals were strange to me (but not to Teri, who steered me through the etiquette), though they are common in African tourist lodges. While guests usually have separate tables, the meal is the same for everyone and served buffet style from a big pot, and everyone has to be there at the same time. Tonight's menu was stewed kudu with beans, which was delicious.

Earlier, I had noticed a penned-off area in the river with a walkway around the edges and jetty leading from the bank. This was the island's "swimming pool." Wherever I go on my travels, I try to do some wild-water swimming, but so far Namibia had been just too dangerous and a bit devoid of water. In South Australia I had trekked along the Murray River, miles from anywhere, a bit lost, and very hot. The river was just too tempting, so a quick skinny-dip was sheer joy. In Canada, both of us swam in the lakes, despite the cold. Very refreshing, although a bit risky due to "beaver fever"—basically a cryptosporidium infection of the small intestine. The so-called wilderness experience for some tourists can include toileting near river sources. This is not a good idea, as feces will be washed down into the watercourse to infect animals and other humans alike. Just dig a big hole away from any water; that's why a spade is really useful in a desert.

Anyway, this swimming pool gave me the chance to chalk up another wild swim, albeit in a penned section of the Okavango. Yes, I was aware of bilharzia (a.k.a. river blindness), caused by an unfriendly parasite that is waterborne. But I didn't intend to be long.

I took our drinks with me in their orange bag-on-a-rope. They would at least get a bit cool for later. The dip was very refreshing, and it was interesting to see all the debris from the river that had been caught up in the wire mesh that walled the pool. Quite a few bits of dead things, I think. I tied the bag to the mesh just under water for retrieval later.

As the sun sank behind the trees, I returned for our submerged drinks to find two young men swimming in the pool. This would save me a job, so I asked them to retrieve my bag for me. They looked quite puzzled at first but duly obliged, then realized what the bag contained. The penny dropped, and their faces lit up. "We're coming to your braai tonight!" one announced, clearly impressed with our new stock of cold beer. Fortunately, they didn't appear later in the evening, as there was not enough beer to go around.

The following morning we returned to the dining room for breakfast. The long banqueting table was unoccupied, and we were tempted to sit at each end and slide the salt and sugar to each other across the polished expanse of wood. Luckily, sense and good manners prevailed, and we sat together to be served a delicious breakfast of eggs and bacon and wurst. We were finally getting used to the barely cooked sausages and bacon (we'd tried asking for it to be well cooked, but the Namibians just carried on serving our food the way they liked to eat it—practically still alive), and had given up worrying about tapeworms and liver flukes.

We made a lot of phone calls to garages within a hundred-kilometer radius, but Botswana was resolutely dry. We then turned our attention to garages across the border, back in Namibia. We located a petrol station, with petrol, about fifty kilometers away. They said that they'd had a delivery the previous day, and if we hurried, we'd get there before they ran out again. We didn't waste time. We threw our belongings haphazardly into our rucksacks, commandeered the boat, and hotfooted it through the border controls to the garage.

Filling with fuel was always a bit of a fraught experience. First there was the lack of any orderly queue formation, with vehicles jostling like bumper cars trying to edge toward the pumps ahead of other drivers. We had to learn to use Up It Yo like a tank and barge it into gaps in the lines of cars. Then there would be a tense conversation with the attendants to see if they would accept a credit card. If they didn't, we'd have to go through our purse (me) and myriad pockets (Lucy) to see how much cash we could come up with. If we were lucky enough to have the wherewithal to fill the truck up, Lucy would get out and do the friendly chat business, while I sat in the driver's seat, bootless (couldn't drive in Doc Martens—too clumsy) and drank water. The first time we were filled up, I was alarmed by a sudden violent rocking of the car. I leapt out barefoot onto the dusty forecourt and looked for the marauding bull elephant that was ramming Up It Yo. Instead, I saw the two garage attendants leaning hard on the car and rocking it about with all their energy to disperse air bubbles in the tank. When you ask for a full tank, they make sure that is what you get.

Scarlet bee-eaters on the Okovango

Chapter 10

Rundu to Ruacana: The Vanishing Cow and Naked Dancing

We set off again with our mercifully full tank and aimed for Rundu. Refueling had been a nerve-jangling episode because the queues were long and more like a rugby scrum than the orderly waiting we are more used to in England. Perhaps everyone was anxious to get to a pump before the fuel ran out. Fortunately, Teri drove Up It Yo like a rhino so we didn't get queue jumped. I left Teri to it while I nipped to the toilet. My guts were still a bit on the dodgy side, and when I needed to go, I needed to go. This is where the ritual politeness of greeting can be a health hazard. Outside the only toilet was a lady attendant who insisted on engaging me in the traditional Namibian greetings while I was desperately clenching my sphincter muscles.

"Good day. How are you?"

"Hello. I am fine, thank you. How are you?"

"I am fine, thank you. My name is Mufunwe."

"My name is Lucy."

"How do you do" (offers to shake hands).

"How do you do" (shaking hands the African way, with both hands, and having to let go of the now-opened door to the toilet, which closes again).

"Where are you going today?"

"We are going to Rundu" (but I'd really like to go to the toilet now).

"Ahh, Rundu. There's not much in Rundu. I never go to Rundu."

"Is the toilet in there?" I said, pointing and attempting to terminate the conversation.

Long pause…then, "Yes, you can use the toilet in there. It is one dollar."

"Thank you!" I said, with my best winning smile to cover up my obvious rudeness and determined to chat when I came out. Fortunately, she was talking to her next victim when I emerged.

With a quick check of all the tire pressures, which involved another scrum, we set off on the road to Rundu. It was the C45 road, and quite new tarmac, so even we couldn't get lost.

Rundu seemed like a bustling frontier town, full of stores to stock up on essentials like food, firewood, alcohol. It even had a bank. If this had been the Wild West, the pickup trucks were the buckboards of out-of-town homesteaders. I even bought a wide-brimmed hat, not out of place in Tombstone. Rundu had little else to offer us, however, so we struck off again, following the wonderfully upgraded C45 to cross the top edge of Namibia: Ovamboland. First stop would be the town of Ondangwa, marking halfway to Ruacana and the next adventure beyond.

Ovamboland sounds rather romantic in an historical, colonial sort of way. The name conjures images of traditional kraals, colorful native dress, perhaps a chieftain or two. This might have been a realistic picture once, but now this strip of land to the north of Namibia, squeezed between the Angolan border and the great salt pan of Etosha, is the old battleground of SWAPO. The Owambo people signed up to SWAPO in droves during the war with South Africa. Reputedly the area is now rewarded with governmental largesse. There was evidence of this from the great concrete canal that seems to run the length of the region from the man-made reservoir across the border in Angola. The canal brings irrigation and farming and seems to be the hub of activity on washdays.

We had come across evidence of the war in this region while in Tsumkwe. The presence of South African soldiers there had abused locals and the environment alike. Here at least the local people appear to have benefitted from the outcome. South Africa "annexed" Namibia while it was South West Africa back in the 1960s, and the rebellious South West Africa People's Organization (SWAPO) came into its own when Angola was given independence in 1975. Angola became a close ally while being conveniently just across the border. In Ovamboland, that means just across the river. SWAPO took refuge in Angola, which was also in the midst of a civil war between UNITA (Jonas Savimbi's "moderates") and the Cuban-backed MPLA. Of course, as this was the Cold War, it dragged in countries from the East and the West, albeit on the sly. The whole thing resulted in a mess of minefields and no-go areas that still exist today in Angola, made famous by Princess Diana appearing on TV news dressed in mine-clearance gear while helping to reduce the casualty list of amputee children. Fortunately for us, and Namibia, there are no minefields south of the river.

My knowledge of Angola, before seeing war footage on the BBC, came from looking at my stepfather's photographs of the place. His "walkabout" journey had him sailing from Lisbon to Luanda (Angola's capital) and then ridiculously driving his twelve-cylinder Daimler across Southern Africa to Port Elizabeth to visit his uncle. The photographs he took that had frequently fueled my childhood dreams were coming to life. Somewhere in my psyche, I had always wanted to replicate his journey, and here I was—OK, not in a Daimler, and not on my own, but what Teri and I were doing was definitely ticking all the right boxes. Somewhere to the west of us, he must have crossed the river and headed south to follow the coast road. Westward was where we were headed.

According to the trusty guidebook, Ovamboland is usually blank on most tourist maps; tourists have little reason to stray this far. Fortunately, we weren't relying on any old tourist map. I'd taken some trouble to source a map from Stanford's map shop in London. This shop has sold maps of everywhere in the world since 1852. For his efforts to the Empire, Mr. Stanford was appointed royal geographer to the queen, no less (that's Queen Victoria, not the current one). Unfortunately, all these royal credentials made our maps no more accurate than a tourist map with blank bits. Our "best" map was fairly up to date, but no cartographer could keep up with the speed of infrastructure development in Ovamboland. The C45 was supposed to be one long, clear road heading westward directly to Ruacana. Not any longer. It turns north toward the Angola border, and the only way west seemed to be back on dirt roads. Nothing is simple in Namibia.

The next leg of our travel from Rundu to Ruacana was more problematic. The journey took us very close to the Angolan border, and once again we got horribly lost. The roads didn't go in the direction we wanted at all, and we resorted to taking directional advice from pedestrians who couldn't understand where we wanted to go, but pointed randomly and helpfully at sandy tracks.

At one point, Lucy steered onto a track as instructed, despite both of us instinctively feeling that it was definitely heading in the wrong direction. I think it was an inherent politeness that meant that we couldn't ignore the helpful pointing fingers and smiling faces and head off in the opposite direction to that indicated. It would be so rude to ignore them, we agreed. So off we headed toward Angola, just to be polite. We turned right, as instructed, and at the junction we drove past a group of five or six young men with an upended cow (dead, thankfully, but with an unnervingly wide-open eye that seemed to stare straight at us) and a collection of knives and machetes. We waved and smiled, again feeling the need to maintain civility despite the gruesome scene. They waved their weapons and smiled toothily back.

In retrospect, this tableau serves to demonstrate how habituated we were becoming. A few weeks ago, a bunch of half-naked young men waving bloodied machetes at us at close quarters would have had us struck dumb with terror, but here we were socializing wordlessly with a bunch of cow rustlers.

We drove on toward Angola, convinced by all our faculties that we were not going to get to Ruacana anytime soon. The maps were wrong, the sun was in the wrong place, the compass said we were going north, and so did the feelings in our bones, our waters, and our guts. After about fifteen minutes, we agreed that we should turn around and return to the previous track, which at least had been heading southwest.

The track was narrow and the sand was deep, but Lucy managed to maneuver Up It Yo in a seventeen-point turn, and we headed back toward the dead beady-eyed bovine. Except that it was no longer there. All that was left of it was an unidentifiable organ (possibly a stomach or four), a small pile of glistening intestines, and a patch of blood on the sand. Two of the smiling butchers were left to kick the dust over the paltry remains; the rest had dispersed, presumably with heavy meat loads. We had been gone about half an hour, and in that time they had managed to butcher, share out, and take home the meat from an entire cow. Impressive.

We drove vaguely southwest along endless sand tracks. It was late afternoon, and I was concerned that we'd still be nowhere as night fell and I'd be making camp by the roadside in the dark. Teri had gone quiet again. Our current route could have been any of the patchwork of tracks marked on the map—or none of them. But it had to go somewhere, surely? As the sun was threatening to disappear, remarkably, we hit upon a tarmac road at a T junction. A big, real, metal road with lines down the middle. There was even a truck going past. Hurrah!

Well, we still didn't know where we were, so, turning right, we headed west and soon came upon a very disappointing road sign. It said Ondangwa was over ninety kilometers ahead. Not even half our journey done. The good news was that it also said B1. This was the B1 road clearly marked on our map, and we could estimate where we were from the distance to Ondangwa. Damn! We were nearer Etosha National Park to the east of us than Ondangwa to the west, or any form of civilization. So we turned round and went back down the B1.

The good thing about being near Etosha was that there would be lodges and campsites near the east gate. A quick scan of the guidebook found a campsite that didn't sound too twee, and it was close enough to get set up before dark. The entrance to Onguma Game Ranch was guarded by an impressive pair of stone pillars and gateway, which led to a very upmarket-looking establishment. However, we were after the Onguma campsite so bypassed the smart-looking lodges and attractive bar area.

Our camp that night was fine, and even quite posh by our recent camping standards. It had a braai, showers and toilets—that actually flushed—and hot water. Yay! I was looking forward to the bratwurst we had brought from Botswana. Or had we? Nope, it was clearly still resting peacefully in a Botswanan fridge. Oh, well, beans would do.

That night, Teri and I were being circled. We both lay in our tents tracking a lion's throaty grunting. I lay there listening. Was it a lion? It sounded very like the lions we heard at the Wildlife Camp. It is more like someone with a bad chest, or a red deer stag calling during the rutting season. Perhaps it was a wildebeest, I told myself. It was behind my tent, not far away. I couldn't hear anything coming from Teri so presumed she was either asleep or so tired she couldn't care less about being stalked by a lion. I turned over and went back to sleep. I was dog tired too. Sod the lion.

I was getting used to the nocturnal animal noises by now and could sleep through most of them. Until this night. It was twilight and dawn was soon to break when I heard a loud, long roar, followed by a diminuendo series of grunts. Very nearby. Then the same sequence again. Strangely, it was the grunts that made the hair stand up on the back of my neck. I unzipped the tent flap and peered out to the direction of the sound. About forty feet away was a midsized male lion with his head raised, and another of the heart-stopping roars emitting from his throat.

For the next hour, I followed his progress around his territory by listening to the roars and grunts moving farther away and then circling until he was finally roaring somewhere over to my left. Amazingly, Lucy remained firmly in her tent. How could anyone sleep through that?

Once the lion was safely heading in the opposite direction from our camp, I decided I might as well get up and have first turn at our ablution facilities. It was barely dawn, but I felt confident enough, now that the lion had moved on, to grab my towel, some clothes, and a washbag and sprint through the dark to the shower.

The water wasn't particularly warm, and the door didn't close properly, but the wonderful thing about really roughing it a lot of the time is that your perception of luxury shifts downward surprisingly quickly. In England, a bathroom shelf collapsing and pitching all of my clothes into the shower stall would have sent me apoplectically to the front desk demanding immediate action! But standing on the dusty ground under a lukewarm trickle of water and watching as my clothes tumbled into the mud, I just picked them up philosophically, halfheartedly attempted to wring them out, and wandered back to my tent somewhat underdressed in just my underwear. I filled the washing-up bowl with water and plunged my muddy clothes in for a swill, and then roamed around our campsite hanging smalls from various accommodating branches. By now Lucy was up, had been warned of the perils of the shower stall, and was washed, dressed, and starting the fire.

We were sitting on small boulders drinking smoky tea and discussing the merits of remaining in the tent in the presence of lions, when a slight movement caught Lucy's eye. We looked across to the dirt track that was the entrance to our camp, and saw a man standing silent and motionless among the trees. He was wearing a uniform, a name badge, and a peaked hat and had a handgun in a holster on his left hip. He also had an empty left sleeve that swung in the light breeze. He was obviously employed by the camp to protect the safety of visitors, but clearly didn't feel he had any duty to protect our privacy! We had no idea how long he'd been there silently watching us, probably half the night.

Determined to maintain Namibian courtesies, we made the usual felicitations but found him to be somewhat taciturn. We eventually established, through a fair bit of gesturing, nodding, pointing (us), and grunting, gurning, and dismissive waving (him), that his main brief was to guard the (rich!) people staying in the lodges on the far side of the camp, but that he was also required to patrol the campsite at least once on his shift. I thought that maybe he had turned up to carry out this duty at 5:00 a.m. due to the fact that a lion had been roaring its head off in close proximity to our tents. But no, he shrugged, he hadn't heard the lion, it was just that our campsite was on his route home at the end of his shift.

We actually felt a bit better about this. It had seemed a bit cushy to have a security guard looking out for us, even if only for the one patrol per night. But as he only had one arm, a gun holster that was ineffectually affixed to his limbless side, and was blatantly deaf too, we considered he was hardly a threat to our independence.

We found the road to Ruacana eventually—helped by the fact that it followed the route of the canal. There were two notable characteristics of this road. Firstly, there were donkeys everywhere—literally hundreds grazing, sleeping, standing, sitting, braying, and generally having a sociable time under the squat trees and in the scrubland. They seemed to congregate in little family groups, with a number of babies and teenagers among their numbers. Their coats were all the colors of the desert: black, gray, white, beige, light brown, and dark brown. They'd occasionally amble out into the road in front of us, and we would happily stop to admire them, trying not to think about their fate. Although, given that they had total freedom to roam over vast scenic stretches of the country during their lifetimes, they were probably better off than most livestock raised for meat.

The other feature of the canal road was all the washing activities that were going on. Women and children were waist deep in the water performing their personal ablutions as well as laundering their clothes, bedding, and napery. The Namibians have a fondness for bright colors in their materials, so where the laundry was stretched out on the banks and over shrubs, it looked like giant psychedelic patchwork quilts. The contrast of the brightness of the laundry against the muted gray-greens and browns of the desert was stunning. When the washing was dry, the ladies would bundle their entire wardrobe of washing into a sheet and carry it home on their heads. Children would also carry smaller bundles on their heads, and we were amazed that they were able to run about without losing their cargo.

Apart from the donkeys and laundry, this journey was pretty dull. I was struck by the overgrazing that was evident for the entire journey. No wonder this was not really a tourist area. The roads and the maps decided to agree with each other for a change, but this didn't make the C46 tarmac road any more interesting. Teri was driving, so I studied the maps and guidebooks. I was quietly planning the next leg of our journey without scaring Teri. She didn't know what I had up my sleeve. Yes, she'd agreed to go the backwoods way to northwest Namibia, but I think she was a bit drunk when I explained what fun it would be. Once we got to Ruacana, our next task was to go across country to the beautiful Epupa Falls. There is an easy route to Epupa Falls, and there's a fun route. If we were going to do the easy route, we would have to turn off soon and head for Opuwo and enjoy an efficient tarmacked drive to northwest Namibia. We ignored the Opuwo turning and continued steadfastly on toward Ruacana, with its rather inferior falls, rumored to be a beauty spot.

We arrived at Ruacana Falls. The falls weren't falling as it was the dry season, and there were no animals in the vicinity, so there was not a lot to do except take advantage of the last bastion of civilization before we headed back to the bush.

We stayed at a small lodge that had motel facilities, a restaurant, and a bar (large gin and tonic—with ICE!). There was also a camping option, or there were about a dozen small huts dotted around the grounds. We decided to stay in a hut.

The little huts were shaped like mushrooms, with domed, cream-colored roofs and brown-painted walls. Our mushroom had a fridge! We'd never had a fridge of our own before, so we delightedly transferred our hot wine and beer from the boot.

We took a walk around the mushroom field and discovered that only five other mushrooms were inhabited, and the occupants were all staff from the lodge. This meant that we had the pick of the rather splendid giant-sized barbeques that were spacious enough to cook an entire antelope (pity we had only sweet corn, tomatoes, and a couple of tinned sausages to cook on it!). We also had the shower and toilet facilities to ourselves, as there was a separate staff ablution block.

We chose a fairly central mushroom, with the bar and restaurant about thirty meters to the left, and the showers approximately the same distance to the right. There was a building, about the size of a small village hall, on the perimeter of the lodge about forty meters behind our mushroom. I peered through the windows; it seemed to be a sort of lecture hall—there was a wooden floor, some long, low benches along the walls, and posters of various Namibian dignitaries on the walls, including the ex-president, who had the splendid name of Hifikepunye.

We watched chefs, waiters, barmen, and hostesses walking through the grounds in their uniforms to go to work and expected that we'd be settling in for a quiet night as all the staff seemed to be on duty. We were wrong.

As we sat on our veranda eating our meal under the stars, the restaurant service started. I'd had a quick look at the menu when we'd checked in, and the dishes didn't seem to be too demanding—mostly steaks from various animals, and vegetables tossed in butter—and there were only a handful of customer cars in the car park. But to hear the Namibian chef's shouting, the crashing of pots and pans, and the slamming of ingredients coming from the open kitchen windows, you'd have thought he was preparing haute cuisine for a clientele of thousands. It was difficult to tell if he was angry or simply loud. Occasionally, a waiter or chef would step out of the back kitchen door for a peaceful smoke. They seemed fairly relaxed, so we assumed that the chef was just being a bit temperamental.

After a couple of hours, things started to quieten down. The lights in the kitchen went off, the customers began to drift from the restaurant to the bar, and the restaurant lights went off too. Staff started to filter across the grounds to their various huts. I went for a dark stumble to the shower block and returned to the mushroom in a fetching combination of gray pajamas and pink Doc Martens. It was about eleven o'clock, and we decided to retire for the night.

Ten minutes later we were up again. It turned out that it wasn't a lecture hall—it was a staffroom, and the staff were ready to party!

First there was a stream of people coming over from the kitchen carrying racks of ribs and trays of sausages. A barbeque was fired up, and the food was soon sizzling tantalizingly close to our nostrils. Great bowls of salads were hauled over to the hall, and a couple of chaps carried crates of beer. Then the party really started. Loud Namibian pop music was blasted out over the barbeque area, and everyone was dancing on the grass in the dark.

We crept out and sat on our veranda, watching the proceedings and slurping drinks of our own. There were a few muffled shouts, but mostly they were all focused on dancing energetically. A few of them beckoned to us, inviting us to join in, but not only did we feel a bit inappropriately dressed, we also wouldn't have had the energy to keep up! Although a rib or two would have been nice.

As the evening grew cooler, they moved into the hall, and things started to get even more interesting. Clearly the hall must have been too warm for dancing, so they started to remove their clothes. We could see topless young men, their chests glistening under the lights, writhing and gyrating with the girls in their short little dresses. It was all too much for us, and we retired back to bed, falling asleep to the sounds of the music.

We wondered afterward if what we had witnessed had been a special occasion—maybe somebody's birthday or a leaving party—or if they partied like that every night. If they did, then no wonder they were all prepared to put up with the shouting chef.

Mushroom hut at Ruacana

CHAPTER 11

THE "ROAD" TO EPUPA—AND PARADISE

There is an area in Namibia described as one of Africa's last wildernesses. Kaokoland has no lodges, no towns, no shops, no petrol stations. It is the land of the Himba, a traditional pastoral people who live off their goats and drought-resistant cattle, and roam nomadically across the vast plains. This area is wild in the true sense of the word. It is also the land of the desert elephant and black rhino, and where lions, leopards, and various dangerous fauna roam freely, giving no thought or consideration to humans, except perhaps as lunch.

The animals pose far less hazard in this area, however, than the flash floods, shifting sands, rock falls, and the dearth of cartographers, who have clearly avoided this part of the world. The guidebook we consulted before embarking on this trip said that the best way to visit this area is by air, using an experienced guide who knows the dangers. It went on to say that, if visiting independently, you would need your own expedition: two or more equipped 4x4s, with experienced drivers, and all fuel and supplies for longer than the planned trip. Obviously, this equates to being told that you can't do something, which leads naturally to finding a way to do it.

The attraction of the wilderness for me is exactly that: it is wilderness, with its own flora and fauna, natural hazards, and the promise of experiencing an environment that is unforgiving but also new. Exploring is about seeking and finding something that is fresh and undiscovered, untested, and unaltered by human hand. A track newly flooded and washed out poses *you* with the challenge, not the previous person who came here; a rock fall blocks your way, and no authority is going come and fix it; your every action on and in the environment is purely your own responsibility, but also your own challenge and reward. When do we ever really get that close to being entirely in control of our own actions, of our own safety, of our own victories? Perhaps this is why we all of us test ourselves in some way, especially when feeling restrained by our usual daily routine. Why do middle-aged men decide to don leathers and buy themselves Harley Davidsons? Why do pensioners go parachuting, or walk the Great Wall of China? Why do my mature students give up their jobs when the children have flown the nest and embark on a degree course and a whole new career?

Why did I decide to drag Teri through her idea of a nightmare because I fancied going off the beaten track? And why did she decide to come with me!?

Our destination for this next part of the trip was Epupa Falls. Teri had read about them in a travelogue magazine, perhaps while waiting in the dentist's. So it was she who proposed this as a goal and, therefore, it was her fault. There is an easier way to get to Epupa Falls than the route we used, but that would mean a huge detour from Ruacana and missing one of the most adventurous parts of the trip. The direct route from Ruacana is a track called the D3700 following the Kunene River, which separates Namibia from Angola. The D3700 is described as a "very rough" narrow and rocky track and can be vague in places, especially when it crosses the numerous dry river beds. The Kunene River is pinioned to the border by the Zebra Mountains, so named not because of the animals that live there but because of the scree slopes that stripe their sides.

We left civilization behind via Hippo Falls, a campsite noted in the guidebooks for its hippo, strangely enough. We only stopped for a cursory look but noted crocodiles rather than any hippos. Was this a sign of the nature of our next adventure? The first landmark for this journey was the remote Kunene River Lodge, a rather upmarket, edge-of-the-wilderness outpost for the more daring tourists. The tarmac road of Ruacana quickly disintegrated into gravel, sand, and then rocks as we climbed over a headland to see the Kunene River winding its way westward into the bush on its way to the sea. We followed the rocky track with dogged gung ho.

Before leaving Ruacana, Lucy and I headed to the nearest garage to top up the tank. We were heading for Epupa, which was a distance of only three hundred or so kilometers, but the maps showed that the route was peppered with those dreaded exclamation mark roads, and anyway, we were expecting to get lost as usual. The garage had a small shop, so we also stocked up on more provisions. I decided that I wanted to make cheesy garlic bread to go with our pasta that evening. The bread was a slightly sweet, thinly sliced loaf, and the only cheese was a pack of processed, individually wrapped slices. I bought them anyway, thinking that I might have to compromise my menu and make sweet barbequed cheese toasties instead. Lucy overcame her previous reticence and purchased a few bundles of wood from roadside sellers, and we lashed them to the roof.

The journey to Epupa started well, with a tarmac road and not too many stray animals darting onto our path. The road soon turned into a chalky track of uncertain boundaries. Our route took us along the Angola border, alongside the Kunene River. It was very scenic, and we were surprised by how different the vegetation on the opposite bank was from ours: Angola was lush and dark green with palm trees and thick rushes, while we were still driving through dry, dusty vegetation, the only greenery being right at the river's edge. The map said that we could follow the river all the way to Epupa, so that was the plan.

On the way to the Kunene River Lodge, Teri and I both foolishly remarked how easy the track was. Clearly marked among the boulder-strewn moonscape of the hills we were traversing, it wound its way up and down the mountain sides. It was well used, even signposted to the lodge—albeit on wooden posts in hand-scrawled writing. There were one or two tricky moments when we had to bounce over rocks while negotiating a bend. Teri had her eyes shut at these moments, as she doesn't like heights and some of the down slopes were vertiginous.

After at least two hours, just when we were thinking the lodge was fictional, we saw a wooden signpost to the right: Kunene River Lodge. There were signs of life—goat fencing, the odd tin can and beer bottle, then the unmistakable cultured "wilderness" trees and watered grass that announces an upmarket African safari lodge. I was getting quite proud of Teri. She had definitely gone bush and now railed against the false splendor of Namibia's best efforts to encourage tourism. It's good that tourism is developing in Namibia. It provides jobs, infrastructure, and investment. But a posh lodge was not for us. Our destination for the day was, if we got that far, a rumored Himba village campsite on the Kunene called Enyandi, fifty kilometers farther on. That doesn't sound far, does it? We kept left and ventured on, leaving the last outpost of civilization in our wake. We were on our own now.

It soon became clear that very few vehicles travel any farther west than the lodge. The track to the lodge had been reasonable. The track after the lodge was insane. It sometimes followed the river very closely, on narrow sandy gaps between the trees, often winding round boulders, plunging across river beds, and looping around fallen trunks. This was beautiful. The river is lined with Makalani palms, which stand tall and elegant like Caribbean sentinels. Underneath their canopies the ground is cool and dappled with little undergrowth, just leaf litter and sandy space. When the river cut into rock, the track would climb up into the Zebra Mountains, winding through loose scree, rocks, and boulders, in between the camelthorn trees, and often over gullies washed into deep gashes by flash flooding. We had to stay in low-ratio four-wheel drive, second gear on these stretches, trying to straddle the gullies while keeping the wheels on the hard rocks either side. Up It Yo was high clearance and had a metal sump guard (I'd checked earlier), but I was mindful of keeping the underbelly well clear of some vicious-looking geology.

We averaged about two kilometers an hour. One problem was going over a summit and descending. Up It Yo had a wonderful long bullnose bonnet that totally obscured my view of whatever was immediately in front of me. On one stretch when we crested a hill, we were faced with a long descent over rough boulders and gullies. To negotiate this, I would have to take a winding route and boulder hop to avoid grounding. But I couldn't see. This is why it's really useful having a navigator. Teri was commissioned to jump out and walk backward down the slope in front of me, watching where the wheels were going and saying, "Left a bit; right a bit," on the way down. Which she did admirably.

Why was I not surprised when the track alongside the river suddenly disappeared, and the only possible option for driving onward led us up a steep, rocky slope? We bounced violently in and out of deep crevasses, lurching and tilting sideways alarmingly. When we'd crested the first ridge, things took a turn for the worse. The "path" down the other side was a mass of deep gorges and sharp, rocky boulders.

"You'll have to get out and guide me down" said Lucy. I looked at her in disbelieving horror, but she was serious.

I staggered out barefoot and scrabbled ahead of the truck—less with the agility of a mountain goat and more with that of a Friesian cow. I surveyed the scene and really couldn't see any sensible route for a car, but I gamely walked ahead beckoning and gesticulating in what I hoped was a confident manner. The slope in some cases was so steep that Up It Yo seemed to be almost standing on its front two wheels in a nose dive. Lucy was wrestling with the wheel with a huge grin. It might have been a grimace, but I was churlishly grumpy with fear and annoyed that she might be enjoying herself when I clearly wasn't. I wasn't smiling. I was too concerned that the truck would roll and either toss Lucy out the window, flatten me on its downward trajectory, or both.

Strangely, while I was wandering about in the mountains guiding a truck down a slope, it never occurred to me that I ought to be vigilant of predators, so I wasn't.

A few miles farther on, we faced the same problem but on the ascent. By this time I was getting a tad overwhelmed by the amount of rocks on a track that had promised to be a sandy riverside drive. We turned away from the river yet again to be faced with a mountainside. There was a vague (I hate that word "vague"!) gap among large monoliths, camelthorns, and crevasses, but as road surfaces go, it was more akin to the side of a quarry. We stopped and had a look. I felt like a mountaineer planning his ascent. Where would base camp be? Where do we need to traverse? The most worrying part was a kink in the route that had a big boulder on the right side, a deep crevasse in the middle and, below that, rough scree on the left side, penned in by the side of the mountain. The approach to the big boulder was a left-to-right traverse from a nasty dip, which would mean Up It Yo "climbing" the boulder from below, rolling to the left into the mountain while having to turn to the right at the same time. Tricky. Frankly, I had no idea how we were going to get up there. I was not going to admit this to Teri, although I was swearing a lot. There was no other way. We were trapped at the bottom of this mountain with no way to turn round, no room on the river side, and the only way was up.

I gave myself a little talking to. Other people must have done this. Yes, but, there has clearly been a flash flood since then that washed much of the track away. Other people may have had Land Cruisers, Land Rovers. Don't be silly, it's just a crisis of confidence. Yes, I had never done this before. I could think of people back at home I admire for their practicality with 4x4s. I wished they had been with us just then. I had to admit to myself I was scared. But that wasn't going to get us out of here, so we would have to go for it.

The first part of the ascent was simple. The scree was slippery, but Up It Yo ground its way manfully up the 1:2 slope. We got to the tricky bit. I had by this time fessed up to Teri and said I was unsure how to tackle this. She offered to guide me up and walked up the track to do her "left a bit, right a bit" stuff. She had no shoes on; the pink DM's too complicated to put on.

Teri turned and beckoned. I lined Up It Yo to get its off-front tire in line with the big boulder. First gear, low ratio, we inched forward tentatively. Too tentatively, as Up It Yo balked at mounting the rock and chose to regard it as a wheel clamp. I had been too gentle. I backed down the slope a little way to get a run up. Going down backward was almost as bad as trying to go up. I cursed myself. Teri descended for consultation. I knew I was scared of bouncing Up It Yo too much in mounting the big boulder and throwing it left into the gully. That would have been very unfortunate. Anyway, I decided not to think of the consequences of getting this wrong and gunned the engine. Teri was back in position, watching the wheels. With a run up, Up It Yo hit the boulder, bucked upward, rolled left, I threw a right for the kink, Up It Yo clung on, back wheels crunching into scree, front wheels clawing at naked stone. The rear wheel hit the boulder, Up It Yo bucked again, its rear bounced, our gear crashed, we tilted farther left, camelthorn scraping at the body. If I faltered now, Up It Yo would tip on its side. Teri beckoned left as I kept the revs up and the front wheels cleared the boulder and bit into the next set of rocks. I was praying, "Please don't slip sideways into the crevasse. Please!" The rear wheel remained on the boulder, cleared the boulder, Up It Yo straightened up, Teri dived aside, and Up It Yo and I cleared the kink. I started breathing again.

I stopped to pick Teri up. She'd walked up the rocky slope in bare feet. She must have cowhide for soles. We ground on to the top and cursed again. The track did a ninety-degree turn to the right around a large camelthorn and descended over pretty much the same kind of terrain. I had to do a three-point turn on more boulders to negotiate the camelthorn, and we then inched our way back down.

The next challenge was at the riverside. The track had been kind for a while, lovely flat sand weaving between the Makalani palms. Teri and I relaxed. Then the track veered to the right. The river was right there, six feet below the bank on our right-hand side, and about six inches away from the track. We stopped for a think. The only available route was *very* close to the six-foot drop to the river, and there was no evidence that the river hadn't washed away part of the bank, or some of the earth beneath. We could drive ourselves into the river and, with the drop, be upended on our roof. The track in front looked solid enough; it was supported on boulders and sand, with trees on the left-hand side, so roots would be supporting the bank.

We set off only to find our way challenged by the big boulder situation again. This time the boulder was on the left side, and we would have to bounce Up It Yo onto the boulder, which would pitch Up It Yo severely toward the river. Gulp! I would have to take it at some speed, as getting clamped again because of my timidity was not an option. We would be suspended on a negative camber, leaning toward the river while I reversed. Not a good idea. So I bashed on, saying stuff like, "Oh, it's not that bad," while Teri went quiet, white, and gripped the door handle in silent terror. We hit the boulder, Up It Yo leaned dizzily to the right, I thought about its center of gravity being, hopefully, very low down, and the suspension bounced us even more toward the river. Teri gasped. I'd never heard anyone actually gasp in fright before. That was definitely a gasp of fear. I am not sure I didn't mutter something at the same time. But we made it. Up It Yo righted itself, we got back on the track, and I said, "That was a bit hairy." I think Teri was ready to kill me.

After the scree slope incident, I foolishly relaxed and enjoyed the lovely sandy track alongside the gently flowing river. The going was still tricky enough to limit our speed to around five kilometers an hour, but the scenery was delightful. Of course, no sooner had we calmed ourselves enough to have a drink and a rusk, than we faced what for me was the scariest part of the journey yet. We were on a narrow, crumbling sand bank that was climbing higher and higher above the river. It then became so narrow that Up It Yo was barely able to get all four wheels on the track—the two nearest the bank were scrabbling for purchase, and I looked down to the river about ten feet below with clenched fists and palpitations. I could barely breathe and definitely couldn't speak. Lucy hunched over the wheel and scrambled along in silence. There was a real danger of us and the truck ending up in the water, and as it was infested with crocodiles, there wouldn't be a happy outcome. I don't know how I survived that episode without having a complete panic attack. If I'd known Lucy was scared too, I'd have leapt out of Up It Yo and left her to it! She seemed to be good at putting on a brave face.

Somehow Lucy managed to negotiate the sand cliff, and I managed not to panic, and soon we were on another of our mountain treks. We climbed higher and higher on the rocky track until we reached the peak. The view was magnificent. Looking northward, we could see Angola on our right and a vast, dusty Namibian plateau on our left. We could see the route of the Kunene River, as it was a line of greenery snaking through arid earth. It was rather a long way away, considering that we were supposed to be following its path.

There was no way we would make the 316 kilometers all the way to Epupa Falls in a day with going like this. We would have to find the community campsite called Enyandi before it got dark, or we'd be sleeping in the back of Up It Yo. Just before we despaired of ever finding it, we spotted a hand-scrawled wooden sign pointing right, announcing Enyandi. We steered right.

What a beautiful place! Beside the river, Enyandi is a sandbank hosting a stand of Makalani palms and grasses along the edges of the river. There was a soft rumble upstream from a set of rapids, and rustling from the palm fronds in the breeze. Once we killed the engine, Enyandi was paradise.

We pitched under a sprawling deciduous tree of unknown species and made camp. As usual, we had the place to ourselves; we hadn't seen a person since Ruacana anyway. I did the usual and cast the drinks bag into the water to cool. Teri organized our rearranged stores, then sat on the grassy riverbank with a book, so I went on a wood-gathering sortie.

It hadn't been the most relaxing day. We agreed to make camp when (if?!) we ever found the riverbank again.

At around 4:00 p.m., we did just that—in a beautiful spot right on the banks of the river, with big old palm trees, some smaller pines, and grassy sand dunes. We pitched the tents, and then Lucy went for a wander while I became a domestic goddess with a plastic washing-up bowl, a crocodile-infested river, and a scourer.

When everything was in order for easy accessibility for cooking dinner in the dark later, I pulled out my book and sat on the riverbank, alternately reading and admiring the view across to Angola. Half an hour or so later, I felt as though I was no longer alone, and I turned around expecting to see Lucy with a bundle of kindling in her arms. So it was a bit of a shock when I saw a brooding, silent Himba chap standing about fifteen feet away from me, leaning on his stick and staring unsmilingly.

"Hello!" I said and smiled at him.

His stare was unwavering, and I felt a bit unnerved, especially as he had a machete in his hand. I wondered where Lucy was and hoped she'd hurry. In the meantime, I tried to read my book nonchalantly and ignore the staring warrior.

After a bit, Lucy came back. She headed to the truck and started to fiddle about with firewood. I coughed discreetly.

"We have company!"

She followed my gaze and did exactly as I had done: greeted him with a friendly smile. She was a bit nonplussed by his unwavering stare and lack of response. I also think she must have felt mildly unnerved, because she went over to him proffering a bunch of notes from her pocket as a camping fee. If she had been thinking more clearly, she'd have offered cooking oil, or sweets or maize meal! Still, the money convinced the chap that we weren't offering anything else and it was time to move on, and he silently glided through the trees with a few backward glances of what looked like venom, but I like to think was curiosity.

We drank tea for a while and sat on the bank admiring Angola. Suddenly there was a lot of waving and shouting from the opposite bank. A naked Angolan youth was splashing about in the water almost directly opposite us, a distance of around fifty meters away. I wasn't sure if he was swimming, or fishing, or making a bid for asylum. I wasn't sure if he was shouting to us or to an unseen friend on the opposite bank. I wasn't sure if he was waving as a friendly greeting or as a distress signal. And then he seemed to go under and disappeared from view. And then I wasn't sure if he'd decided to do some underwater swimming, or been eaten by a crocodile, or drowned.

I looked across at Lucy, and clearly the same series of alternatives was milling around her mind too, judging by the perplexed expression on her face.

It was rather a disturbing incident, and we didn't really discuss it much at the time, probably as there was nothing we could have done even if the worst scenario was in fact the case. We were willing to bathe at the edge of a croc-infested river, but only after a thorough inspection of the area, and always within jumping distance of the bank. We certainly couldn't have taken the risk of swimming out to the chap in the water. And if we had done so, and he was merely swimming or fishing, it would have been quite difficult to explain why a couple of middle-aged women were swimming out to join a naked teenager in a bit of frolicking in the river. So we did nothing.

Since we've been back from our trip, we've considered this event several times, and we're still not sure if we watched with a cup of tea in our hands as a man drowned.

Our next visitor that afternoon was a young man of about twenty, who again crept up to take us unawares. I don't think the Himba creep about deliberately—it's more that they are silent and stealthy people who walk vast distances quietly to catch their prey, so a gentle, fluid gait is adaptive for them. This young man also stood about ten feet away and stared brazenly, but by now, we were feeling Himba-like too and adopted their social mores, so stared back quite unabashed. Ndomu was of a more friendly demeanor than his predecessor, and we soon progressed from staring to smiling. He squatted down companionably, and I admired his animal skins, horns and feathers and quills, and even his little Manchester United bobble hat.

I offered him some of my water. He took a swig and then spat it out—it was a bit tepid, having been lying in the sun, but still! He waved the bottle in the direction of the river, implying that I had filled it from the murky swirls of the Kunene. I protested indignantly, and we all laughed—our first Himba joke!

Ndomu spotted Lucy's phone and indicated that she should take his photo. He had a special "having my photo taken" face and put on a serious, almost arrogant expression. Very much like a Himba warrior, not so much like the smiling Ndomu who'd been squatting and smiling for the last half hour. He then grabbed my hand and entwined his fingers with mine, black, white, black, white, and then put his face on again for Lucy to capture the image.

We admired the photos, and Ndomu looked at himself for a long time with intense, rapt attention, and then he went back to his silent, staring squatting, so we got going with fire and food preparations, leaving him to eventually get bored and amble off into the bush with a wave.

This interlude was a classic example of the clash of culture and tourism in Namibia. Ndomu had the accoutrements and social skills of the Himba but could adjust his behavior to accommodate, and even enjoy, modern technology. He didn't pose for those photos for material gain; he posed for the pleasure of looking at the photos and admiring his image. We all took mutual pleasure in each other's appearances and idiosyncrasies, and there was an innocence in the encounter that enriched all of us. But this innocence needs to be preserved somehow to prevent the nomadic Himba in Kaokoland becoming beholden and pathetically dependent on the largesse of tourists as we had experienced in Tsumkwe.

Our final camp visitor arrived before seven the following morning. We were up, and fumbling about silently and blearily—neither of us is very sociable in the morning. Lucy was lighting the fire for tea, and I was doing last night's washing up.

And there he was. Out of nowhere appeared the oldest and thinnest Himba man we'd come across. He had the requisite stick and machete, and also a piece of paper that he proffered to Lucy. Apparently it was a medical document. Quite why he felt the need to show us his medical history was unclear.

I now think that the medical card was, to him, an indication to us of who he was. It was his way of communicating to us who he was, written down in our language and culture.

He was clearly malnourished, and pointed at his stomach several times while repeating a word that sounded like "semse." We didn't need a Himba dictionary to work out that he was telling us he was hungry.

The difficulty was that we'd lost all our maize meal on the track back at Khaudum. The best I could do was to give him half a loaf of sliced bread and the processed cheese slices—both items that he had clearly never come across before. The bread, in perfect, neat little squares, didn't resemble the porridges and gruels and dumplings that he was used to. And the sliced cheese didn't look like something that you would want to put in your mouth. I had to break off a bit of bread and chew it encouragingly, nodding and smiling with delight, and then I unwrapped a slice of cheese and put a bit of that in too, chewing and nodding a bit more. It seemed to work, and he took the unusual picnic and wandered back to wherever he'd come from. I'm not sure if he intended to share the food with others in his village, but I was amused to imagine him doing a party trick of stuffing a plastic yellow square into his mouth and chomping on it to encourage the others that it was, surprisingly, actually edible.

Ndomu at Enyandi

Chapter 12

Reaching the Nadir

Shortly after our ancient Himba visitor left us, we headed off again in a second attempt to get to Epupa Falls. We were more prepared for the arduous trek this time, and were enthused by the hope that we may actually get to Epupa Falls by nightfall.

We bumped and bounced up and down the mountain, lurching to the left, rolling to the right, and occasionally I got out to do a bit of pedestrian guiding. After an hour or so of plunging about on top of a mountain, we felt that Up It Yo seemed to be listing a bit to the right. There was a strange clattering sound too.

We had a seriously damaged tire.

And so began Lucy's finest hour.

Next day gave us our biggest challenge yet. After an hour's driving across more moonscape, the weird thrumming sound from the back of Up It Yo got my attention. I looked in the wing mirror and saw flapping rubber. Stopped and out of the driver's seat, I saw the disaster that was the off rear wheel.

"Have we got a puncture?" Teri asked from the passenger seat.

"Er, you could say that," I said. The tire was *shredded*. The smell of burning rubber and dented wheel rim signaled major damage.

Teri came round the back of Up It Yo and swore.

Then she went quiet.

I was disappointed.

Teri was nervous.

I see such events as part of the adventure, one of those challenges that present you with the sense of achievement when you overcome it through your own resources. Yes, I was anxious about changing a wheel on a strange vehicle, but I have a sense of self-efficacy about mechanical things, thanks to my stepfather. The time we spent bonding when I was a child involved stripping down a Morris Minor and changing the cylinder gasket, building a kit car, tinkering on Sunday mornings with plugs and points, brake pads, petrol pumps, and all the like. I had no aptitude for mechanical engineering per se, but when someone nice gives you loads of attention, you tend to take notice. I learned the principles of combustion, the nature of oil rings, the difference between leaf springs and torsion springs, and I developed confidence in wielding spanners and screwdrivers and knew what to do with a pair of mole grips. Very usefully, for a girl who went to a convent school and never had a physics lesson in her life, I learned the principles of leverage, torque, and what happens when the irresistible force meets the immovable object.

I suspect Teri does not possess my sense of autonomy when faced with a broken wheel, but she's very good at not panicking. She clearly put her trust in me (what option was there?) and helped with the task.

We had two spare tires. One was under the vehicle somewhere inaccessible. The other was in the back of Up It Yo and had been beating a rhythm for hundreds of kilometers thanks to its rubbish strapping, as if to say, "Let me out of here!" So now it had its chance. Unfortunately it was very much at the back of Up It Yo, so all our gear had to come out first. Teri put the camp mattresses (which we left inflated) on the roof to keep clean. The rest—food boxes, camping gear, backpacks, tool box—all got strewn about the ground.

I found a bottle jack and appropriate tools under the back seat, as promised (thank you, thank you, Value Rentals!), with added wooden block to raise the jack in order to compensate for Up It Yo's high clearance. The winding arm for the jack was fairly flimsy rubbish, but Teri and I took it in turns to gradually wind the thing up to meet Up It Yo's sill. I expected the nuts on the wrecked wheel to present the usual problems that all pneumatic drills give to lady wheel-changers: being on too tight. I tried, rather feebly. Nope. Teri enquired if I was turning it in the right direction; another thing I learned to the point of instinct in my childhood. To her credit, when I said, "Definitely," Teri didn't doubt me, she just jumped on the wheel brace with her DMs and loosened all the nuts.

The jack was too short. Even with the wooden block, when the jack reached its zenith, we had enough clearance to take the wrecked wheel off but not enough to get the inflated spare on. So here's a dilemma I've never had on a normal road: either we'd deflate the spare to get it on (then hope the air pump worked) or reduce the road surface. I got the spade out. The track was hard-baked gravel, but, through chipping and scraping with the spade, I managed to make a hole underneath the axle deep enough to slide the inflated spare in place. Phew! Another test successfully met! Teri and I were both relieved; I was soaked in sweat with the exertion in ninety degrees of direct sunlight but had been supplied with water by Teri throughout.

We looked at our wrecked tire. It was not a pretty sight. What on earth would Value Rentals think when we arrived back with a tied-up windscreen wiper, a piece of wood jammed behind the cab, a filthy vehicle, and a burnt, shredded wreck of a tire and wheel? We'd have to worry about that later. Next stop, Epupa Falls. Oh, if only!

I did my bit by stowing a lot of our kit up on the roof to clear the way to the spare tire. I fiddled a bit with the jack, and leant a bit of weight to unscrew the screwy bits and then again to screw them up. But mostly I drank water, had a comfort break that startled a mountain hare somewhat, and made lots of encouraging rallying noises while Lucy did all the work.

After an hour or so, we headed off again. We'd gone about a kilometer when I had a sudden thought.

"Did we remove the stuff from the roof before we started out again?"

"I didn't. Did you?"

Neither of us had, so our inflatable sleeping mats were somewhere up a mountain. We needed to get them back before a Himba snaffled them for cozying up his hut. I told Lucy to stay in the car, and I'd walk back up to collect the stuff. I'd got a little way up when I heard the engine start up. Lucy was attempting to reverse the truck up the narrow crevasse of rock.

I nearly had hysterics. "Stop! For heaven's sake, just stop!" I had visions of a smashed, punctured exhaust pipe as well as three more shredded tires. And we had only one spare left. Lucy heard the panic in my voice, and although I think she'd have enjoyed a bit more 4x4 reverse mountaineering, she stopped and waited patiently while I continued back on foot.

It was fortunate that both mattresses were bright orange. Teri found the first one among some camelthorn. The second, being the first to depart the roof, was nowhere to be seen. The track behind us was a steep, rocky slope up, which had been much easier coming down. I was keen to reverse back up it, but Teri volunteered to walk the next bit. The second mattress finally located and retrieved, we set off again.

The going had got easier, as much of the track ran along the river on the level sand. We just had to weave between palm trees and fallen trunks. We relaxed and enjoyed the beautiful country. It was worth the struggle to get here as this was paradise. There couldn't be more than fifty kilometers to Epupa Falls, we reckoned, but we had learned by that stage not to cross bridges, or riverbeds, before we got to them. The land had opened out and flattened. We'd lost the mountains and ran alongside the river with just flat plain to our left. We'd crossed a lot of omiramba, riverbeds that fed flood water from the mountains to the river. Most were straightforward, some were shallow fords with gravel beds, but the next one was blocked.

This omuramba had steep sides along its length, with one narrow crossing gap, just wide enough for a vehicle. Right across this gap was a large tree trunk, obviously washed there by the last flash flood. The trunk was about three feet in diameter, not a palm tree but some sort of deciduous species that grows a fine girth. And it was right across our path, all twenty feet of it. We got out. Hmmm. There was no way we could shift it, but a bulldozer might. We didn't have one of those. We had Up It Yo with bull bars the size of a rhino, but they didn't look up to the job either.

We walked either side of the riverbank to find an alternative route, but the bank was steep all the way along as far as we could see. The river end was boggy, and we didn't fancy getting stuck in deep mud. The tree trunk lay across the path, blocking nearly the whole track, but with a gap of about three feet on one side. The trunk was also angled toward us, with the gap nearest our side of the ford. I had an idea. We did have Up It Yo, and we also had a towrope—at the back of the pickup part of Up It Yo—holding all our gear in place.

Out came all the gear again. Out came the towrope and its linkages for the hook on the front of the Toyota—which Up It Yo didn't have. Teri set about finding a point on the tree trunk to secure the rope, and I brought Up It Yo as close as we could get without getting tangled in branches. With one end of the rope round a branch at the nearer end of the tree, I had nothing to secure the other end to except the bull bars, and no linkages would fit, so I tied a granny knot. Well, it might have been a reef knot, who knows. I wanted to try a fancy bowline, but I'd forgotten how to do them: "The rabbit comes out of the hole, round the tree, and back down the hole"—that's what I remember about bowlines. I also remember that they are easy to undo after you've pulled them tight. Not so with granny knots.

Having secured Up It Yo to a tree trunk, I inched back, with Teri doing her "left a bit, right a bit" stuff. The gap grew as we pulled the trunk toward us, like opening a door inward. Because of the angle of the tree and the fact that Up It Yo was restricted to pulling only directly backward down the track, we were soon in danger of blocking the gap completely with the tree. There was a finite space we could make with this operation. Would it be enough?

We inspected the gap. It had grown. Up It Yo might squeeze through if we either took the doors off or climbed the bank a little bit and swung hard right and then left. Teri untied her end of the rope, passed it through her window, and got in. We went for it, up a lump on the bank, branches scraping at the windows, hard right to maximize the gap, hard left to chuck Up It Yo's backside round, and through! Up the other side, we stopped to get the towrope off the bull bars. Oh. The granny knot had shrunk to the size of a pea. There was no way that was coming undone.

So we trucked on, wrecked wheel in the back, string holding the windscreen wiper on, branch squeakily jammed behind the cab, and towrope trailing from the bull bars in through the passenger window.

We reckoned we had ten kilometers to go before Epupa Falls, a bath, a bar, and a comfy bed. We started to see signs of habitation: a wooden sign to a clinic down a rocky track, goats in the undergrowth, falling-down kraals. Must be there soon. We slowed for another omuramba and got flagged down by an eager Himba adolescent boy, resplendent in sarong and plaited hair and with the ubiquitous walking/prodding stick. Teri groaned. I stopped. He grinned.

"Epuwa?" he said, then chatted on gleefully about something, with us nodding incomprehensibly.

I thought he said Epupa. Where else was there to go?

"Yes," I said. Teri muttered. The teenager grinned and shouted to an invisible person under a tree. A loud conversation ensued, Teri made impatient signs at the teenager, he reassured, then shouted louder and more urgently at the tree.

Eventually, two people emerged with bundles—another teenager and a man, both also dressed in their finest Himba garb and sporting the usual sticks and machetes.

By this time, we had given up putting our gear in the pickup section of Up It Yo and had stuffed most of our food and clothes in the back, with seats carefully folded away to make more room. Somehow we got three Himba warriors and their sticks and bundles into the back, sitting on the floor, in between our food boxes. They giggled and squeezed and wriggled in. We set off.

Adolescent males are the same the world over. Put them in a compromising position with two mature women present, and they find everything hilarious. They also tend to laugh like hyenas; high-pitched whinnying kept coming from the back every time we went over a bump. We heard the word "English" every now and again, accompanied by more whinnying. I wondered how many women had been annoyed by the inane giggling of a young Himba warrior scrunched up in the back of her car.

At least they knew the way, except their way was not ours. We said "Epupa" and pointed, and they nodded and pointed. We were encountering the occasional fork and crossroad in the track, but they were quite insistent on directing us. We thought this was an advantage. Eventually we came to civilization. Well, we came to a gravel road, of C class. Clearly this was the "long way round" road to Epupa, as we should have come to Epupa first. Our guides had taken us a different route because, as it came clear, they wanted to go to Opuwo, down the road, while we wanted to go to Epupa, up the road. To our Western ears, these two words sound very similar. Never mind. We dumped them by the side of the road to get lifts and waved good-byes. Relieved of our passengers, with gear all topsy turvy in the back; smelly, wrecked tire; filthy mattresses; and feeling like we'd survived a war, we turned onto the C road and looked for civilization. Our day was not yet complete.

We soon found "civilization" in the form of a police roadblock. No sooner had we settled onto the road than we spotted a police car and fluorescent cones up ahead. We were flagged down. Now what? Then we realized that neither of us had our seat belts on. Seat belts? Are you kidding? We'd just been through hell in the wilderness and were being pulled over for not having seat belts on!

Finally, the tire was fixed, our belongings gathered, and we were on our way again. Following an incident involving a tree, a tow rope, knots, grapples, and a bit of shouting and swearing, we were able to make reasonable progress on flat, sandy terrain. We'd seen horses, cattle, goats, abandoned huts, and lots of beautiful birds, but no people, and more worryingly, no River Kunene. Clearly, no vehicles had been this way for a very long time; what track marks there may have been had long since been obliterated by dust. So we were just meandering along, heading in what we thought was a northwesterly direction and enjoying the scenery.

After an hour or so, we found that there was a watercourse on our left. It couldn't be the Kunene—that should be somewhere to our right (unless we'd somehow managed to cross over it and gone into Angola without noticing, but this was a bit unlikely, even for us!), and anyway, it was way too narrow and shallow. Suddenly a glistening body came crashing out of the water, dripping wet plaits and shouting whatever is the Namibian equivalent of "Oi! Stop!"

We stopped. He approached the truck, hung on to one of the handles to keep us stationary, and started yelling to his friends who were the other side of the water.

We sat patiently and waited to see what would unfold.

Think about this now. If, anywhere else in the world, a complete stranger waylaid your vehicle and yelled incomprehensively to his accomplices, would you stop? Would you wait indulgently to see what they wanted? I've traveled quite extensively, even lived abroad for a couple of years, and have always felt reasonably safe, but I would never allow myself or my vehicle to be accosted in such a way, even in somewhere innocuous like Tenerife, or Malta, or even Bognor! That's what makes Namibia such an unusual place. Instead of racing away from putative danger, we were relaxed enough to turn the engine off and curious to see what our next adventure would be.

Two more Himba crossed the river, and we had a "conversation" with the one that "spoke English."

"Opuwo!" he said.

"Epupa!" we said.

"Opuwo!" he said again.

"Epupa!" we said again.

Clearly his English was as good as our Himba, so we weren't going to get far with this conversation. The easiest thing to do was to try to make a bit of space in the back seats and let them hop aboard. Presumably they'd hop out again if they weren't happy.

We took turns to drive for several hours. Whenever we were unsure of our route, we would shout "Epupa?" at them, and they would point enthusiastically left or right or ahead and shout "Opuwo!" back at us. We must have traveled about twenty kilometers in this way, and however many times I glanced into the back, I couldn't get used to the vision of fur and bones and spears and big happy grins.

Eventually, we emerged onto a tarmac road in a north-south orientation. We knew that obviously we needed to head north (we were only about fifty kilometers off course), but the Himba Hitchhikers' chorus were off again:

"Opuwo!" they shouted, pointing left.

"Epupa!" we shouted back, pointing right.

The penny finally dropped. Opuwo and Epupa are distinctly separate places, about 150 kilometers apart. But to our ears, the Himba pronunciation made them sound the same.

We left them smiling and waving at the roadside and headed, finally, to our intended destination. We were relaxed and happy in the knowledge that we had successfully traversed eastern Kaokoland and were now heading toward Epupa, where a shower, bed, cold drink, and stunning scenery awaited us. If we'd been the singing type, we'd have been singing "She'll Be Coming 'round the Mountain" or "Show Me the Way to Go Home" or something of that ilk at the tops of our voices. As it was, we simply celebrated with water and biltong and bounced our way happily northward.

We hadn't seen a car for a while when suddenly, from the right, a policeman strolled out into the road ahead of us and flagged us down. We pondered aloud to each other as we approached, and decided that he was probably after a tin of corned beef and the price of a bottle of Windhoek beer.

We were wrong. He peered into the car and noticed that neither of us was wearing our seat belt. We'd dispensed with them early in our travels, as the uneven terrain meant that every bounce caused a friction burn on the shoulder, so we were a bit sore within days. We'd also reasoned prosaically that if the truck was going to roll down a mountain or crash into a river full of crocodiles, a seat belt wasn't going to make a great deal of difference to our survival prospects.

The policeman was unimpressed with our explanations and told Lucy, who was driving at this point, to "Step into my office!" We looked around in amazement, wondering why there would be a police station way out here in the sticks, and more to the point, why we couldn't see it.

The "office" was two long wooden benches under a tree at the side of the road, surrounded by another seven or eight policemen.

We got out and went to sit penitently on our bench while the "arresting officer" told us off for not adhering to Namibian highway regulations. He said that we were going to be fined N$1,000 (about sixty pounds). This would probably pay the entire northern Namibian force's salaries for a month, so we didn't feel too bad; we felt we were contributing to the provision of law and order. It seemed a bit rich though. What about all those trucks, lorries, tractors, and donkey carts driving all over the place with human cargoes bouncing about unfettered? They didn't get any sanctions!

The fine took a long time to process. There was the policeman whose job it was to flag us down and explain why we'd done wrong. Then he vacated the bench, and another one sat down to record the details of Lucy's driving license on his form. He was replaced by another policeman who asked to see our car-hire paperwork and recorded the details on his form. A fourth then occupied the bench to ask for our credit card details, which he duly recorded. A fifth took the bench with a machine to process the payment. A sixth took his place and wrote out a receipt for our fine. The seventh stood about throughout the procedure looking mildly bored. He didn't have any role at all.

"Are you the boss, then?" I asked.

They all laughed uproariously. He was very young; maybe he was a cadet. Or maybe his job was to carry the benches back to the station at the end of the day.

When we'd first arrived in Namibia, we were amazed at the sheer volume of staff in any venue. Shops had more staff than customers, restaurants had waiters and waitresses lining the walls, hotels had four reception staff to every guest, museums had more staff than exhibits, and garages were so well staffed that they provided seating for twelve alongside the two petrol pumps. There was a purpose behind this overstaffing policy: Namibia has a very low unemployment rate because everyone who wants a job is recruited. They are paid very little and may only carry out one miniscule duty in a sequence. (Pity the poor waiter whose job was to place the drink mats on the bar table. His more elevated colleagues were allowed to provide the drinks: one to carry the tray, and one to lift the drinks off the tray onto the table.) But they are employed, contributing to the economy, and feeling valued as a productive member of society. We had originally thought that this subdivision of tasks to share out the labor only applied to the more menial jobs, but after our encounter with the traffic policemen, we realized that it's a policy that operates at all levels.

It seems like an excellent way to reduce unemployment, but I'm not sure if it would work in Western cultures. Namibians have generations of inherent patience and watchfulness in their blood. They walk for miles and for hours to achieve the minor goal of buying their flour, or wait for days for transport to get them to the doctor. They live in cooperative communities, hunting together, building their huts through collaborative effort, collecting water and butchering cows as a team. So to sell a T-shirt as a six-strong team isn't as frustrating as it would be to impatient, self-sufficient Westerners.

One wrecked tire!

CHAPTER 13

Epupa Falls: Andrew, Vertigo, and the Red Doll

And so we return to Chapter 1, in which Teri and I stood on the border between Namibia and Angola, perhaps a foot in each, astride the Kunene River at the Epupa Falls. Our sense of achievement knew no bounds because we had made it the hard way, testing ourselves with experiences we neither understood nor anticipated; we simply knew that "out there" somewhere, we were going to meet challenges neither of us had ever met before, and we would have to find new resources to overcome them. To some extent I was a little disappointed that we had emerged, dusty, dirty, a bit tattered but definitely upbeat, to find people who had traveled the "easy" way up the C road. The respect we commanded when our journey became known soon helped me realize what two mature English ladies more at home in their gardens had achieved. We'd emerged from the wilderness, like Livingstone and Stanley, having overcome not just a few physical obstacles but situations in which we'd had to rely on our wits and self-belief. And it was nice to be able to have a bath and a cold beer.

Lucy and I were delighted with our accommodation in Epupa after the excitement and exhaustion of the previous two days. Omarunga Camp was a collection of canvas huts with thatched roofs strung along the bank of the Kunene River and a central reception/bar/restaurant area that was also thatched but open on all sides.

Our hut was so close to the river that we could take just two steps from our door to paddle. But as we could see at least three crocodiles lying in the sun on rocks in the middle of the river, we forbore to dip our toes. We had twin beds, a veranda, a wet room, and electricity. There were even little sachets of shampoo, conditioner, small bars of soap, and soft, white towels. Very Holiday Inn! And if the toiletries seemed a bit incongruous with the sandy, dusty floor of our hut and the punkah wallah air-conditioning fan, we weren't complaining.

After a short stroll through the grounds to get our bearings, unsurprisingly, we quickly adjourned to the bar. With the thunderous roaring of the falls a little way downstream, we decided we would visit them at sunrise the next day to appreciate their full glory. The owner of the lodge, Andrew, poured a glass of wine and pulled a bottle of beer from the fridge. I sat at the bar unable to lift my drink, being struck both mute and immobile by the sight of glistening condensation on the outside of the glass and the promise of icy alcoholic nectar within. I looked over. Lucy was staring at her glistening beer.

"It's too good to drink!" I said eventually. "Just let me look at it for a bit longer!"

Andrew laughed but very kindly got a chilled bottle from the fridge, plonked it on the bar, and suggested I look at that while drinking my wine while it was still cold.

We talked at length with Andrew over our drinks and found him to be a thoughtful, wise, and perceptive host. He was born and raised in Botswana before crossing the border to start his tourism career in Namibia. He was passionate about the country and its potential and fervent in his enthusiasm for his innovative, inclusive staff recruitment policy. Like the rest of Namibia, he seemed to employ twice as many staff as he realistically needed, but more interestingly, he was employing Himba from the local area to fill key roles in the lodge. The ladies and gents were required to wear the lodge uniform, but they kept their intricate hairdos and red-dye makeup, so their appearance was a compromise of cultural integrity and modern tourist sensibilities. The chefs cooked the sort of food that they would eat at home (kudu stew was delicious, as were the various vegetables and pulses) so that the waitresses felt confident and comfortable to serve the tourists. The staff were well trained and had the relaxed demeanor and social confidence commensurate with a comprehensive hospitality tuition program. This helped them to be approachable to the visitors who—unlike Lucy and I, who had had plenty of proximity to the Himba—may have left the country without having the opportunity or self-assurance to get into conversation with these charming and friendly people.

Tourism is one of the world's fastest-growing industries, and there's no reason why African countries shouldn't benefit hugely from it. Really, there are more reasons why they should. Teri and I had already encountered some of the problems with, and the responses to, increasing tourism in Namibia, and on the whole we'd been impressed by the efforts to help the country and its people benefit without destroying the very thing tourists come to Namibia to see.

UNESCO reports that tourism helps alleviate poverty, generates jobs, brings in foreign currency income and internal income from taxation, and improves infrastructure, provision of education, and health care. You can't develop tourism without a skilled workforce, and you need people to read and write and have information technology skills to service the tourism industry. To my limited toe-in-the-water experience of seeing change in progress in Namibia, one thing that seems to be happening is a developing ownership of Namibia PLC by locals, rather than a multinational takeover where the resources are exploited and the profits go elsewhere. It is to the credit of Namibia and her governments that there is little evidence of that kind of takeover happening.

The threats from tourism in vulnerable places like Namibia of course are legion. Uncontrolled tourism development threatens the environment for wildlife and local communities alike. Teri and I had already seen how projects to protect both were working hand in hand in Bushmanland. In Kaokoland, we discovered the community guards program in operation here too, delivered by the Himba and protecting the vulnerable, free-roaming wildlife species like the desert-adapted elephant and black rhino from poachers. This is a simple approach to a big problem, but it is shown to be a model for other African countries to manage their environment. When we arrived, Namibia was about to host the Adventure Travel World Summit, a conference on responsible and sustainable tourism. Apparently, Namibia was described then as an example to the world as an unspoiled destination.

The concern for us was that the very unspoiled nature of the country and the rich heritage we were witnessing and enjoying be protected without being exploited unequally. We had witnessed the begging in Tsumkwe, which contrasted so much with the efforts of the Bushman ladies at the village; we had seen extreme poverty and problems with unemployment mixed with a ready supply of cheap alcohol, and seen the effects of overgrazing in our journey across the northern edge of Namibia, a sea of dust, goats, and donkeys. People like Andrew are perhaps part of the solution as much as the problem. In working with the local communities, offering employment, training, opportunities for spreading the gain of the benefits of tourism, local people will see the benefits of protecting the environment they live in. Or perhaps it merely creates "us and them" divisions between those who benefit and those who don't, those who gain power and those who are dispossessed. Time will tell.

After a rather upmarket Treetops-style dinner of kudu in the dining area with some lively Germans, we withdrew to our tent-chalet, drew up the chairs on the front porch, and watched the sun set over the Kunene River. The weaver birds flew in to roost in the trees around our chalet, while plops and ripples from the river suggested creatures going to bed or stirring for the night-time feasting. Strange birds cawed and shrilled in bedtime farewells, and a cacophony of insects made up the background music that is rural Africa. The sun set in glorious red, the moon glazed the river with glittering beams, and the stars came out above us. We'd arrived.

From our porch, hugging sundowners, we tried to spot what was making the splashing sounds in the river in front of us. It had to be crocs or hippos, from the racket they were making. Teri had night-sight binoculars that shone a green beam at whatever you pointed them at. I think she'd brought them following the episode in Canada when we hadn't seen hide nor hair of a beaver but one night they came out in force, running across the island, bumping into our guy ropes, crashing and splashing and swearing at us. Did we see them? Did we buggery.

As with the beavers, we saw nothing in the Kunene that night, which is probably good because, whatever they were, they sounded very large and only about twenty feet away.

Nighttime in Africa is when things get eaten, including me. Teri had supplied herself with gallons of various lotions of baby oil, sunscreen, body moisturizer…you name it. I had sunscreen and deet. Our tents had in-built mosquito nets, and our chalet was made of fine mozzie-proof mesh, but being outdoors was always a risk, especially near water. That evening, I slapped on more deet in anticipation of being mobbed by all the mozzies in Epupa and prayed my yellow fever jab and malaria pills were working overtime. You can never tell when you're being bitten; you just find out the following day when the itching starts. I had already gathered a fine collection of bites on my feet, legs, and arms and was a touch past caring at this point. According to a documentary I'd seen on the BBC, mosquitoes hone in on the carbon dioxide from your breath and then manage somehow to determine which is the feet end. They then head for the ankles. This explains why I get bitten most on my lower half. I guess the arm and neck bites are because the mozzie couldn't get at my feet. I had asked my doctor why I needed a yellow fever jab if just going to Namibia for a few weeks. He gave me a gleeful smile as he drew out his favorite riposte:

"Do you know why they used to call Africa 'the white man's grave'?"

"No," I said.

"Because during the Empire days, that's where the British died in their thousands of yellow fever, malaria, sleeping sickness, and cholera."

Fair enough. I had the jab.

Which is good, really, because throughout our whole trip, I was pretty much eaten alive despite being layered in DEET, while Teri, sheened in moisturizer, didn't get a bite. I suspect DEET is a bit overrated.

The following morning Lucy and I were up and dressed before dawn. We followed the sound of the crashing waterfalls for about ten minutes, walked a little way up a hill, and turned around a rocky bend. We were rewarded with the most incredible sight.

Ahead of us the aqua-green water of the Kunene met the first rocky cliff of the falls and plunged hundreds of meters down in a thunderous white froth. From our perch atop the rocky Namibian bank, we could turn our heads and see a series of spectacular falls stretching as far as the eye could see from east to west and across the full width of the river to Angola. We leapt about like mountain goats trying to get the best viewpoints to take the photos that inevitably could never do justice to the extraordinary experience.

I have suffered from vertigo since I was very young. I think I was about ten when I became paralyzed with fear halfway up the Eiffel Tower. I stood rooted to the spot on the first landing, and my mother and sister decided they wouldn't waste the chance to carry on up to the top to admire the views, so they left me poleaxed with fear on my own while they went on upward to explore. After an hour or so, they returned, prized my white knuckles from the railings, bundled me into the lift contraption, and returned me to ground level.

It seems incredible behavior now, looking back. Leaving a minor alone and in the grip of terror would probably be classed as child abuse these days, but back then I just accepted that my phobia wasn't important enough to interfere with other people's enjoyment. This has been my attitude to my vertigo ever since. My husband likes to teeter on the edge of cliffs, glaciers, waterfalls, and mountains, and I have learned to stay well away, avert my eyes, and let him get on with it. Usually, if I try to climb a mountain, I burst into spontaneous and embarrassing tears, so I try to avoid triggering my fear.

I am aware that avoidance in phobic states is very attractive, and very dangerous. Avoiding the small things turns into avoiding the bigger things, until avoidance becomes essential. But there's a balance to be had. I once heard of a man who had a spider phobia so bad he couldn't leave the house (yes, the house is where there are lots of spiders—no one said phobias are logical). He decided to do something about this, so he signed up for some cognitive behavioral therapy and embarked on a course of exposure therapy. Pictures of spiders, real dead spiders, then real live spiders in safe glass containers were part of his graded exposure to the feared object. He was doing very well and overcame being housebound and having to avoid social and work events in case there was a spider about.

His life became "normal." Then he wanted to keep pet spiders, but his wife put her foot down. His flight to health had become a bit obsessive. His wife won, and there is an example of balance: So long as it doesn't interfere with your life, why put yourself through hell to cure a phobia? Good point. So long as you don't find yourself avoiding the small things, they won't escalate to the big things, and life can continue without stressing out.

In Namibia, we had taken Up It Yo up and down a few mountains and through some vertiginous passes. On these occasions, Lucy was required to take the wheel, and I stared resolutely into my lap or at a map. So it was a surprise as much to me as to Lucy that I was able to conquer my fears at the falls in Epupa and cavort quite confidently on the rocky cliffs. I even managed to get halfway up a steep mountain path to gain a better vantage point before having to admit defeat and leaving Lucy to climb higher on her own.

I think it's a testament to the sheer beauty of the scenery that I was determined to make the most of my unique opportunity to admire a view that so few people have had the privilege of seeing. We also both felt that the unspoiled nature of the area would soon be destroyed by development. Currently, there are no resorts on the Angolan side of the falls, and only two on the Namibian side. The falls are barely accessible by road, even using the C route, but there is a small airfield nearby, and tourists tend to take the easy option of flying in for a day or two with a guide and ticking Epupa off on their itinerary. Andrew told us that his company alone is planning a further two lodges in the area, and he's fairly sure that as the political situation in Angola stabilizes, they will start to invest in the tourism industry to exploit their natural resources. For this reason, we were so pleased to have taken the opportunity when we did.

We left the falls eventually and returned to the lodge via a small shack manned by Himba ladies offering various trinkets for sale. One of the ladies had a baby of maybe ten months old that was wearing a miniature leather thong with bits of fur attached, and his few tufts of hair were teased into waxy braids. It didn't look much fun being a Himba baby. He would occasionally struggle to his feet, fall flat on his face in the dirt, be hauled back into a sitting position by one little arm by his bored mum, and then repeat the process again. Clearly his developmental steps were going to be achieved under his own steam. No motivational parenting for this little chap. No toys either. We in the West have the idea that toys are a necessary educational tool to encourage our children to develop and refine their motor skills, but Himba children seem to manage perfectly well with the stones and bones and nonchalance that surrounds them.

We wandered around the little stalls and had to decide which of the ladies to purchase from. This was a constant dilemma for us at markets, craft stalls, and the like. They all had virtually identical stock, so it was awkward to purchase from one and not another without it appearing to be some sort of favoritism. The worst case of this was on the road to Ruacana, when among the donkey fields we spotted a long line of ladies displaying their produce on little thatched stalls. We were desperate for fresh vegetables and fruit and pulled over eagerly, only to discover that every single one of them was selling tomatoes. Either a large bowl of tomatoes or a small bowl of tomatoes. But just tomatoes. I like tomatoes, but I'm no connoisseur, and one bowl of tomatoes looks very much like the next to me.

The Himba ladies at Epupa had selections of bracelets and necklaces made from natural items gleaned from their locality—shells, bones, horn, porcupine quills, and mysterious little bits of metal. And then Lucy spotted a truly hideous doll in the likeness of a Himba lady, with bare breasts, braids, and goggle eyes. I have no idea what it was made from; possibly it was wax, but it was covered in the trademark Himba red dye. This ugly little effigy spent the rest of the trip residing on the back seat of Up It Yo, melting and sweating and leaking in the heat like a malevolent mascot, turning everything (and everyone) in its vicinity dark red.

Returning from the falls, only slightly hung over and with fresh red lumps on my legs, Teri and I went to the dining area for breakfast, which was a very civilized buffet of teas and toast and waitress-served cooked breakfast. I tried to dress respectably by putting on the zip-off lower halves of my shorts to make some slacks but found the legs part was now a shade lighter than the smoke-stained top half. It was clear that Andrew's lodge habitually catered for the higher end of the tourist market through the personal guided trips to the falls; hence, my resolve to look clean. When I'd finished investigating the muslin doilies with weighted beads around the edges covering the sugar, we sat on the table next to an elegant elderly couple who were obviously English. They were quiet, deferentially polite to the waitress, genteel in their manners, and clearly purchased their clothes in London's West End. We managed to breach the barrier that is English reserve and etiquette through that age-old ritual of borrowing the sugar. Well, actually salt, but it works just as well. Besides, I was desperate to find out who they were and what they were doing in Epupa.

They were from Sussex. I might have guessed, as I too hail from those parts of feudal England, though I am a Saxon serf, and they were clearly of Norman stock, and hence the ruling class. They were the people we'd seen at the falls the day before with the guide and had traveled up through several countries in Southern Africa. We soon got to swapping travel stories and reminiscing of Blighty. They used to live in a very distinctive house I remember from my bus journey to school and passed twice every day. Teri muttered that if anyone said, "Well, it's a small world," she would poke their eye out, so I stifled it as soon as it occurred to me.

This couple were, however, endeared to me, and they soon had Teri purring when we explained the route we had taken to get to Epupa. The gentleman commented regretfully that that was the proper way to do it, how adventurous we were, and how they were only touching the surface when we were delving deep into the experience. He didn't put it that way, but that's what he meant. Although it struck me that he had the quiet air of someone who had been there and done, that in his youth, probably while being shot at during a war, but of course never mentions it. His wife voicelessly conveyed the wisdom of her years as his support through thick and thin. They gave us credit for having a go. And yes, the gentleman was right. This is why Teri and I had come to Namibia and chosen to travel off piste with Up It Yo. By taking risks, being adventurous, and going beyond the safety nets, we'd been on a journey that so far had not only given us great insight into the country and its people but shown us our own capabilities too. I think this couple "got" this and I felt, well, vindicated somehow.

Later that morning, after we'd packed our gear, I spoke to Andrew about the Himba and how they make use of the resources that development was bringing. I was really interested in mental health and how this is seen in Namibian culture. The World Health Organization is putting resources into making better access to mental health care in countries with low or middling income. While the WHO is pressing for more psychiatrists with medication and generally a medical approach to mental illness, there is also quite a bit of concern that this may bring along some of the stigma and disabling aspects of diagnosis with it. People on heavy medication struggle to hold down jobs in industrialized countries, so what impact might this have in countries where "work" is much less easily defined?

I was at that time in the middle of a research paper exploring mental health problems in what's termed "the Global South" (as opposed to Europe and North America, I suppose). Anyway, the issue is whether exporting Western ideas of what mental illness is into cultures that operate with different values may threaten the conventions of those cultures. For example, Western counselors who turned up in Sri Lanka to treat people for posttraumatic stress disorder after the 2005 tsunami found that people weren't distressed by the event itself. Perhaps natural disasters are more accepted or even expected. However, what people were concerned about was the loss of a social role: what they did in their society was gone. Being a farmer, husband, or shopkeeper was a valued social role. This distress didn't lead to posttraumatic stress disorder but to depression. So, people are affected by events differently depending on their culture, and assuming the same values apply in the industrialized West and the Global South may be a bit erroneous. What could happen, however, is that if people are told they have schizophrenia, depression, or whatever, it is quite likely that the symptoms of those labels will become important. This has happened in Tanzania, where people were told that a behavior called "high expressed emotion" (that is, doing a lot of shouting, complaining, and throwing your weight around) is part of schizophrenic families, so, lo and behold, that's how people started to behave around people diagnosed with schizophrenia. This may have been in order to get a diagnosis for a "problem" relative, get a pill, and therefore get a "cure." People do the same thing in England when they see their general practitioner and want antibiotics for a sore throat. Who hasn't hammed it up a bit to really get the message across that they are not well?

So I was interested in what the Himba do when they get depressed (that is, what *I* would call depression). According to Andrew, there is no division between physical health, mental health, and spiritual health. If a member of the community gets sick (with a wide definition), he or she will consult the community witch doctor first. This is the matriarch of the community, and Andrew used the term "witch doctor" to describe this person. It this matriarch will decide what is wrong and tell the sick person what to do. This may mean going to see a doctor or nurse, or something else, but the matriarch is the gatekeeper of access to health care and the one in the role of assessor.

I added this insight into my paper as an example of how mental health or illness may be seen completely differently in different cultures, and that expecting people to comply with the Western notion of biological illness is problematic. Thank you, Andrew.

Leaving Epupa was rather sad because it felt as though we had arrived at our ultimate destination: the farthest reaches of Namibia on our journey. After the D3700, anything was surely going to be an anticlimax. We were also turning south, in a Windhoek direction, and so eventually back to the airport. Not so fast though. We had two more wildernesses in our sights, and perhaps those for which Namibia is most renowned: its desert and the Skeleton Coast.

Teri negotiates with Himba and Herero craftswomen

CHAPTER 14

AQUA AND HIS CATS

We left Epupa a bit reluctantly. Apart from the spectacular scenery, it had the luxury of beds and cold drinks, but it was time to go bush again before we went soft.

We'd read about an irrigation system set up by a Greek immigrant at a place called Warmquelle, southeast of Epupa. The ingenious Theodopolos had harnessed some underground natural springs and created an extensive network of overground pipes to facilitate the growing of fruit and vegetables. Lucy and I both liked the idea of the natural springs and were also keen to sample fresh vegetables, so we headed southward.

The road was long and straight and tarmac, so I was happy to be at the wheel. We passed the spot where we'd had our police interrogation and noted that the "office" was no longer in situ. Presumably they'd reached their fiscal targets by imposing our fine, so were taking the rest of the month off. We planned to go to Opuwo, where our Himba friends had tried to take us a few days before, to fill up with petrol and provisions before driving on to Warmquelle.

Driving through Herero country provided a fashion show of ladies wearing their Victorian-style, full-length, fitted dresses and ornately contrived horned hats. Whether they were walking along the dusty roads or riding in the back of pickup trucks, they managed to look cool and clean, which was remarkable really, as Lucy and I seemed to be permanently covered with a film of dust. It seemed a bit unfair that the ladies were required to wear what almost amounted to fancy dress, but the men were dressed in casual shorts and T-shirts.

We had several discussions about whether we'd prefer to be a Herero lady or a Himba lady, and we tended to vacillate between the two. The dreadful, claustrophobic Herero dresses would be so uncomfortable in the heat, but on the other hand, you'd feel as though you were permanently dressed for a glamorous evening out, and the hat would come in useful on bad hair days. The barely there Himba-wear would be lovely and cool, but constantly smearing yourself with red dye and wax would be time consuming and messy. Eventually we decided that if we were to be reincarnated as a Namibian, we'd prefer to be a bloke.

The outskirts of Opuwo were announced by the usual plethora of cuca bars and shacks advertising booze, hairdressing, and various personal services. It was a bustling place as we drove through the well-populated streets to the center of town and pulled into a crowded carpark next to a supermarket. I sat in the truck while Lucy went off to find some cash. I had the door open and was putting on my boots when two youngsters aged about twelve sidled up.

"We can look after your car!" they said, holding out their hands for cash.

I assured them that I was more than capable of looking after my own car.

"Sweets?"

"Fruit?"

"Drinks?"

"Plastic water bottles?"

I replied that I had none of those things.

They were persistent and trying hard to see what was in the boxes in the back seat, but they were thwarted by my refusal to budge.

"Money?"

By now I was starting to feel a bit besieged and asked them to go away, saying that I had no intention of giving them anything, as I don't believe in encouraging beggars, especially well-fed beggars.

They continued to hang around with their hands out, and then a youngish man strode out from the supermarket and headed toward me purposefully. Oh Lord, I thought, another person coming to harangue me for a handout. But it turned out that I was lucky enough to have encountered probably the only person in Opuwo who not only had a university education but could also speak fluent English. Not only that, but his studies had been in tourism and economics. He proceeded to reprimand the children, telling them, "*It is peasants like you and your lazy families that diminish tourism in our country. You give us a bad name and a bad reputation. You should go to school and learn to earn a living! You should be ashamed of your laziness, your insolence, your rudeness, and your bad attitude!*"

It seemed a bit brutal but had the desired effect, and the children slunk away. He was now on a roll and proceeded to give me a potted history of the economic situation in Namibia, the prospects for tourism, and how the only way for Namibia to progress economically was to stamp out the "peasant underclass."

Blimey.

This all seemed a bit too radical and excessive for a downtown carpark in Opuwo, so I was glad when Lucy returned with the cash. She was expecting to have a quick look around the supermarket, but I couldn't face any more sociopolitical lectures, nor indeed did I particularly want to leave the truck unattended when the two thwarted children probably weren't far away, so I started the engine and, with a cheery wave, set off for the fuel station for a top-up without a backward glance.

The petrol station was a bit of a cultural eye-opener. It seemed to double up as a sort of community meeting place, and there were some very disparate groups hanging out together.

Herero ladies in full dress stood about chatting to seminaked Himba ladies; young male warriors leaned on their sticks and fiddled with their bones as they talked to conventionally dressed youths in T-shirts and flip-flops; young women in full makeup and miniskirts stood alongside the red-dyed and waxed young Himba women, and there were several albinos with yellow hair and pale, coffee-colored skin to add to the mix. One of them had a tiny yellow-haired baby that was being passed around affectionately.

As I watched this diverse population, I couldn't help wondering how they managed to relate to each other so effectively when they were from such different heritage. When a Herero lady is sweltering in her heavy dress, doesn't she look at her nearly naked Himba friend with envy? Conversely, doesn't the Himba lady feel a sort of sisterly compassion for the woman dressed up to the neck and down to the ankles in the midday heat? And the Himba with her breasts on display in the company of overdressed friends, does she not feel a tad underdressed? I also thought that the teenage boys must have a fair bit of cognitive dissonance going on. The boys we'd come into contact with in the course of our chauffeuring duties had all seemed typical of youths around the world. A little bit giggly and shy in female company, a little bit macho, and on the cusp of sexual awakening. So how on earth did they equate the joyously liberated, virtually naked Himba girls with their girlfriends who wore the cut-off tops, miniskirts, and hot pants? Clearly a topless young woman walking down the high street in any English city would attract extensive male attention, but the young men in Opuwo seemed immune to the braless Himba.

This tolerance of differences was also extended to the albino women we saw. Again, in England, any outward differences tend to attract attention, and an albino is a rare enough sight to be noteworthy. However, in Opuwo, the albinos were absorbed into the population with no apparent stigma whatsoever. In fact, I was probably the only person looking slightly longer than I should.

Opuwo was unlike any place I have ever been, even in Namibia, and although I usually celebrate new and unique experiences, I found the place a bit peculiar and was quite glad to leave.

I was also glad to get out of Opuwo but very proud of my new possession. A quick dive into a shop while Teri wasn't looking led to me emerging fully equipped with a precious machete. Everyone else had one; I didn't want to be left out. What I was going to do with it, I had no idea, but I'd been envious of the one I'd seen with our mysteriously quiet visitor at Enyandi and had felt covetous ever since. Mine was very sharp, about a foot long, and sheathed in a canvas scabbard. Teri was aghast but trying not to show it.

"What are you going to do with it?" she asked in an "I'm going to deal with this very calmly" sort of voice. I imagine she uses that manner a lot in prison.

"Cut up wood?" I suggested.

"The wood breaks easily," she said. "You just stamp on it."

"Well, it will be useful at home in the garden." I was trying to sound convincing.

"Hmm," said Teri. Not impressed.

I thought it had better go on the back shelf with my doll, which she also found offensive but deigned to ignore, while I quietly sought opportunities to wield the thing at some opportune moment.

We drove on, aiming for the next camp in our sights, chosen after much thumbing of the guidebooks and map. Despite two years of school German, it didn't occur to me that our next destination, Sesfontein, must have six fountains, or at least one or two springs. The trusty guidebooks both reported this with throwaway references as if it was beneath them to mention it. Having become used to indigenous place names, the switch to German had thrown us. I have found a similar effect when traveling from West Wales, where everywhere is unpronounceable, to East Wales, where everything is understandable, even if it's spelt bizarrely. I mean, Cardiff is just Cardiff. Why does it also have to be Caerdydd? I intend to discover if other bilingual countries are the same; how about New Zealand? I don't think Teri had noticed the language change either. And she speaks French. In Canada, we had driven across a bridge from English-speaking Ottawa to French Quebec, and suddenly she was having to translate the traffic signs. She also ordered breakfast in a diner in fluent French-Canadian, but the waitress soon switched to English, probably for my benefit. Shame.

The campsite we were aiming for was in Warmquelle, nearby. The guidebook said the campsite had a waterfall and deep pool that few visitors could resist diving in. Sounded good!

After a few drive-pasts when both Lucy and I missed the painted wooden sign, we eventually found the well-disguised track to Warmquelle. We'd tried asking the way at a roadside shack, but our pronunciation was way off, we discovered later, and we were met with blank stares. Understandable really—we were asking for "Warm quell" when in fact we should have been looking for "Valum-kell."

We saw Theodopolos's irrigating water pipes and inspected the vegetation with interest. Sadly, there was no abundance of vegetables for sale. In fact there was nothing for sale, but this didn't stop whole families rushing from their huts at the sound of the car. They would wave the car down, and we would stop to see if they had any goods for us to purchase, but inevitably they just stuck their hands out in appeal. Even tiny children of about three or four would speed through the undergrowth with their arms outstretched. We found this learned behavior quite depressing, and eventually, for our own equanimity, we stopped slowing down. It would have been useful to have my graduate friend from Opuwo in the back seat. He could have berated the idle "peasants" and lectured them on their national responsibility not to tarnish the reputation of Namibia with their indolence, in a way that we clearly wouldn't dare to!

After a winding route through chalky rocks and the occasional boulder, we found ourselves at the entrance to the campsite. The track pretty much disappeared, and the path turned into a steep downward slope that didn't look big enough to accommodate a Mini-car, never mind a great big truck. Wordlessly we swapped seats; this was clearly Lucy-driving territory.

It was so isolated that we half expected the site to be unattended, so it was a nice surprise to see a young man bounding up the hill toward us with a huge grin on his face. He gesticulated that we should progress down the slope and through a fairly deep ford, which we did, watching him leaping athletically from rock to rock.

There were no other visitors, so we had the pick of the campsite. Aqua (for that was his splendidly appropriate name) encouraged us out of the car and down a narrow path. We were stunned as we stepped through a gap in the rocks, and there was the natural spring and pool, with built-in shower waterfall. The pool was deep and blue and surrounded on three sides by steep, ferny rock faces; on the fourth side, a fallen tree lay picturesquely and invitingly at the water's edge. There were a few goats grazing alongside the spring, some dragonflies flitting about, but apart from them it was a still and calm oasis. We loved it, and Aqua clearly loved it too, because he couldn't stop smiling at our obvious pleasure.

We chose a site as close to the spring as possible and set up camp quickly. We'd checked with Aqua, and we were welcome to use the spring for washing and bathing as long as we didn't use any chemicals. So we took the opportunity to rinse out our smalls and hang them from the upper branches of the fallen tree. Lucy put all of our drinks into a bag attached to a rope and plunged them into the coolest part of the spring near the back where there was a bit of a rock overhang. We swam for a bit and then stretched out in the sun with our books, I on the tree trunk and Lucy on a large, smooth rock.

About half an hour later, Aqua returned with four Germans in tow. We'd told him that we liked the isolation of the place, so were a bit put out that he'd brought more tourists to "our" spring! I think it was a combination of Aqua's offer of the cheaper sites farther from the spring and the sight of our smalls drying in the sun that persuaded them to drive back up the hill to a site nearer to the entrance.

That evening we were assembling the food for our evening meal (I was trying to make a pasta sauce from the dozens of overripe tomatoes we had, reduced with red wine and garlic), when we were paid a visit by two domestic cats. We hadn't seen small cats in Namibia until then—lions and cheetahs, but no domestic moggies. We nicknamed them Herero-cat and Himba-cat—they were really good at begging—and Lucy proceeded to trawl through our provisions to see if we had anything they would like. She made feeding bowls by cutting the bottom off plastic water bottles and fed them a two-course meal of tinned tuna followed by strawberry-flavored porridge. Himba-cat helped open the tin with her face in the way and reluctantly shared the spoils with Herero-cat but really couldn't take to the porridge for afters. Lucy's strawberry porridge smelt sweetly synthetic and was the texture of cat sick, so I couldn't really blame either of them. I offered a slice of plastic cheese, but they were as fazed by that as our old Himba chap had been.

We left them to roam around the fire for a bit, and then they wandered off into the night, and we adjourned to our tents.

Warmquelle was heaven. I even got to use the machete! The only drawback was a lack of wood, so I had a long search for a suitable piece, which was actually a whole tree, downed by some long-departed storm. The tricky bit was getting it back to base, where I found Teri and two cats that had emerged from nowhere and taken up residence. The tree was brittle and dry, and I was disappointed to find I only had to stand on it a few times to break it down to sizable chunks for the fire. No machete wielding required.

I'd snaffled the drinks bottles into the pool earlier by swimming around to find the coldest spot, placing the orange bag underwater, and trailing a rope from bag to shore for easy retrieval. So we had the perfect spot and were set up for a relaxing evening: cool beer, fire, pool bath, and cats for company.

The two cats were so appealing I had to give them the tin of tuna we'd had bouncing around in the back of Up It Yo for days. I had a tin opener of sorts on the very useful Swiss Army knife, but it was no match for the tin of tuna. Ah-ha! Out came the machete. I thought I heard tutting coming from the chef, but Himba, Herero, and I engaged in the business of opening the tin. The machete was perfect! I knew it would come in handy. Herero and Himba were very appreciative of it as well and downed the contents with more purring than two industrial sewing machines.

A few hours later, after Lucy and I had retired to our tents, I awoke and became conscious of a heavy weight lying on top of the tent against my right hip. I wondered if there'd been a freak storm and the weight was a tent load of water resting on me. This had happened in Canada, and I knew to my cost that if I wasn't very careful, the water would seep through and drench both me and all of my belongings. I tried turning over onto my back, but the weight just sort of readjusted itself onto my stomach. And then it started purring. Himba-cat was using me as a mattress. This was fine for a while until Herero-cat decided that he'd like to share her bed, and I ended up being more of a wrestling ring than a cat bed. I tried pushing and poking at them through the canvas, but Namibian cats are obviously hardy, and they ignored my muffled protests and squabbled on. Eventually I decided I might as well get up and go and see how the spring looked in the dawn. Luminous and unearthly was the answer. I was glad I'd looked.

Warmquelle is still in Kaokoveld, but by heading south we would be entering southern Damaraland. Our next stop was to be somewhere near Brandberg, a mountain range in a geologist's heaven, apparently, but its treasures were likely to be lost on us. Neither Teri nor I had paid much attention to science in school. However, the landscape would change from flat plains to red rocks and mountain passes, and Teri would be challenged again by precipices and steep tracks.

We left Warmquelle and the refreshing pool behind, with a sad wave to Aqua, Himba, and Herero, though they would soon be entertaining their next visitors, we were sure.

The route south was straightforward. The C43 was clearly marked on all the maps, and even tarmacked in places. Everything was going swimmingly until we reached the mountains and the road turned into gravel and loose scree and wound its way snake fashion up and down the sides of the mountain range. Teri did well until we faced a long, slow climb with a sheer drop on her side of the vehicle, so I took over. She was soon distracted by road signs with exclamation marks (surprise ahead), bend warnings (no, really?), and pictorial elephants (where?!).

We aimed first for diesel in Uis, which is a small mining town, largely closed. We entered along its gravel high street slowly, like thirsty homesteaders arriving in Tombstone. It was quiet. Too quiet! There was no traffic, no parked-up pickup trucks, no goats, no other tourists. An air of forboding grew in Up It Yo's cab. Where was everybody?

Nearing the "town center" (there was a crossroads), we noticed loafers: young males hanging around, sitting on steps, leaning on street corners, congregating. Hmm. Teri was driving, so I consulted the guidebooks for warnings like "Do not go to Uis."

According to our more socially switched-on guidebook, Uis had been a large tin mine, with a small town that grew up alongside. When the mine closed in 1990, most of the population left, and those who remained struggled for survival from the tourist attraction of the "White Lady," a rock painting of many figures, including one character painted white. This figure excited its first European discoverers, who dreamt up all sorts of ideas of early visitors from the Mediterranean in classical times. With a bit more sense, the figure is now thought to be either a medicine man or someone disguised as an animal. But that is less attractive than a bit of Eurocentric interpretation, especially as the painting is a rather classy piece of primitive art.

Regardless of any possible ancient Greek visitors, the history of Uis in modern times results in a destitute population who struggle to find an income and rely on selling semiprecious rocks to tourists. So, when we turned in to the gas station, several likely lads approached with their wares, and much to Teri's disgust, I bought a few lumps of crystals and rocks, which nearly caused a riot between the vendors as soon as I paid for one item. This is where Teri's ability to draw boundaries around her personal space shows up my inexperience in these matters. We both of us are aware of our role in tourism and local economies, and the negative and positive impact our behavior can have. The beggars in Tsumkwe and Opuwo were a good example, but here were people at least trading something that was part of the resources of the area. Of course, I could simply have been fueling a dangerous and illegal trade in my naivety. I checked up on this later at home and found that Namibia definitely has rich resources of gems and semiprecious stones that local people can exploit through small-scale and independent mining and panning (called "artisanal" mining, apparently). Swedish experts have established a joint relationship with this group of independent entrepreneurs, connecting up miners, polishers, and vendors to help create a more sustainable (i.e., safer) source of income for local people. So they're not so much "blood diamonds," but rather more income support. I now look on my little collection of amethyst, rose crystal, and green garnet with a bit less anxiety.

Finding ourselves in Uis was ringing another alarm bell in my head, and I finally worked it out as we drove away and calmed down after being besieged by the growing crowd I'd attracted. When we collected Up It Yo—and sort of lied about where we intended to go—the chap sorting our vehicle out, Andy, decided to tell us a story of tourists who get a bit overenthusiastic with the exploring bit.

According to Andy, a group of German fellows had ventured out this way with their Toyota HiLux loaded with camping luxuries, satellite phone, GPS gizmo and, the bit that made us jealous, a fridge. Now, the fridge obviously works off the car battery. OK, great while you are traveling. Unfortunately, these chaps left it plugged in and running overnight while camping somewhere remote "near" Uis. Next morning—flat battery. Their Toyota was now nothing but a stationary store cupboard of luxury items. They used their phone to contact Andy, who was happy to go and rescue them and asked where they were. They had no idea (near Uis?). The description, "off a dirt road west of Uis" was not helpful, as there are many dirt roads, some not on any maps. Their GPS coordinates were not the same as Andy's system (something about which satellites you use and not to use the Russian ones?). Whatever, they were gobbledygook. Several days went by, and the Germans saw nobody for a tow or to get clear instructions on where they were. This reminds me of an American folk song sung by Michelle Shocked. When the lost traveler asks a local farmer if the road goes to the town, the farmer says, "Been here all my life, and it ain't gone nowhere yet." As Teri and I had discovered, sometimes locals who walk everywhere have a different concept of roads and directions from tarmac-trained Europeans.

After a couple more days, with Andy being phoned by the Germans' better halves from back home, a helicopter was hired (by the better halves) to search for a white Toyota somewhere west of Uis. At the same time, Andy had arranged for a garage owner in Uis to set up a search pattern. This person had systematically driven his breakdown truck along various dirt roads out of Uis and by day six spotted a white Toyota off the road. He'd beaten the helicopter to it. The Germans were fine, as they had lots of supplies, including warm beer. The better halves were reassured and, we suspected, busy plotting their revenge when their wayward husbands got home. So, rule one for exploring independently in Namibia: look after your wheels and they will get you home. Good old Up It Yo!

Brandberg is a big mountain, nicknamed the Matterhorn of Namibia, and people go especially to climb it as it's quite a challenge. The Brandberg Massif also has craters that attract the hardier visitors and require guided expeditions. Our destination, however, was the Ugab Valley where desert-adapted elephant were reputed to hang out.

We gave the area's many attractions a miss this time because we fancied a relaxing day at the campsite instead of hastily thrown-up tents and a thrown-together dinner. Arriving early meant being able to explore and just chill.

Brandberg White Lady Lodge and camping was just one of the White Lady–branded accommodation choices, but this one was in the Ugab Valley and had reasonable tent sites nestling under large camelthorn trees, according to the guidebooks. On arrival, we found hardly anyone else there (always a bonus) and well-equipped sites with braai, tap, and an ablution block with outdoor shower.

We decided at one stage to head up into the mountains via the Boshua Pass to see the long-legged desert elephants. Well, no. Actually, Lucy decided we'd go the mountain route to find the elephants. It was a slightly scary journey to get there, involving sheer mountain passes (during which I made close examination of my grubby fingernails) and hairpin bends (ditto). I am sure there is a less arduous way to get there, but perhaps less adventurous. We ended up on a steep, narrow track of deep sand. Lucy drove determinedly in the single-file tracks while I hyperventilated at the thought that we might meet an oncoming vehicle and need to back all the way down and start the whole blessed trek into the mountains all over again.

The lodge was surprisingly upmarket and had an eclectic selection of purchasing opportunities. There were glass cases full of jewelry. Not the gaudy baubles with which we'd delighted the Bushwomen, but ornate and intricate filigree pieces and bangles set with semiprecious stones. There was a case filled with carved wooden animals at five times the price we'd seen them in street markets. And there were T-shirts, hats, bags, and bandanas, all printed with the name of the lodge and a few long-legged elephants. There was also a counter that sold gourmet camping provisions: hermetically sealed packs of beef stroganoff, pad thai, sweet-and-sour chicken and chicken chow mein.

These packets reminded me of a surreal situation I found myself in at the prison where I had once worked. In the weeks preceding Ramadhan, the catering manager, the imam, and a representative group of Muslim inmates would meet to discuss the arrangements for the delivery of hot food to the wings after sunset. I was drafted in to take the minutes and generally to add my two pennies' worth. We held these meetings in the prayer room, with the Muslims comfortably lolling or sitting cross-legged on prayer mats on the floor and me perched politely shoeless on the only chair.

Security restrictions in prison meant that transporting the food after darkness wasn't possible. This meant that when Ramadhan fell in the summer months, we had to find a way of keeping the food hot for several hours from leaving the kitchens at around 6:00 p.m. until the daily fast ended at around midnight. After discussing the relative merits of flasks and heated trolleys, someone had the bright idea of getting packs of dehydrated food that could be reconstituted with the hot water urns that were available on the wings. We decided that we needed to assess the quality of what was available from our authorized supplier.

Thus it was that I came to be sitting barefooted, surrounded by the Muslim inmates lounging at my feet, all of us scoffing reconstituted halal meals out of foil bags, discussing the relative merits of chicken korma, spaghetti Bolognese, and vegetarian pasta. At ten o'clock in the morning.

Anyway, Lucy and I decided that we wanted none of the various items on offer in the lodge. If there had been a hideous tribal doll or a giant spear or suchlike on offer, I daresay Lucy would have been tempted. And if there were any fresh fruit or veg, I would have been enticed, but overpriced trinkets and prepacked food weren't our thing.

We set off away from the lodge and followed directions to their campsite. It was mercifully quiet, suitably isolated, and very scenic, with big trees, flowers, and shrubs. We set up camp. Lucy laid the fire and put up the tents, while I organized the larder and washing facilities and made the tea. We were becoming so attuned, like a long-married couple.

Once we'd quickly thrown up the tents, Teri and I set off for a walk along the riverbed to look for the famous desert elephants. Considering we just wandered off on our own, it is a good job we didn't find any. These creatures are a bit more aggressive than their savannah cousins, perhaps a characteristic that comes with the "desert adapted" logo. They are more able to survive without water and have long legs and a bit of a temper, for shooing off competition at waterholes, we supposed.

Having trekked along the riverbed for a while, seeing nothing, we were getting a bit disheartened when we saw the large dinner-plate circles in the sand all around us that are elephant footprints. They were everywhere, along with large mounds of fresh poo. We'd just missed them (by a day or two). But there were clearly signs of lots of animals in the vicinity. We thought that early morning would be more promising, so we made a plan to go on a walking safari at daybreak.

We got back to our campsite to find a hornbill family tucking in to our rubbish bin and goats wandering between the tents. We shooed the goats off but enjoyed a meal in the company of the hornbills. These comic birds are one of the main joys of Namibian wildlife. They often appeared at our campsites as soon as Teri and I got any food out, hopping around on the fringes and waiting for us to retire. Then they were quick to move in and make the best of any food spillages and crumbs we'd left behind. Pity they didn't do the washing up too. We were told later that the female retreats to a hole in a tree, wads up the opening with whatever's to hand so that only her head pokes out, and remains there during child-care season, while the male does all the hunting, feeding his partner as well as any offspring that may appear through the hole. This sounded like a great idea to us: get hubby to do the shopping to feed "The Mrs."!

The next morning, after a night of scurrying, chirruping, growling, and snuffling noises, I got up at dawn to go trekking. Teri was going nowhere at that time in the morning, apparently, so I trekked off on my own for a bit of quiet stalking. Early mornings are lusciously cool and devoid of insects, and a good time to spot wildlife on their way back from waterholes. I walked as quietly as I could, stealth being the watchword, avoiding snapping twigs, rustling leaves, and squeaky boots. I found the tracks we'd seen the evening before, but no fresh ones. There were signs of rhino poo, and it occurred to me that I could walk into one by accident, and then what would I do? One of the problems of being stealthy is that the animals don't hear you coming, so you take them by surprise, and they get frightened. The sensible ones run away, and the bigger ones probably attack you. Ah. Since I wasn't an expert at spotting gray rhinos or elephant in the brush, and they really are hard to spot among the trees, no kidding, it would be safer to announce my presence. Oh, what the hell, I decided. I'd keep quiet, and I might have a close encounter to tell people—if I survived it, of course.

I trekked on but saw nothing. I heard the odd rustle a way off, probably kudu or gemsbok, but no elephants. So I turned for home and had to track my footprints back in places, as I found forked paths look quite different in reverse. As I was looking down, a sudden movement by my foot made me jump. A "branch" suddenly shot across my path, whipped around a small tree trunk, and disappeared into the brush. It was a long, dark gray snake shooting off for cover as my stealthy approach disturbed it. It must have been less than a foot from my boot, and I'd nearly trodden on it, with all my creeping about. At least I'd seen something for my efforts, especially having gotten up really early. I had no idea what type of snake it was. None were featured in our guidebook, but the only one I'd heard of was a black mamba. At least it wasn't one of those because this one was definitely gray.

Later in our trip, we found a bookshop, and I perused a book on Namibian wildlife. I looked up snakes. It had great pictures, and there was mine from Brandberg, a long, dark gray snake. I read the description. This snake is rather misnamed because it is really dark gray when its name implies it is black. The name comes from the color of the inside of its mouth. Its venom will kill a man in twenty minutes. It is one of Africa's fastest, most deadly, and feared snakes. The black mamba. Holy bejesus.

The following morning, when I crawled from the tent, I saw that Lucy's walking-cum-fire-prodding stick was gone, so I assumed she was wandering somewhere in search of elephants. I had made myself a smoky cup of tea and was standing half asleep and vague next to the tents admiring the view, when I heard a strange rumble in the distance. A drumming of hooves accompanied by frenetic bleating. And it was getting nearer. I stood stock still in amazed awe as a massive herd of goats bore down on me. They had evidently been released from wherever they had spent the night and were in a hurry to get to their chosen grazing. I was directly in their path but acted as no hindrance whatsoever. They swarmed around me, left and right, and occasionally head butting my knees, bleating and stampeding their way to their grub. The dust flew for what felt like ten minutes but was probably only one. I wasn't frightened exactly, but I felt a desperate urgency to stay on my feet. How ignominious would it be to go to Namibia and suffer death by marauding domestic goats? Lions, elephants, even Lucy's black mamba—but goats? Way too embarrassing.

Aqua and his lovely spring pool at Warmquelle.

Chapter 15

Ignatius, the Cheetahs, and Why We Thought It a Good Idea

Teri and I both studied psychology with the United Kingdom's Open University, and one module involved studying biology and animal behavior. This was fortunate because comparative psychology, as it is called, was something I really took to, and studying meerkat sexual promiscuity was interesting enough to give me a good honors degree. Thank you to the BBC and the then contemporary wildlife programs called *Meerkats United* and *Meerkats Disunited*. *Meerkats United* showed how these cute African mongooses live in desert conditions and survive by being fiercely loyal within their own family groups. They look out for each other, play nanny to others' offspring, and fend off any other meerkat group, so protecting their own gene pool. Basically, they don't like to mix—a bit like Manchester United fans and Manchester City fans. The second program, *Meerkats Disunited*, featured a very saucy minx in one meerkat group who rather took a fancy to a sneaky male from another group. They called him Bandit; it suited him. These two would meet up in secret behind a bush when no one was looking (except a camera crew), get up to naughty mischief, and then carry on in their respective rival groups like nothing was going on. The naughty minx then brought Bandit's babies up in her own meerkat group, like cuckoos in the nest.

So my thesis was about genes and the importance of promiscuity. The meerkats are potentially threatened with inbreeding if their strict group loyalty is always obeyed; the group becomes a family of cousins with very little genetic variation and develops high vulnerability to disease or infection. In short, they would die out as soon as a nasty virus came around.

One interesting feature of the northern European plague in the Middle Ages is the answer to the mysterious question, if everyone exposed to the plague died, who buried the bodies? Answer: the people who proved to be immune to the plague. Plague in northern Europe then had 100 percent case mortality: if you got it, you bought it. The same virus did the rounds for more than three hundred years, killing an awful lot of people. That does something to a population. In northern Europe, it is thought to have created a selection pressure on the population so that those who carried genes that made them immune were the ones who spread their genes to the next generation. The population developed resistance through genetic mutation and natural selection. Of course, improved medicine and a tin of flea spray helped in the long run as well.

So what's this got to do with promiscuity? Well, not a lot really, but it's an interesting example of how it's really important that a population—humans, meerkats, cheetahs—consist of individuals who vary in their genetic makeup, and they need to crossbreed every now and again, to spread the word genetically, so to speak.

OK, lesson over. I knew a bit about meerkats and a bit about plague before Teri and I set off to find a place advertised in our guidebook called the Cheetah Conservation Fund, CCF for short. It said in our guidebook that it was near Otjiwarongo, had a thriving visitor center, and we could see cheetahs close up. The guidebook gave it the "thumbs-up" ethically and said that it needed support. OK, we were up for that.

There is a cookbook by Laurens van der Post (him again!) called *First Catch Your Eland*. This could apply to the CCF: first find your conservation fund. It was clearly marked on the map in the guidebook, but directions were from Otjiwarongo to the south. We were coming from the northeast, so we thought we'd be clever and take the north road on our map and come along a different route. This took us several hundred kilometers away from the guidebook route, but hey, we knew best.

So, after finding you can't get to it that way, we went to Otjiwarongo and followed the directions in the book. From the big C road, we had to take the first right. We saw a BIG sign to CCF by a little track that went to someone's shack, so presumed the road to CCF was the next right. Nope. And, yep, it was the little track. This took us to a heavily guarded army barracks where we were viewed with interest by Kalashnikov-wielding uniformed types who weren't strong on smiling. After a lot of gesticulating, arm waving, Teri smiling as though her life depended on it, and me hiding in the well of the passenger seat, we headed off up a highly unlikely dirt track littered with, well, litter. And the odd burnt-out vehicle, bottle pile, and shacks made of tin and cardboard. This scenery was typical of land immediately outskirting the towns, we'd found.

The track went on forever, and we persisted only to avoid going back past the army guys and the dodgy neighborhood. Several kilometers later the land turned to more cattle-grazing country, and eventually we reached a rickety metal gate and a hut. After the customary ritual of "how are you," et cetera, with the man on the gate, followed by the noting of our registration number, we were off for another long drive, at least reassured we were heading the right way.

It was worth all the hassle. Teri and I both agree that of all the places to visit mentioned in guidebooks and leaflets picked up at lodges, the Cheetah Conservation Fund headquarters is top of the list.

A little oasis opened up on arrival: beautiful buildings with sweeping, low, thatched roofs around a sandstone-cobbled atrium with garden beds and mature trees. Very civilized. We were met by the star of the show, Ignatius, a Rasta-hat-wearing young man with whom Teri was obviously going to bond immediately.

Ignatius is a Rastafarian with an angelic face and a gentle voice. He is a guide at the Cheetah Conservation Foundation, and we were charmed by his demeanor and his passion for his work. I liked him immediately.

The cheetahs, like the lions at the Wildlife Camp, had been given names. Some were named after the person who rescued them, so had human names like Peter and Angela and Brian. But some were given a name according to the conservationists' interests or political persuasions, so there was Hifi (named after the ex-president of Namibia), Blondie and Marley (for musical tastes), Paprika and Ginger (gastronomic tastes), and even Alexis. Not really sure about that one; perhaps the conservationist was a fan of 1980s television soaps.

Ignatius was a bit of a "cheetah whisperer," and rather than call them by their (sometimes rather idiotic) names, he encouraged the cheetahs toward him with a softly murmured "Kom! Kom, kom, kom!" This seemed to work, and they approached to his gentle croon rather than having to be enticed with lumps of dead donkey the way the Wildlife Camp animals were.

But at lunchtime, when the big enamel bowls of donkey meat were set out for them, they ran into the feeding enclosure with their legendary speed. They ate as though ravenous, starting with their own bowl, but periodically checking each other's to see who had the most left. If a neighbor was eating too slowly, it was fair game for him to be elbowed out of his bowl, and the bully would continue to eat the bigger portion, while the slow eater would have to make do with the bully's meagre leftovers.

The quick and the hungry indeed!

We were intrigued that they were fed from bowls, as this seemed a rather domesticated conceit at odds with the authenticity of the rest of the foundation's practices and philosophy. But Ignatius explained that cheetahs are in fact quite fastidious eaters, and greatly dislike having dust, grit, or sand on their food. In the wild, they would eat their kill from the top down, but the side that had lain on the ground in the dirt would be left to scavengers and vultures.

This knowledge actually caused us angst at a later date when we visited a lodge that homed rescue leopards and cheetahs. We were upset to find that, unlike the foundation, this lodge used their animals as entertainment, taking tourists into the enclosures and throwing pieces of meat into the air to encourage proximity. The poor things leapt to catch the meat, trying to catch it before it fell into the dust, as they preferred their food dust free. The entire spectacle offended us greatly.

We visited the foundation's museum, where I was quite mesmerized by the "Poo Sample" section. Feces from a variety of species had been collected, put into appropriately sized jars, labeled, and displayed. Since I'd been in Namibia, I'd started to consider myself a bit of a poo expert. Driving through the bush and the reserves, Lucy and I had taken great interest in the spoor that we came across, as this was the only way to know if there were any animals in the vicinity. We could tell the species (elephant dung being particularly distinctive), we could usually tell the direction of travel of whatever had left its calling card (look away now if this is TMI, but the dollop tends to be more pointed at the front than the back, or in the case of bucks, there was a lower density of pellets at the front), and we could tell how old the sample was by its level of desiccation and dehydration. We'd even shared the truck with a large specimen of old rhino poo (the poo was old—no idea about the rhino) after Lucy had decided that it would make excellent and free fuel for the campfire. She was wrong. It was undoubtedly free, but it refused to ignite. I was secretly relieved, as I really didn't want to spend the rest of the trip jostling for space with mountains of old poo.

We had an informative and interesting tour with Ignatius, during which he didn't limit himself to cheetahs but also pointed out birds, plants, and insects. He was extremely knowledgeable about all sorts of things, and we trusted his wisdom implicitly. So when he pointed out a huge tree with long, pendulous fruits about the size of large marrows hanging from it and told us that it was an African sausage tree, we believed him. It's only since we've been back and I've failed to find any reference to African sausage trees in any of my books that I wonder if he was teasing us.

Our tour included the education center. Teri was particularly captivated by the examples of "spoor"; looked like poo to me. The CCF train border collies to scent cheetah "scat" (that's poo to the rest of us), which they can analyze and tell which individual it was and what it's been eating.

I am usually allergic to "education centers," but I couldn't prize myself away from this one. Did you know that cheetahs don't have collar bones? They get in the way of running fast. We saw a skeleton—no collar bone. They have fantastic eyesight, with wide-angle lenses that allow them to keep their eye on the prize even when it's jinking sideways. This, and their great speed, is very advantageous in wide savannah but puts a dampener on their efforts where there are too many trees about. Cheetahs tend to run very fast and may not see the tree they run into until it's too late. This means their territory is rather specific and limited. Pressure from humans and overgrazing pushes the cheetah into denser bush, where they get injured running into obstacles. Ignatius explained that the CCF rehabilitates a lot of injured cheetahs, but the "tame" ones we'd seen were permanent residents. They were often brought in as cubs or young "pets" that had been rescued by locals and hand reared as cubs when their mothers were shot. Unfortunately, hand-reared cheetahs don't get the essential minerals they need from gnawing bones and end up with skeletal deformities. Ignatius pointed out one of their cheetahs that had a distinct waddle in her walk: the result of well-meaning hand rearing.

The CCF supports a lot of research into cheetahs. So, back to genetics. Apparently a major problem for cheetahs is, they are all related—to each other. There are two groups in the wild, those in East Africa and those in Southern Africa, and you can barely put a cigarette paper between them. The same goes for those in captivity. There may be loads of cheetahs around the world, but they all stem from the great bottleneck. A long time ago—we're talking last Ice Age here—the cheetah population suddenly shrank to only a small, related, population. This is the genetic pinch point from which the cheetah population increased by inbreeding but without developing genetic diversity. So, all the cheetah in the world are cousins, which is not healthy for any population and something the meerkats have managed to avoid by diversifying into separate groups that officially do not speak to one another but occasionally share the odd gene or two illegally (like Minx and Bandit). If the two cheetah groups remain separated for a few thousand years, they might develop diversity enough to strengthen the species, though this might be difficult because (a) they tend to need a rather narrow type of environment to live, which doesn't add environmental diversity; and (b) they're starting from a position of large similarity. So genetic drift is a bit tricky. The other problem this represents is that those in captivity are difficult to breed from, and even if there were a breeding program, they'd have to be very careful not to interbreed animals with different gene types. This sounds a bit strange, as surely that's what cheetahs need. Apparently the meerkat promiscuity solution is a bit premature for cheetahs, as cousins still breeding from cousins would create an even more homogenous world population; they'd all be the same, and what little diversity there is would be lost. So there are now strict laws about where rehomed cheetahs can go and a total ban in Namibia on breeding cheetah in captivity.

Somehow I managed to understand quite a bit of this from Ignatius and the education center, and I did a bit of looking stuff up when I got home. Of course, the biggest threat is not from natural disasters like viruses or droughts but from humans and loss of habitat. The Cheetah Conservation Fund were onto that too. The answer is sheep dogs!

Ignatius showed us the Turkish sheepdogs. The CCF has a livestock dog guarding program to stop farmers shooting cheetahs in order to protect their goats. The Anatolian shepherd dog is a big beast that looks like a mastiff and thinks it's a goat, especially when brought up with goats rather than people. This has lots of advantages because the dog will wander off with the goats as they graze and will defend them with its life if need be against predation. Any self-respecting cheetah, leopard, or not-too-hungry lion might think twice about tackling one of these huge hounds; hence, no goat killings and no cheetah or leopard shooting. Predation of goats drops to 0 percent when there's an Anatolian shepherd dog around. That sounds like a success!

The CCF has a model farm where they breed the dogs and teach local farmers how to manage the dogs with their goats. The dogs are placed with the farmers, but CCF makes checks regularly and provides veterinary assistance when needed. There's now a waiting list for puppies.

Education about the wildlife in Namibia is desperately important. Many town-dwelling youngsters are distanced from their own natural environment and believe that any big cat is a "tiger," which they are taught to fear, perhaps in the same way Western children are taught to fear the bogey man. Ideas about the wildlife being an asset to Namibia are getting through, however, and Teri and I had seen several programs by now, formal and informal, to help local farmers and visiting schoolchildren realize the potential of their own resources and get the message of ecotourism over to people. This place and organization was the best example we'd found so far. And when we think of the first "wildlife center" we encountered on first arrival—no comparison!

Anyone visiting Namibia: Go and run the gauntlet of the little track, visit the CCF, and spend money in the little shop. I bought a shirt that Teri approved of, an Herero doll that Teri disapproved of, and an ice cream made from local goats' cream. Marvelous!

Ignatius and the Sausage Tree.

Chapter 16

THE CASE OF THE MISSING SHIP AND SEALS, SEALS, SEALS

After a long drive through sandy desert, a bit of an altercation at the conservancy border (pesky tourists), and a race with an ostrich (we won, but only just), Lucy and I arrived at the Skeleton Coast. We intended to have a pit stop at Toscanini—a curious name and not at all in keeping with the German history of the country, so we were interested to find out its origins. We also planned to have a look at the *Winston*, a ship we'd read about that was marooned on the beach between Toscanini and Cape Cross. We were thwarted on both counts.

Toscanini was marked on our maps as being a coastal place approximately the same size as Warmquelle, which had been a reasonable-sized town with a couple of shops, a bottle store, some dusty huts, brick bungalows, and a small school, as well as Aqua's lovely campsite, of course. Toscanini had no shops, school, campsite, or even huts. Toscanini was one small brick house. And it wasn't even on the coast; it was about two kilometers in from the coast, perched on the edge of a wadi. We stopped the car in disbelief when we saw the sign proclaiming the house to be Toscanini. Is that it?! How, and even more curiously why, had it made it on to not one, but all three maps?

We again remarked on the idiosyncratic nature of Namibian cartographers before heading on toward the ocean.

It was a welcome sight when we arrived at the coast: beautiful blue glistening sea, with surprisingly strong waves. We meandered along the coastal road, admiring the dunes with their wind-induced ripples and swirls and the little clumps of flowering desert succulents with their startling, acid-bright colors.

We were less admiring of the many beer bottles that littered the roadside. There were a few rangers' vehicles patrolling the roads in the desert. We have no idea what their role was, as there were never any traffic jams, no road signs (apart from the occasional helpful "Sand" reminder), no pedestrians, no animals that we could see, no streetlights or potholes. The rangers seemed to drive aimlessly and stop randomly. We thought that it may be a good idea if litter picking were added to their job description; it would have made their working day a bit more purposeful.

After the disappointment of Toscanini, we were looking forward to the shipwreck. From what Lucy had read, it was a substantial vessel that had run aground. Except that it wasn't substantial enough for us to find it. We followed the directions on a little wooden sign and drove right out onto the beach, along the wet tide line, coming close a couple of times to marooning Up It Yo in the deep sand. As the going got tougher, I abandoned the driving seat to Lucy, and she doggedly drove up and down long stretches of sand, determined to locate the wretched ship. Eventually we agreed that it wasn't to be found, although we couldn't work out why not.

Since our return, we've remained baffled. Yes, the maps are rubbish, and the wreck may not be exactly where they suggested, but ultimately we drove the length of the Skeleton Coast and never saw anything that looked remotely like a bloomin' great ship. We've come up with a few explanations, but nothing definitive or even plausible. Maybe it was dismantled over time by souvenir hunters until there was nothing left. Or maybe it had been removed to a more secure site, such as a museum. Or maybe it had washed back out to sea. But in any case, why was the signage still there?

Yes, the mystery of the missing ship bothered me enough to look it up on the return home. It is still there but we missed in in the sea mist. I also looked up Toscanini and discovered Teri and I had found it after all but didn't realize what we were looking at.

But first, back to the bit Teri skipped over because it put me in a huge sulk. We had to pass through the conservancy border post before we could enter what is a national park. Nearly the whole length of this strip of coastline is a protected site. It is the famous Skeleton Coast, and to the eye, it is one hell of a long beach. The boondocks behind are desert of the real desert variety: sand dunes followed by more sand dunes. There are omiramba threading their way to the sea, but they mostly run underground, and inland there is the occasional wadi that sustains the desert-adapted wildlife. It is also famous for its diamonds, and there's one end of the coast that is strictly verboten because, they say, you can pick diamonds off the beach like seashells. I don't believe that, but if it were true, it would soon knock a hole in the diamond market if everyone helped themselves.

The border post was manned by a laid-back Namibian who moved at snail pace (malarial anemia?) and appeared to be unfamiliar with the paperwork and rules of the job. While we'd become accustomed to being almost the only tourists in Namibia, it was annoying to find another party at the post. In retrospect, this shouldn't have been surprising, because it took so long to process each party that Father Christmas would probably still be there come Easter.

We queued behind a group of young German chaps while they diligently filled out copious forms like all day would be fine for them. Then a retired South African couple arrived behind us, and the man of that party simply took over. When I say "retired," this does not mean an elderly Darby and Joan with sticks and "walk all over me" labels on their hats. No. This couple were used to getting their own way by force of personality and taking charge. This had advantages and disadvantages for Teri and me. Dressed like a Great White Hunter, the man, I'll call him "Jens," pushed past all of us, marching into the back office and getting out the forms he needed. He filled them in while I fumed in my English way about people pushing in front of an orderly queue and presumed he thought Teri and I were with the Germans (still dutifully bent over their forms and consulting together on every detail). Jens then leaned over the desk at the poor chap officiating and told him to give it the appropriate stamp. The Namibian official just backed off, politeness getting the better of him, while Jens then told him to stop faffing and get the Germans on their way.

By this time, Teri was nattering with Mrs. Jens outside while I watched the proceedings, making some attempt to get relevant forms. Words like *boarish* sprang to mind while I watched, but a creeping admiration emerged as I realized that Jens, with his fishing-rod-festooned 4x4, was in fact turning a bureaucratic nightmare into efficiency itself. Mrs. Jens then came to our aid, after Teri's chatting-up skills, telling hubby that we were English newbies needing similar aid through the paperwork. Jens went to work with a vengeance on our behalf. With Germans finally packed off on their way and a warning to the official not to try anything on with us regarding "charges," he thrust a short form under our noses and told us not to pay anything as it was all a con, and that you had to tell "these people" or you'd be there all day.

With a robust and cheery "good-bye and good luck" wave, they shot off in a dust cloud, fishing rods swinging on the roof like aerials, and Teri and I were faced with our form and the Namibian official. The Jens treatment had the poor man subdued into surrender mode, and he couldn't get us gone fast enough. No paying, no faffing. Brilliant. Thank you, Mr. and Mrs. Jens! I felt a bit steamrollered by Jens myself, and annoyed that Teri and I had been dismissed at first as the Germans' female add-ons. Still, it speeded things up and cost us nothing. Just the guilt of the bullied official to cope with.

The Skeleton Coast in Namibia is about five hundred kilometers long, or three hundred miles if you prefer imperial, from top to bottom. And Teri and I can verify that from the coast road it all looks the same. You have to take a special interest in sand, desert plants, and lichen to really appreciate the landscape. The coast itself, though, is awesome, and the beach simply goes on forever—as far as the eye can see and then some. We stopped en route at interesting inlets to explore and found flocks of waders on sandbanks, footprints of jackals (called "strand wolves" on the coast), and skeletons. I'd always thought the Skeleton Coast was so called because of the numerous wrecks: wooden hulls rotted down to bare spokes of planking that make them look like ribcages. I've now changed my mind. Whoever named this place must have been awed by the number of skeletons littering the beach. There are skulls, ribs, vertebrae, and quite a few unidentifiable bits all along the shoreline, scattered and broken up by scavengers. I scratched my head quite a bit trying to identify them. Animals, certainly, but nothing I've ever encountered before. The skulls were like dogs with sharper teeth. The lack of limbs was puzzling, and trying to analyze only bits of bodies made it confusing. Finally I found an intact "hand": long, narrow bones almost fused together on a shortened limb bone. Like a flipper. Ah-ha! Seals!

The road is salt, hardpacked and shiny, very flat in places, and verged with occasional succulents that are bright green or red. Our trusty guidebook explained that the landscape is very fragile, and driving off the road is very damaging to the lichen that films the sandrock terrain. We could see tracks running off the road across the dark brown scree that made up the landscape. Some of these could have been there for fifty years, according to the guidebook. We suspected they were more likely to have been made recently by tourists who couldn't resist a quick spell of off-road driving and bugger the lichen. Teri and I stuck obediently and respectfully to the road.

Our landmarks of Toscanini and the wreck of the *Winston* failed to appear, but we did come across a huge rusting structure on our left in the sand drifts. We stopped for a look round this skeletal monstrosity, trying to make out what it had been. Since neither of us have any engineering experience, the tangle of rusting struts and walkways meant nothing to us. It was some kind of mine/factory/drillhead thingy. The footprints, droppings, and skeletons of animals and birds told us something about how this barren-looking place was really quite inhabited. We wondered if they all come out at night. We only found out later that *this* was Toscanini, an exploratory mining site not long abandoned but quickly being reclaimed by the sea and the sand.

Lucy and I had spent most of the day looking for a town and a ship that didn't exist, so we were feeling a bit jaded and needed to find somewhere lovely to stay. The campsite we found was a bit of an oxymoron, being at the same time appalling but perfect.

The two men at the entrance shop accepted our N$15 fee and informed us that this entitled us to use all of the facilities. The shop contained a few dusty packets of crisps and sweets, bottles of bright orange soft drinks, and a few bundles of firewood. Not a lot to interest us there. We drove off the concrete path and onto the sand and remarked on how ugly the shower blocks and toilets looked—just gray cement squares with holes where the windows should be. We thought it would be a good idea to camp reasonably close to the facilities to save a long walk if we were caught short in the night, so, pulling up a hundred or so meters away, I went to inspect the facilities. I ventured into one of the toilet cubicles and was amazed to see that it had a toilet, a cistern, and a hand basin. Unfortunately none of these were plumbed in; they were just lying uselessly on the dirt floor. I checked all of the cubicles and found that they were all in a similar state: fully equipped but unplumbed. Next I checked the shower block. Again, it had a dirt floor, and I wondered how we were supposed to get clean, as presumably the floor turned to mud when the shower was turned on. I needn't have worried; although the shower head was attached to the wall, which was a step ahead of the toilets, there was no water. So much for our N$15 worth of facilities.

The chaps from the shop had gone home, and there were no other campers on the site, which stretched for about half a mile along the white sand beach. We were totally alone, with just seagulls and waves to listen to. The beach was littered with shells, sun-bleached driftwood, and curious bits of skeletons of small birds and beasts. The sea was clear enough to see small fishes dashing about in the shallows. There was evidently wildlife in the area, as we'd seen a couple of jackals as we were driving in, and there were other interesting animal footprints that required investigation. It was perfect!

We set up camp quickly and dragged an empty dustbin down to the sea to fill with water to act as our fridge. Then we put our swimsuits on and had a long swim in the sea. Who needs showers?

That night, as well as the waves breaking on the sand about fifty meters from our tents, we heard a lot of strange, snuffling, rustling sounds. Then some howling and barking and shrieking shattered the peace of the night. Our tents weren't close enough for us to talk to each other, so we just lay in the darkness listening to the noises getting nearer and hoping neither of us was being eaten. The shrieks were high pitched and prolonged, and although I have never heard Lucy shriek, I can't imagine she would scream so dramatically, and anyway, she's an alto in her choir, not a soprano, so I was fairly sure that she didn't need rescuing. A mosquito had managed to get trapped in my tent, and I really wanted to open the flap and let it out, but I wasn't going to brave the unidentified beasts that were out there. At least the mosquito took my mind off all the howling and creeping about.

The next morning we were awake at dawn as usual and crawled blearily from our tents to try to poke a bit of life into the dying fire. We were stunned to see lots of footprints all around the camp. Strand wolves (for that is what they were, according to our book of footprints) had been wandering about around the fire, stepping over our guy ropes, tipping our "fridge" over, and generally having a jolly vulpine party at our little campsite. We found out later that strand wolves are partial to bones, and as neither of us is particularly meaty, we felt we'd done well to avoid becoming the main course for a pack of wolves.

We continued our meander down the Skeleton Coast, heading for Cape Cross. This is where the world's largest seal colony resides, and we wanted to fit in a few more animals before visiting the large townships of Walvis Bay and Swakopmund.

The road curved inland for a while, and we couldn't see the sea for a few kilometers, which was a bit worrying, but eventually there was a track leading coastward that indicated the route to the colony. We parked the truck in a surprisingly organized car park—gravel chippings, a small entrance kiosk, and a visitors' toilet—and headed toward the distant barking.

As we drew closer, the barking and vocal yawning became deafening. And the smell! It was the most extraordinary stench of fetid fishy breath, brine, feces, and decomposition. As this was the birthing season, there was also added to the mix the unmistakable metallic tang of blood. The spectacle assailed all of our senses, and we were speechless as we tried to accustom ourselves to the cacophony and the dreadful pong.

What plan existed for the next leg of our journey involved heading south toward civilization and finding a hotel with a bath. On the way, we'd check out any likely looking points of interest. Personally, I was reluctant to leave the wilderness, because you get used to having a place to yourself—and by "place" I mean what seems to be the whole wide world. The map showed the whole of the Skeleton Coast devoid of place names, roads, buildings, anything. Short of Toscanini and Camp 108, we could have been in the Sahara—apart from having the Atlantic Ocean to our right. But south, the map became too busy for comfort, and Henties Bay, Swakopmund, and Walvis Bay featured map signs for Beauty Spot, Hotel, and even Airport. Before that, though, was Cape Cross Seal Reserve marked with nothing but a red dot. That would serve as our last serving of wilderness.

We had no idea what to expect. The trusty guidebook had a picture of a few seals on some rocks and a short write-up that commenced with access details and instructions that put us off reading any more. Pity really, because we arrived unprepared.

Parked up, and rounding a bluff on a rocky peninsula, firstly we saw a few seals. Great! Then the entire vista opened up. The whole coastline was just seals. And not just along the coast. There were seals up in the rocks, on the headlands, on the beaches, and the sea was black with seals, like a giant oil slick from a supertanker. There must have been hundreds of thousands at least. And all braying and stinking of fish. I rarely blaspheme but, really, OMG! So much for having the place to ourselves.

I was totally unprepared for the sheer numbers of seals that day. We visitors were confined to wooden-decked walkways with waist-height wooden railings along the perimeter of the colony. The seals were packed together tightly over an area of about half a square mile. They were swimming in the sea, lounging on rocks, and flailing along in the sand. The huge males in the sea were roaring at their comrades on the banks, and their comrades roared back.

There were seals giving birth in among all the activity, which left us fearing for the newborns' well-being. Seals aren't the most elegant movers, and the huge, great males waddling their way down to the sea with their heads swinging from side to side as they barked their seniority to all in their path were in imminent danger of flattening the poor, helpless babies. We watched one seal as she circled in the sand, clearing a spot for her labor. She wrenched and strained and pushed for around twenty minutes, and eventually the little chap appeared. He headed for her teats as she tore at his birth sac with fairly scary-looking teeth. Then she picked him up by the scruff of his neck and carted him off to somewhere less exposed.

Clearly some of the babies hadn't fared so well in their entrance to the world, and interspersed with the heaving, living mass were tragic little dead bodies. They were left where they died, to be disposed of by the ecologically friendly system of scavengers and the tides. We saw a jackal weaving its way through, nimbly dodging the big, lively bodies and homing in on the tiny, dead ones.

The cubs weren't neatly arranged alongside their respective mothers as I would have expected. Instead they seemed to be parked in large "nurseries" where up to twenty or so cubs lay together in rows in the shadier parts of the colony while their mothers were sunning themselves or swimming with their friends. The mothers seemed to know exactly which baby was theirs and kept in touch with their offspring with long-distance grunts and calls, to which the cubs squeaked back.

Some of the cubs had managed to crawl through the wooden railings or onto the ends of the walkways to get underfoot. Most of them were bright enough to waddle along the short paths until they got to the end, plop onto the sand, and waddle back to their nursery. We came across one of them who hadn't worked out an escape route, His mother was calling with increasing anxiety from the beach below. The baby seal was squeaking back piteously while trying to squeeze his fat little body through the railings, which were clearly too narrow. I tried nudging him gently with my feet, hoping that if I pointed him in the right direction, he'd head off. But he was determined to persist with his hopeless endeavors.

I looked around to see if there were any staff or tourists in the vicinity. There was no one. The staff were in the office avoiding the heat of the day, and the only two other tourists had left after less than five minutes, complaining about the smell.

I looked at Lucy.

"Well, you'll just have to pick him up and drop him back over the railings!"

"Why me?"

"Erm…because you're stronger than me?"

I have no idea if this is true or not, and in retrospect, I have no idea why Lucy didn't argue a bit more. We peered down at the cub speculatively. We peered at each other. We looked again at his teeth and decided that they could give a nasty bite…and we didn't even want to imagine the dreadful germs that were being harbored in his smelly little mouth. I agreed to pinion him by the neck with my foot to stop him turning his head and biting his savior, and Lucy braced herself and grabbed hold of his wriggly body. He was surprisingly heavy, and as he went over the railings and she let go of him, he made a clumsy landing, before lolloping across the sand to his relieved mother.

Teri and I separated in order to, basically, gawp at the bedlam that is Cape Cross Seal Reserve. I couldn't say it was interesting, exciting, astounding even. My feelings were a mixture of awe and shock. The drama of life and death that was all contained in this mass of bodies along the coast, the tragedies of separated mothers, crushed cubs, bullying bull seals, and, most distressing of all, the cubs trapped by the visitors' walkway, built to provide safe viewing for tourists. I wanted to kick the whole structure down. It was unnatural and interfered with the process of mothering and nurturing that was part of the life of this colony. Cubs could enter the walkway at either end but had no way of understanding that their way out was to go back the way they'd come. They moved up the beach to lie under the walkway and around the staff hut for shade. Once on that walkway though, they were in peril. I watched a German couple trying to shoo cubs back to the open end. I saw dead cubs lying on its slats, dehydrated by the sun and from their efforts to reach their mothers.

Teri called me down to one end. A fat cub was making a huge noise trying to squeeze through an impossible gap. She wanted *me* to lift it over—and she was the one with the rabies jabs!

I have done many dangerous things in my time but picking up that cub has to be top of the list. OK, sleeping with lions lurking in the bushes is up there somewhere, and grizzly bears by my tent in Colorado is one, but those were only in hindsight. Hiking solo in the Grampians mountains in South Australia was close, and let's not forget I ride a motorbike to work every day. However, a bite from that cub would easily penetrate my hand through to the muscle, bones, veins, and arteries beneath the dermis. The bacteria in that mouth would keep a bio-plant running for years. Sepsis kills pretty quickly without intravenous antibiotics, but necrotizing fasciitis kills within hours. I didn't fancy the job at all. My only chance was to grab it like the seal mothers do—round the scruff of the neck, firmly so it couldn't whip round and fang me. Teri was instructed to stand on its head when it was between the walkway bars. Then I made a lunge, one hand grasping its slippery neck (all oily—yuk!) and one under its flipper to lift it, and I hoicked it over the barrier. It landed on its mother, who growled ferociously at it, at me, Teri, and the rest of the world, while the cub brayed for all it was worth, I think explaining to mum that it wasn't his fault he was late home.

Just some of the seals at Cape Cross.

Chapter 17

Civilization, the Namib-Naukluft, and Dunes, Dunes, Dunes

Swakopmund is an unlikely sort of place. It's a town on the run from the desert. Like Syrinx fleeing Pan, it raced west to the Atlantic Ocean till it had nowhere else to go. As it is surrounded on three sides by desert, the naive traveler would expect a frontier town, relying on its own cunning to keep the inevitable advancing dunes from its backyard. And yet it is the playground of Namibia, where people go to party. You can surf down sand dunes, drive sand buggies, go on balloon rides, paraglide, go night clubbing, cycle, horse ride—hell, shoot pool, I expect. The unlikely bit is that Swakopmund is halfway down the Skeleton Coast, teetering on a strip between the longest beach in Africa and the oldest desert on the continent. I guess it is the Las Vegas of West Africa, an oasis in the desert, with two lifelines to feed it: the B2 road and the railway line to Windhoek in the east.

Teri and I turned up at the Hotel Adler like dusty cowpokes arriving in Dodge City. You would think people in Swakopmund would be used to this sort of visitor, but our jokes about sand to excuse our appearance (and possibly smell) seemed to fall flat. Swakopmund is Germanic to its core, and messy things like dust and sand do not enter the vocabulary. Maybe this is how its citizens cope with their predicament. Just deny everything. Desert? What desert?

Swakopmund! Civilization! A town! Shops and running water! I was very happy to get to Swak. Lucy and I drove around for a bit trying to locate hotels from the maps in our guidebooks, only to discover that those very hotels had been burnt down, dissolved, gone bankrupt, or been turned into offices since the books had been written.

We cruised about and eventually came across the Hotel Adler, a gorgeous little pension with hanging baskets, a decent-sized car park, the promise of a yummy German-style breakfast, and a BATH! We happily decanted our dusty belongings into the spacious and abundantly hot-watered room. Lucy did her weird inventory thing and unpacked the entire contents of her backpack. I did my weird lounging-in-a-bath thing and lounged for hours in a bath. We were both very happy. I was delighted with a brand-new plastic bottle of water. So delighted that I insisted on taking a picture of a pristine plastic bottle of water next to a desert-bedeviled bottle of water. Bonkers? Who, me? Later that evening we went for a walk through Swak. It was a bit like walking through Bournemouth. Or Rüdesheim. Best described as a mixture of both. Before we could get too fixated on the vagaries of Swak, we decided to find somewhere to eat.

We chose a seafood restaurant that was located in a shipwreck hovering over the sea. Fun! We shuffled in wearing ridiculously scruffy clothes, as we discovered that Swak is a veritable fashion metropolis. All the bright young things from Swak uni were dressed up in the latest cutting-edge clothes for a sophisticated night out. Old colonial types were wearing the sort of clothes that wouldn't look out of place at a royal garden party; there was even one lady who wore her hat throughout the meal. Listening to the conversations ebbing and flowing was fascinating. There was German-accented English and a bit of German speaking; there were African accents and South African; two of the students were French and chatted happily together (from what I could translate, they were geologists, so were in the best place for their studies). Namibians conversed in their native dialects. I can only imagine that the waiting staff were multilingual—the hospitality industry is tougher than you'd think!

We were ushered to a table and perused the menu. Fish, most definitely. Kingklip? Yep! Lucy chose a subtly herby-flavored dish. I chose a fiery fish dish. But it wasn't fiery enough. I glanced at the table to our left. An elderly, bony, white colonial lady was picking at her green salad. Next to her was what we assumed was her "walker"—a beaming, handsome African teenage boy who was happily scoffing snapper and chips with a generous helping of hot pepper sauce. My sort of a bloke! We shared a look. I raised a Rasta-bangled wrist. He did likewise. We bumped knuckles. I pointed toward the bottle. We shared hot sauce. Everyone was happy.

The next day Lucy and I decided to do some souvenir shopping. Thankfully no hideous dolls were purchased. But rather bizarrely, I got a bit carried away and bought a huge punnet of unripe peaches. I think I imagined that they would ripen slowly over time, unlike the tomatoes that were overripe within a day. I was wrong. They stayed as hard as cricket balls and just shriveled and wrinkled until they resembled little shar-pei heads. At which point we threw most of them away. We sat for a while at a roadside café and drank the first cup of coffee we'd had for a week or so. It was all very civilized. And we felt like fish out of water.

It was time for us to return to the desert, but to do so we needed a permit, so we drove to the other end of town to the tourist board office. I parked at the end of a wide road and was surprised to be approached by a young man in a high-vis jacket and carrying a clipboard. He informed me that there was a parking fee (equivalent to about thirty pence), which was payable to him, and in return he would look after my car. I wondered if this was an upmarket city version of the "indolent peasants" scam in Opuwo, but he was wearing an official-looking tabard, so I gave him the money and left Up It Yo to his ministrations.

The lady in the tourist office was magnificent! She was swathed in all manner of brightly colored materials, her massive headdress was twisted and knotted intricately, and her hands were bejeweled with thick gold rings and finished off with shocking-pink nail varnish. She was of quite substantial girth, so the effect was jaw dropping. Lucy recovered herself first and got down to the tedious business of paperwork in triplicate, proffering passports, and paying premiums. I was drawn to the big framed photos of various dignitaries on the walls. They all bore themselves haughtily and with authority, which was just as well, as they had to live up to some pretty spectacular Christian names. Apart from (my favorite) Hifikepunye, there was Theo-Ben, Tjekero, Lempy, Pohamba, and Pendukeni. The lady government ministers seemed to have had much more prosaic parents and were called Doreen, Priscilla, Angela, and Sara. I've no idea what the lady in the tourist office was called, but I hope it was something splendid like Magdalena-Azaria and not plain Mildred or Maud.

Permits organized, we headed back to the truck, relieved the parking man of his caretaking duties, which seemed to comprise wandering about looking into shop windows, and headed south.

While Teri was waxing lyrical about the bath, the shops, the comfy bed, and having clean feet, I was studying the map. Well, maps. Our trusty charts were looking the worse for wear and had to be carefully refolded so that the next bit of the journey was uppermost. The creases were now just tears. We had become adept at appraising the information from all maps and amalgamating it into our own mental data bank. Cross-referencing maps in Namibia is very important, as the roads have several different numbers and can go in diverse directions depending on which map you have. This we were now used to, though I was a bit worried about the next trip because we were entering the Namib-Naukluft National Park. The desert. This actually made reading the map easier simply because there are very few roads. The tricky bit was being able to tell if you were actually on a road.

The Namib-Naukluft is about fifty thousand square kilometers—which is meaningless to me, but it is apparently bigger than Switzerland. I am not sure if that is surface area, as Switzerland has a lot of ups and downs. So, apparently, does the Namib. The big dunes are called barchans. These are the crescent-shaped mounds that "march" inexorably leeward as the wind piles up sand on the crest until it cascades down to be the foot of the next windblown pile. The guidebook says they can be quite high. There are also mountains, or inselbergs, of granite or limestone that collect dew from mountain mist and support a whole ecosystem of things that hide in crevices and nooks. I was soon to encounter some of these and have another near miss with the hazards of safari. Oh dear.

Our plan was to enter the northern section of the Namib and head south to the edge of the barchan dunes. Here there are roads for which a permit is required, and the trusty guidebook states, in no uncertain terms, "Warning! Please note—no water and no firewood available in the park." And I guessed no shops or petrol stations either. So a supermarket stock-up in Swakopmund included firewood, *gallons* of water (most of which Teri would drink), strange food tins for Teri to experiment with, and more rusks to keep my guts happy. I should at this point explain.

Since Epupa, my digestive system had been rioting. It started quietly at first. Just a few complaining rumbles, some earlier-than-usual toilet breaks. I fed it, thinking it was not used to long breaks between eating. I am a grazer rather than a binger. Teri is a binger—well, actually she eats very little until evening, then goes to sleep after her main dinner. I do the reverse: big breakfast, slightly smaller lunch, snack for tea, and a light supper, with elevenses, brunch, high tea, and a "tide me over" snack before supper to keep me going. Grazing. I was starting to need the toilet more and more. I was passing fluid, my guts were always on the go—churning, rumbling. I drank Dioralyte to keep my salts up, and I tried to drink more, as I drink very little compared to Teri. A big dinner would silence everything for a while, but then we'd be off again, my guts and me. Warmquelle was the limit of my endurance, as I spent far too much time on the bog instead of having fun, so I rummaged in the field-hospital-style first aid kit and found "bung it up" tablets, which did the job for a bit. Rusks helped. I could graze on these all day and give my guts something to work on. Hence the rusks at the top of my shopping list.

We didn't really have a plan for the Namib. There were several 4x4 trails, according to the map in the guidebook, with designated camping places marked along its winding route. The book added that to break down here would result in a long wait for any rescue, as very little traffic ventured out that way. This kind of reportage was music to our ears; it meant we'd have the place to ourselves. Our rough plan was to venture out and see where it led.

The landscape rapidly changed from the usual tatty scrub that is suburban Namibia to empty tracks, sand, and vague crossroads that weren't marked on the maps. It was lucky we didn't have a plan so we could say we were never lost. We were just where we ended up. We headed south, following one of Teri's favorite straight tracks, crossroads and side turnings all ignored. We think we were headed for Homeb, the most southerly campsite in the northern section of the Namib. After that would be dunes. The land was flat, gravel and sand terrain, quite barren of vegetation or wildlife. Not even a goat. We stopped for a brew and a pee, and Teri amused me by trying to find something to squat behind—"in case someone came along." I think she settled for a dried-up tuft of grass in the end. Supping tea, we watched dung beetles busy maneuvering their larders hither and thither, greeny-pink lizards playing stand-on-one-leg games on hot rocks, and basically, nothing else. Not even a mosquito. Too dry. There were mountains in a shimmering distance, and this was our destination, so we hoped for some relief from relentless red sand. We struck up and carried on.

Our track trundled forever toward a distant blob on the horizon that gradually got bigger, redder, and more distinct. Eventually we could make out, bizarrely, in the middle of nowhere, a white tower nestling under a giant red barchan dune. It grew as we approached. The tower was tall, but the dune dwarfed it. We could then make out white single-story huts within a high enclosing wall. We debated. A military lookout post? An airport? A secret CIA spy station? The road led right up to it, so we went to investigate, hoping no one was about to start shooting at the intruders. Gobabeb, Namib Woestyn Desert, a sign said. It didn't say much else. Why would it? Who would read it? We'd parked outside the wall and stared. Teri suggested we call in, say hello. I said, "Go right ahead. I'll wait here," clearly being the more paranoid one today. We searched around and found a shiny information board, all metallic with lots of tiny engraved script and colored insignia splattered all over it. Gobabeb Research and Training Centre. An internationally recognized center for desert research. Ah-ha! Yes, that figured, and explained why someone had decided to build the place right in the shadow of a thirty-foot barchan dune. Investigating later, I found that Gobabeb had been founded in 1958 by an Austrian entomologist who had a fascination for beetles. Good for him. Since then it had developed to study climate change, desert landscapes, and renewable energy. I guessed that meant solar power rather than hydroelectric. They were also really into studying desertification, desert-adapted animals (including the lizards that dance foot to foot, I supposed), and tested the air for carbon dioxide, sending data back to Colorado, where global data is analyzed. So, I'm guessing, those guys measuring carbon dioxide levels in the atmosphere causing global warming get their data from here then. Cool! And there were Teri and I, keeping Up It Yo's engine running (in case a quick getaway was required) and buggering up their readings.

We hung around outside for a bit but didn't see a soul. All huddled away in their nice solar-powered, air-conditioned laboratories probably. Lucky them.

Time to move on. Our next camp was to be Homeb, listed in the guidebook as an excellent place to view the dunes and not far from Gobabeb. The guidebook also mentioned that it was near a small village. Teri and I should have read this bit more carefully!

We could see the great dune that was the start of the Namib Desert as we followed a fairly clear track that led to Homeb. The campsite was situated by the Kuiseb River, a mostly dry course that runs east to west to the sea and cuts the Namib-Naukluft in two. The riverbed was obvious from the well-grown camelthorn and ebony trees that marked its course.

Homeb was certainly a contrast to the cushy few days we'd spent in Swakopmund. Lucy drove us to a rocky outcrop that was only definable as a campsite by the broken-down concrete picnic bench and a rather rickety toilet shed that was little more than a three-sided, well-ventilated windbreak. I went to inspect it and got a bit of a shock when I encountered a massive set of horns attached to a lump of a beast sauntering out from the tatty wooden shed. I gingerly ventured into the depths, picking my way through heaps of dung. Clearly the local cattle enjoyed the use of the latrines too! Still, it added to the excitement of the experience: not only did you have to worry about local tribespeople peering in at you through the gaps in the walls as you sat on the loo, but there was also the possibility that a bovine bum would deposit something in your lap.

Lucy went for an explore and then a snooze under a great big tree with branches spreading to provide her with welcome shade. I, on the other hand, took my book and stretched out on a rock in the sun. After a bit I became aware that I was being watched. Three scruffy little boys no more than eight or nine years old had sneaked out from the homestead that was about a quarter of a mile away. They were creeping from tree to rock to patch of scrub, stalking me as if I were a prey. I pretended not to see them until they reached the picnic bench. They clambered onto it and saw Lucy sleeping under the tree for the first time. They seemed mesmerized by the sight of two middle-aged white women, one sleeping and one reading. They stared at me, then at Lucy, and then back at me, all the time whispering behind their hands and giggling. I suppose it's not such a common sight in the outback of Namibia, but eventually I got a bit fed up of being treated like an exhibit and got up to rummage in the food box. I came upon the cricket ball peaches and offered them to the children. They weren't impressed and took themselves off back home for something more appetizing.

After a bit of exploring down the riverbed, admiring the glossy, healthy-looking cattle and avoiding the giant millipedes that were thicker than our fingers and twice as long, we ate our meal under the stars. We were a bit surprised to see headlights in the distance and hoped we wouldn't be invaded. But no, the truck turned off toward the homestead. After a scant ten minutes, the truck roared off again, headlights lurching away in the darkness.

We were unused to all this vehicular activity in the bush and were intrigued by what happened next. About fifteen minutes later, two trucks appeared in convoy. Evidently the first had been dispatched to recruit his mate. The villagers poured out of their various huts and shacks and began to unload the two vehicles. From the first they pulled crates of Windhoek beer, boxes of wine, and bottles of lager. Pallets of soft drinks and trays of indistinguishable foodstuffs were all carried into the homestead to an open area where a fire had been lit. From the second truck, the men were all lugging a huge stereo system with cables and speakers and all the paraphernalia of a noisy night. By now it was about ten o'clock, but we could see that an early night was going to be out of the question. So with a resigned "if you can't beat 'em, join 'em" look at each other, we each reached for another drink.

The Homeb townsfolk certainly know how to party! We'd seen the horrible pink bus kids having a bit of a rave, and we'd enjoyed the staff party with naked dancing up in Ruacana, but Homeb was a whole other league! Every member of the village turned out, from the youngest babies who were passed randomly around the group, to children who ran and shrieked, and older villagers who sat by the fire. The music blasted out into the night air, bottles clanged together in raucous toasts, meat was spiced and grilled and devoured. They sang, they danced, they screamed, and they shouted. All night. Marvelous.

As with the party at Ruacana, we wondered if this was a special occasion, or if Homeb rocked under the stars every night. Sadly, I suppose we'll never know.

We had arrived at Homeb early in the day, giving us a chance to relax, explore, and chill out. Once the tents were up, I left Teri to her book and hiked up the nearest mountain, a low tor of hard rock that a geologist would wax lyrical about, I've no doubt. The rock was certainly of interest even to me, as many stones were brightly colored and often shot through with crystal. The mountain was on the tent side of a tree-lined omuramba— the course of the Kuiseb River when it flows. On the other side of the Kuiseb was the Namib Desert. There was no gentle transition between the mountain area and the desert. The river divided the two like the Berlin Wall. The river was the only thing stopping the sand engulfing the valley we were camping in. The regular flash floods washed away the creeping sand. Behind the omuramba, the desert was present ominously as a huge barchan dune of yellow-red sand that dominated the valley. Rising over two hundred feet, the barchan was higher than the mountain and called temptingly to me. I had to see what was on the other side.

Why did I think that was a good idea? I had no idea how hard it is to walk up a real sand dune! After hacking my way through the dense bush around the riverbed, I reached the foot of the dune. Its steep sides rose away from me toward a windblown pinnacle, and I set off slowly, one foot in front of the other.

I've read stories about Everest climbs. It can take a person fourteen hours to stagger up the last stage to the summit through the deep snow. The lack of oxygen doesn't help, but at least they don't have to do it in ninety degrees of sunbaked heat. The explorer Ranulph Fiennes described his experience of walking up Everest. He advised that, rather than thinking "Just a few steps more," it is better to think that it will go on forever. That way, you don't raise your expectations and will feel the pain less.

I can now understand what he means. For every step up, I slid down half a step. The sand got in my boots; the sweat poured down my face. Every time I looked up, the ridge seemed just as far away as the last time I looked. I am a fit person. I am a member of a running club, and I still compete in cross-country races in my age group, but this was bad! I couldn't believe this was such hard work. When I got to the top though, I didn't care how grueling it had been. The view to the south was awesome! As far as the eye could see, the land was a sea of yellow-red barchans; like waves on an ocean, they stretched to the misty horizon. There were no trees, hills, or plains. Just waves of sand. To the north, the hard-rock mountains; to the south, sand. A real desert. Very impressive. I waved at Teri miles below. A speck, and the only person I could see in all this land.

Returning to the campsite, I dived, exhausted, under a spreading camelthorn tree and went to sleep. It was a good job, as I wouldn't be sleeping again anytime soon. It was bizarre that Teri and I had driven into the desert wilderness and were kept awake by a party. For some reason we didn't mind, because it wasn't other tourists or urban dwellers but a rural community doing what it usually does on a Friday night. In the middle of nowhere.

The next morning all was quiet. The visitors had roared off in their trucks before dawn, and the only sounds came from the cattle in the undergrowth.

Dressed to kill: Teri at Groot Tinkas.

Chapter 18

From the Sublime to the Ridiculous

The Namib-Naukluft National Park has basic campsites accessed by 4x4 only. This is according to our more pessimistic guidebook. The idea of campsites in Namibia varies between those with the full set of amenities to those that are merely a patch of ground by some trees. The "campsites" in the Namib-Naukluft National Park are of the latter variety but all the more attractive for that. Homeb was a space under a few trees with a shed over a hole for a toilet. Our next campsite was a grade above that by having a stone table in situ. Groot Tinkas is a delightful spot hidden away in a green valley. A water source nearby promises wildlife and, as usual, there was no one there. We only saw one other touring vehicle in the distance in the whole park, so having the camp to ourselves was no surprise. This time there was the added bonus of no "small village" nearby.

In this out-of-the-way place, Teri chose to glam up for the evening and wore her ball gown for dinner. Well, why not. I am not sure how she managed to pack it, as her backpack contained all her sleeping gear and books. I think it once belonged to Mary Poppins. I had a backpack for my own stuff and still lacked a change of clothes after a week.

We had arrived at Groot Tinkas via a waterhole at Gemsbokwater where we watched a jackal trying to circle in on a family of warthogs. They were having none of it and trotted through the grasses with their tails up, a troupe of piglets following mum and dad. On our travels we were frequently seeing herds of gemsbok, hartebeest, zebra, springbok, and impala, but this had become normal. We no longer squealed to each other, pointing insanely, trying to take photos. We were becoming fascinated by the other creatures we encountered. In her reading, Teri had discovered the "little five" of the desert: chameleon, sidewinder snake, gecko, cartwheeling spider. So we thought we'd aim for an alternative little five: pink lizard, dung beetle, centipede, scorpion, rock hyrax. We'd found some of these already, but we were in hyrax and scorpion country now, and I was determined to find them. We discovered that the pink lizards we'd seen are actually geckos, but our list was a hierarchy of cuteness (yes, dung beetles are cute when you get to know them). I was starting to turn over stones in my search of scorpions. A nature program had suggested that the fatter the tail of a scorpion, the deadlier it is. This is useful information, but I'd forgotten this in my bid to spot the alternative little five; besides, I wasn't planning to cuddle it.

I decided that, as it had been a while since my wash in the sea at the Skeleton Coast, and my long bath in Swakopmund, it was time for a bit of beautification. I filled the washing-up bowl with water from the tank in the back of Up It Yo, grabbed a change of clothes, and wandered off up the hill.

I stripped off and had a lovely time swilling off the grime in the open air, fairly content that there were no eyes upon me. I'd not taken a towel, so I lay on a large white rock to dry off in the sun, taking the opportunity for a short shut-eye.

I opened my eyes some time later and was slightly alarmed to find a donkey eyeing me from a distance of about three feet away. I hoped that he was a free-range donkey and that he didn't have an owner somewhere in the vicinity, but I thought it best not to push my luck on the naked-gamboling front. I pulled on my pink Doc Martens, my bejeweled evening gown, and my bush hat and strolled nonchalantly back down to our tents. Lucy looked mildly bemused at my outfit but said nothing except to offer me a cup of tea.

Groot Tinkas was a strange sort of a place. We'd driven for hours and only seen a single vehicle heading in the opposite direction. Of course, it's possible that we were surrounded by hidden locals and leopards, but we'd seen nothing of particular interest.

There were three "Tinkas" sites among the hills. The only way of identifying the first two of them was the fact that they had large, brightly colored recycling bins that stood sentinel, looking incongruously brash against the drab greens and grays of the bush.

Groot Tinkas also had the psychedelic bins, but at least they were mostly hidden by a dilapidated toilet hut. We didn't fancy camping in what felt like a recycling center, so we pitched our tents well upwind. The "toilet" was so rundown that we would have had no use for it anyway.

The lower part of the valley was carpeted with acid-green succulents, while the slopes were mostly thorns and tufts of yellowed grass. We had a brief look around, and I became convinced that I could see an expanse of water in the distance. Lucy agreed that that is what it looked like, but surely, we reasoned, water being such a rarity in Namibia, it would be on the map?

We decided to head off that way to investigate whether it was a lake or a mirage. The going was undulating, and at some points deep sand. We would occasionally lose sight of our mirage on the lower sandy slopes, but then it would reappear as we crested the next slope.

Teri and I set off to check out the little lake at the head of the valley. Our campsite was in a valley of large boulder-type rocks with smooth sides that had been worn by eons of water erosion. They were easy to clamber over, and from the top we soon spotted furry animals scurrying away under clefts in the rocks. One or two remained outside their dens, so we got a good look through binoculars. We'd found the hyrax. Like little rabbits, they were high on the cuteness scale. We sat till dusk on a vantage point by the lake to see what would come to drink.

Everywhere we went, sundown was always spectacular. The wide vistas allow for the great splash of red to fill the whole of the western sky. Tree silhouettes stand stark against the glowing background, and often a rumble of distant thunder was the only sound. Living in England, it is impossible to go anywhere without man-made noise. Even the tops of the Pennine hills will rumble with airplanes high in the sky, the clouds streaked by contrails and distant city lights polluting the darkness of night. Namibia's sky is a joy when the slanting sun rays cast relief on grasses, trees, rocks, and distant mountains and bring out the spectacle of the Milky Way, the planets, and the moon when night falls. I have never seen the stars so clearly than in rural Namibia. Never has the moon seemed so close or the planets so bright. The first night I confess I was confused and thought myself drunk when the constellation of Orion was not quite right. There were the three "belt" stars, framed by the four corner stars, but where was Sirius, Orion's dog? I hadn't had that many beers, surely? But stupid me. I'm used to looking at the sky in the northern hemisphere, so Orion was upside down. I'd forgotten we were now nearer the Tropic of Capricorn than the equator.

I was anticipating another night show as the sun touched the far hills when a massive squadron swooped over our heads at full throttle. Not jets. Birds. Thousands of them. Bomber Command was coming home to roost. Teri and I ducked as waves and waves of formations flew at breakneck speed into bushes, reeds, and the tops of the trees around us. And the noise! A million twittering, chattering gossips all shouting at once set up echoes off the rocks in the hills. As one squadron settled, another would arrive, swooping, swerving, and diving into the roosts, setting up another shouting match. Branches swayed with their weight, the lakeside thickened with thirsty drinkers, the trees bowed under the bobbing burden. They swooshed over our heads like fighter jets on a mission. We have still no idea what sort of birds they were—small sparrow-sized brown things with very loud voices, and clearly very sociable!

As the sun set, the mosquitoes came to life and smelt blood: my blood. We left the birds to their roosting and beat a hasty retreat back to camp, where I got a smoky fire going to dissuade the little critters from using us as dinner.

The next morning, from the limited comfort of our sleeping bags, we heard Bomber Command taking off in waves at the crack of dawn. A repeat of the earlier arrival but more subdued, like sleepy early-morning commuters—just the swooshing noise of thousands of wings heading off for the day. We had thoughts that we would soon be doing the same as we packed up our last wild camp. I went off into the bush to attend to the normal morning ablutions and found a nicely sheltered nook among the rocks. I'd forgotten I was looking for scorpions when I rearranged a few stones to dig a small latrine and nonchalantly picked up a stone with my bare hands to find a fat scorpion nesting underneath. I jumped out of the way for some reason, acutely aware that my hand had been in striking distance, as were my bare legs. It scurried away rapidly under the rockface, and all I can remember of my brief glimpse of it was the back-curving tail with its sharp needle on the end. My close encounter with another of the alternative little five.

Our journey was now steering us toward Windhoek and civilization, but Lucy and I wanted to have one last camp experience. A farm mentioned in the guidebooks promised us sightings of leopards and cheetahs. Since our trip to the Cheetah Conservation Fund, we were particularly interested in supporting concerns that helped to preserve these animals, so we made the detour.

We drove past a stylish German colonial house and on to the reception building, where a beautiful young Namibian lady offered us a pitch for our tents, the use of a toilet block, an afternoon trip to visit the cheetahs and leopards, and an early-evening drive to see the rest of the animals. All at a reasonable price, so we happily accepted the offer.

We drove to the camping area, which was enclosed by a chain-link fence and had about six individual pitches, separated by trees and small bushes. A lone eland lurking in the trees close to where we were intending to put up our tents was a bit perplexing, but he seemed reasonably disinterested in us, so we decided to stay where we were.

We went back to the reception area to meet with the guide who was to take us to see the big cats. We were somewhat discombobulated to find two Moke-type vehicles surrounded by a number of middle-aged be-suited gents and ladies wearing name badges on their lapels or around their necks.

They turned out to be delegates from an international conference being held in Windhoek. The conference had ended after a week of worthy discussions about climate change, ecology, and other green issues. As a recreational conclusion to the event, the conference organizers had arranged for those delegates, as wished, to leave the sanitized confines of their hotels so that they could have a look at the "real Namibia."

We all clambered aboard the vehicles and set off in convoy along a dirt track bordered on either side with high chain-link fences.

By this stage of our trip, Lucy and I had developed a convention that we would speak sotto voce, if at all, when out among the animals. This meant that not only did we have more chance of seeing them rather than scaring them away, but also, we got to hear the sounds of nature as well as seeing it.

So it was infuriating that the delegates persisted in shouting to each other, not only within our vehicle but also to their colleagues in the second truck. They had clearly got to know each other fairly well over the past week, and sniggered over various "in" jokes, made raucous comments about absentee delegates, and flirted outrageously and embarrassingly with each other.

Lucy and I scowled at each other and hoped the guides would shut them up. Unfortunately, the guides clearly felt it unnecessary to censor their guests, as they knew that they had some entertainment lined up that would temporarily quieten them down.

We traveled along the track for a while and eventually reached a gate in the fence. Our driver jumped out, sprang the catch, and drove us through. He then climbed out of the truck and up into a tree carrying a sack of meat. He proceeded to attach small lumps of meat to the branches. The second driver then opened the gate of an adjacent compound, and in came a young male leopard. He was clearly both hungry and well trained in what was expected of him, as he immediately climbed the tree and began eating, moving among the branches eating mouthfuls of food and paying no heed to the stationary vehicle less than twenty feet away, nor the second vehicle that was driving straight toward him with its cargo of beer-swilling tourists.

This was clearly maladaptive behavior for a leopard and would make its release back into the wild impossible. Leopards need to preserve a wariness of man, as he is their main predator. Farmers shoot leopards to protect their livestock, and villagers shoot leopards if they perceive them to be a danger to their people and property.

By training the leopards to ignore noisy people with flashing camera lights and loud voices, the "conservationists" on this farm were preventing any chance of effective release.

We drove on into another compound, and almost immediately Lucy and I spotted two cheetahs in the far corner of the enclosure, crouched watchfully. The delegates by this time had started taking selfies. I couldn't even look at them. The real Namibia? Nope. Not a chance.

In sharp contrast to Ignatius's softly uttered "Kom! Kom, kom, kom!" to encourage the cheetahs closer, the guide just drove the truck straight toward them, stopping about twenty feet away. And then things took a turn for the worse.

The guide started throwing lumps of meat into the air, and the hungry cheetahs ran forward to leap and twist in an effort to catch the food before it landed in the dirt. After an initial hush, the ghastly delegates all started shrieking and pointing cameras and laughing.

Lucy and I were horrified. As I write now, I still feel sick thinking of how such majestic and beautiful creatures were reduced to circus entertainment for the baying, ignorant tourists.

After this distressing spectacle, Lucy and I really just wanted to go back to the camp and get away from the exploitation. We left the trucks and meandered down to our tents, walking around the grazing eland as if he were no more than a garden ornament, surprising ourselves with our insouciance.

Over a cup of tea, we debated giving the early-evening tour a miss, but as this was our last night, we decided, despite our misgivings, to go ahead.

So a few hours later, we again headed to reception, past the eland whose impressive horns were an arm's length away as we detoured around him. We were relieved to find that we would be in the company of a different set of delegates. There were only half a dozen, and these were girls who would hopefully have no need to try to recapture their lost youth, as they were still young.

And heavy in one case. In fact she was so large that she didn't fit into the Moke and had to perch up front with the driver, half hanging out of the vehicle. As she launched herself into her seat, the Moke veered precariously downward on one side. I whispered to Lucy that at least I wouldn't worry if the tire was flattened by the weight, as I knew she was up to the task of tire changing.

We set off and bounced up and down the slopes of the farm. By now, Lucy and I were pretty good at spotting animals, and we felt forgiving when the guide had to point out impala and gemsbok to the girls when we could see them quite clearly. We also felt tolerant of their excitement about seeing these animals at quite a distance and taking pointless photos which, when viewed later, would be an expanse of sandy bush with a brown dot in the distance.

Our patience began to evaporate with one of the group, a myopic lady who shouted, "Where? Where?" increasingly plaintively as all the animals were pointed out to her.

When she shouted, "Where? Where?!" when shown a giraffe that was less than thirty feet away, we knew that she was beyond help, and decided not to bother even if we spotted an elephant.

Toward the end of the evening tour, we drove up to a large pool and were encouraged to de-Moke and walk onto an elevated walkway that overlooked the sandy shores of the pool. Our driver handed out bottles of beer and soft drinks and then drove himself down to the water's edge. He chucked a bale of hay onto the sand. He was clearly agitated and kept casting a nervous eye into the water. He had three large bales to dispense, and he was only a little fella. He finally heaved the last one off the truck and then legged it back into the driver's seat and drove hell for leather to the walkway.

Ripples had appeared in the water as soon as the first bale hit the ground. Firstly just three sets of eyes were visible on the waterline. Then bigger ripples until finally three enormous hippos lumbered out of the pond and ran with astonishing speed toward the food.

We were given a fantastic close-up from above of a family of hippos feeding. We gawped. They grunted. We gawped a bit more. They scoffed a bit more.

They were the only close-up hippos we saw in Namibia.

We should have been offended by the fact that they were manipulated so that we could see them. But we weren't.

I have two explanations for our equanimity.

Firstly, hippos are the clowns of the bush—big, cumbersome, and clumsy, with goofy grins on their enormous faces—so we didn't see any compromise of dignity. They don't have any.

But secondly, and more satisfyingly, our guide was scared of them. So, despite the undignified taming of the magnificent cats, man was still awed and intimidated by wild beasts. Small vindication for the cheetahs.

CHAPTER 19

RE-ENTRY TO CIVILIZATION: ADJUSTING TO THE "NORMAL"

Our return journey had started in Swakopmund. That outpost, in all its Las Vegas–style energy, still had the feel of defensiveness. It wore its civilization like armor to keep the desert out, as if all the hectic effort that went into its shopping malls, its fresh paint and swept streets was there to fool everyone that the hundreds of miles of sand and mountains between it and the nation's capital did not exist. Swakopmund had been a soft landing for us as we emerged from going "bush" for what seemed weeks. The peaceful Naukluft was a reprieve from the reminder of having to return to cities, airports, baggage carousels, and trains home. The colonial game lodge was where the horror of reality kicked in.

Here we crossed paths with tourists having a taste of the romance of Africa. Only a stone's throw from Windhoek, the United Nations delegates were on a trajectory a world away from ours. From their busy conference, discussing the major issues of desertification, drought, sustainable development, they were there to play at safari and let their hair down. I am sure they were aware that this reserve was a fiction of Africa, somewhere that city dwellers and short-time visitors could pop out to from Windhoek for the day. Unfortunately, the delegates arrived the same day that Teri and I were struggling to catch up psychologically to the norms and values of everyday life after feeling like we'd had Namibia to ourselves. Like long-term prisoners on day release, we were not ready to tolerate its brutal commercial pastiche of African wilderness and so, blinking in reality's light, we both felt hugely frustrated at the imposition of these norms from the thoughtless delegates. But it probably did us good.

Our exploration gave us some insight into the development, and exploitation, of Namibia's rich resources. While many could list its diamonds and other precious stones, what we had experienced firsthand were the ecological gems. Namibia is one of the most sparsely populated countries in sub-Saharan Africa. This is significant because its natural treasures are still there, largely unspoiled and not yet measured, cataloged, and commodified. Yes, Namibia is being discovered by tourists; it has been a go-to place for many years for outdoors-loving South Africans and adventurous German speakers. It is following in the footsteps of Kenya and South Africa in exploiting, and protecting, its wildlife, but unlike those countries, it does not have other major economic drivers to support its development. It does not excel in exporting cash crops like coffee, wine, and fruit. It does not have fields of oil and gas, or mines of coal, copper, or uranium. It does not have the population size or the infrastructure for major manufactory. What is does have, still, is biodiversity.

Two German economists have made a study into the role of nature in economic growth—namely, Andreas Freytag and Christoph Vietze from the Friedrich-Schiller University. They calculated that having great natural assets does not in itself improve the number of tourists visiting a country, but it does improve the quality of those tourists: how much they spend. Andreas and Christoph suggest that a sustainable tourist industry has a knock-on effect on wider economic development. In other words, high-value tourists are more likely to visit areas with rich biodiversity, and their money leads to increased national economic development. So, sustaining high-quality biodiversity pays off: look after the ecology that rural communities and the wildlife need, and the people who want to experience authentic Africa will pay to see it. This appears to be what Namibia is doing right.

As I write this chapter, I remember the global fuss made because a Minnesota dentist paid US$35,000 to be guided to shoot a well-known lion, Cecil, in Zimbabwe. The debate around this incident swung from the barbarity of a rich Westerner killing a lion with a bow and arrow for fun, and the money it imports to a developing country for conservation. It doesn't help that an American dentist can be seen making a lot of money out of the vanity and profligacy of the West; he's not a doctor working for Medecins Sans Frontieres, nor is he a San or Himba protecting his livelihood. It is also unlikely that this sort of game shooting will reinvest funds for conservancy, unless you call conservancy the keeping of specially bred animals in private game reserves for customers to come and kill for trophies.

It is an argument, however, that grouse, red deer, and partridge are still living wild in England, and trout and salmon abound in its rivers, because hunters and fishermen value them and the ecology they depend on. The morals that come into play in this debate go beyond the rational economics of sustainable tourism. Some of the hunting areas in Namibia can cover thousands of square kilometers of unfenced conservancy land over which migrating and freely roaming wildlife will cross. Is it the money from the hunters that sustains interest in conserving this land, or people like Teri and me who will not be spending anything like thousands of dollars to take a photo of a leopard, let alone shoot it?

Teri and I were certainly put off when we saw advertisements for taxidermy outside private game reserves. We were encouraged (if a bit scared) to meet our Kalashnikov-toting game warden guarding the waterhole in Khaudum National Park. But are we being hypocritical by valuing the Namibian wilderness and enjoying having it to ourselves, while not appreciating what sustains its unspoiled nature, or why we were not tripping over buses full of camera-clad tourists.

While I instinctively disliked the feel of this overcrowded, colonial-style game lodge, I was not rational enough to mentally articulate all this debate. After our disastrous game drive to see the undignified spectacle of captive cheetahs leaping to catch lumps of donkey meat, I simply felt grumpy. Teri did too.

The contrast between the sensitive efforts of the Cheetah Conservation Fund to save the cheetahs and the insensitive practices of this lodge to exploit the cheetahs was rather depressing. Anyone who has seen big cats in the wild would never feel that they had experienced even an iota of their magnificence when seeing them captive and used as circus entertainment.

Part of the problem is that as a society, we have become very demanding. We have become used to immediate gratification, whether it's using a search engine to answer our queries in seconds, or wanting to buy our cheese ready grated and our salads ready washed. We haven't the patience to wait and act for ourselves.

Lucy and I spent many hours in the bush, sitting in the truck acclimatizing our vision to be able to spot ostriches (they look like small trees in the distance), lions (which blend beautifully with dry grass), and even elephants (which spend a lot of time impersonating trees). This patience paid off because our peaceful watchfulness meant that we got close to many of the animals, which would have legged it if they'd heard noisy tourists hooning around.

But Namibia also wants to cater for those visitors who want the sanitized conveniences of the capital city and want to see as many of the animals in a short space of time. So the game lodge that guarantees close-up sightings of big game is fulfilling a need of sorts.

Another tourism venture that seems counterintuitive to animal welfare is the big game hunting industry. In my youth I was vehemently antihunting. One Boxing Day, when I was a hotel duty manager, one of my duties was to take the stirrup cup out to the huntsmen gathered at the front of the hotel in their scarlet jackets, surrounded by milling hounds. I appeared at the top of the hotel steps with my silver tray loaded with tumblers of port and sherry, walked down the steps…past the huntsmen, down the drive, and over to the hunt protesters to distribute warming cups of port into their mittened hands.

So I can't imagine the allure of hunting. Why would anyone want to stand grinning over the bloodied corpse of a magnificent lion, leopard, or buffalo when they have the option of watching them living their lives and interacting with other animals in a stunning environment?

However, there are clearly many with a different mindset to my own, who enjoy the thrill of the chase and the courage and marksmanship required to bag a lion. Namibian entrepreneurs have tapped into this market and created breeding programs, whereby lions are bred in relative captivity before being released into secure reserves where intrepid hunters can take potshots at them.

Namibia Way Beyond the Comfort Zone

Except that the majority aren't intrepid; they have no courage and, in many cases, no skill in tracking or shooting. These hunters are driven to the location of the lions by local guides in the comfort of their air-conditioned jeeps. No spoor tracking required: the compounds are enclosed, and lions are fairly easy to locate, being creatures of habit. The "hunter" then aims at the animals and pulls the trigger, or possibly draws back his bow in a rather pointless anachronistic approach to hunting. If he is inept and the animal is merely wounded, the guide is armed and able to finish it off. The hunter can then proudly pose with his prey, unaware that, far from having been a brave, skilled adventurer, he has been shooting fish in a barrel.

Our campsite was a cramped little space too near the toilet block, the footpaths, the main building, everything. But it was next to a Swiss gentleman with a neat little self-contained camper van that had clearly seen some action. Spotting a fellow explorer, we soon got an invite to inspect his custom-built wheels. It had obsessive neatness written all over it. There were pullout stoves and cupboards; folding this, that, and the others; hooks for hanging useful things; and batteries and generators to run everything. While I fought to make smoky fire in the prevailing sundown wind for our dinner, the neat smell of self-contained and vented frying from his vehicle just about did the trick for me. The notion that we would be sleeping in a bed and eating in a restaurant the next day was suddenly looking attractive.

However, I was thinking how lucky we had been. If Teri and I had stuck to the tourist routes and camped in lodges along the way, what would we have missed? Would we have enjoyed seeing the wildlife and finding out about life for Namibians? I am sure we would. After all, we got stupidly excited seeing baboons on our first day, and I worried that we wouldn't see any big game at all. But it wasn't what we came for ultimately. We came to extend ourselves and go beyond our comfort zones. We didn't stay in lodges or enclosed campsites that ensured animals were kept away from the guests. Well, only by necessity occasionally. We didn't stick to tourist routes or travel the easy way. We didn't even have all the comforts we could have easily afforded ourselves. A fridge would have been nice. There were times I longed for a chair to sit in! No, we came to Namibia to do something else. Teri, I suspect, wanted to do something she had never experienced before. All the luxury hotels in the world never give you a true sense of self-responsibility and risk. For me, I wanted to test myself as a true adventurer and prove that I could look after myself in a pretty scary environment. The wildlife was a bonus! So, I reasoned that being grumpy about this campsite was unfair because it was only a means to an end for us, just somewhere to camp.

The following morning, I decided it was time for a bit of a clearout. There were some children playing close to where we were camped. Probably they were with the maintenance man who was walking around the chain-link perimeters of the lodge with a pair of pliers, doing a bit of desultory twisting.

We had finished our final meal in camp before our return to Windhoek. The children looked at me curiously when I held up a bag of sugar, Lucy's pink porridge, and a packet of pasta. One of the little boys came over shyly and was rewarded with an armful of foodstuffs. The children got the idea, and then it became like a moneyless auction.

I held up my cup, plate, knife, fork, and spoon, and another little boy darted forward to claim them.

T-shirts and a pair of sparkly sandals went to a little girl who would take years to grow into them. My watch went to a tiny girl who was delighted with its purpleness, but who I doubt had learned to tell the time yet. Pajamas, towels, pillows (which we'd snaffled from the airlines on the way out), socks, tins of tuna, and everything else that I could offload, all were accepted with shy smiles. (I should admit here that I had no smalls to give away, as they had been burnt on the fire as we traveled.) I thought about trying to palm off Lucy's leaky red Himba doll, but she was watching my reckless giveaway with an eagle eye, probably to stop me chucking out the contents of the toolbox and the tent bags in my enthusiasm.

Thus relieved of most of my holiday belongings, we headed back to Windhoek. To a hotel with a bath, copious amounts of hot bathwater, cold wine, clean sheets, and food that didn't taste of smoke. So why was I feeling a bit glum? Was I actually already missing roughing it in the wilderness? Surely not!

After the colonial game lodge, Teri and I were unusually quiet on our drive back to Windhoek, but it came as a less painful withdrawal from the wilderness than it might have been. We were back to tarmac roads and baboons and warthogs cavorting on the roadside. There were trucks laden with people standing in the back in their finery; there were wood collectors by the road and picnic areas with disgorged saloon cars with no suspension.

I, for one, was looking forward to a cold beer, a plate of food cooked in a proper kitchen, and a comfy bed.

Wreck on the Skeleton Coast.

Chapter 20

Reflections

I've never been a fan of December. There's not a lot to love about it as a month: It's cold in the northern hemisphere, the days are short and dark, and what light there is has a dreary, gray tinge rather than a sunlit blue. Even worse, as the month progresses, the constant bombardment by Santa, seasonal adverts, sleigh bells, the Snowman, and Slade turns me from a benign pagan into a psychopathic agnostic.

So leaving the white, sun-splashed airstrip of Windhoek and landing on the gray, wet tarmac in Zurich and then going onward to the grayer and wetter tarmac in London in mid-December was a dispiriting experience.

Our return to England was an assault on the senses in more ways than one. Apart from a squad of petrol attendants in Kunene who sported Santa hats, complete with a sprinkling of incongruous snow, the festive season had so far mercifully passed us by. I had expected to feel a bit discombobulated by the stark and sudden contrasts of climates and cultures, but having to contend with the hypercommercial dash to the tinselly, tawdry end of the year left me somewhat overwhelmed. I would imagine that a prisoner, released after a long sentence, would undergo the same rehabilitation anxieties that I did. The sheer pace and volume of my new world was astonishing. I had previously lived life at this speed for fifty years, but after a few weeks of crawling through my days at five kilometers an hour, in relative silence (apart from the incidents of cackling hyenas, lions roaring from a distance of a few meters, or elephants trumpeting and crashing about in the vicinity), getting back into the swing of things was alarming and exhausting.

The first trip I made to the supermarket on my return was an analogy for the contrasts between pared-down life in Namibia and pampered life in England. I stood in the entrance aisle with a huge trolley (not many big trolleys in Namibian supermarkets; not many people have enough money to purchase vast amounts, nor the means to lug it all home) and surveyed the multitude of choices of cereals.

Even now, a year or so after this initial rehabilitative trip to the shops, I can (almost) understand that as consumers we want to have a choice of textures and flavors. So biscuity cereals, chocolate-flavored cereals, banana-flavored cereals, cereals with nuts, cereals with honey, airy-ricey cereals, square cereals, round cereals, cereals with sugar, cereals without sugar, cereals with salt, cereals without salt, and cornflakes all have a place on the shelves. But do we need seven sizes of biscuit cereals packs? Ranging from an idiotically overpackaged two-pack to an equally idiotic 172-pack? And do we really need five brands of chocolate-flavored cereals? There's the cheap own-brand one, the deluxe own-brand one, the sugar-free one, the big-name-brand one, and the organic one. I rather longed for the Namibian cereal option. A sack of cornmeal or a sack of oats, both of which would be turned into a glutinous porridge. And I don't even like porridge.

As I wandered from aisle to aisle, surveying huge selections of crisps, jams, toilet rolls, baked beans, and cheeses, I felt nostalgic for the randomly displayed and often rather paltry offerings of the small township stores and stalls. Shopping is so much easier when it's a choice of cheese or no cheese.

The other downside of this rampant consumerism that sets us so far apart from the Namibians is the effect it has on our environment.

The sheer volume of packaging from our extravagant purchasing habits means that we are subjected to urgent recycling campaigns for our rubbish. This leads to the unedifying sight of town and village verges blighted by an assortment of variously shaped and colored boxes and bins, not only on collection day, but often left in unsightly situ all week.

Conversely, the Namibians have very little waste and are naturally inclined to use and reuse whatever resources they have, which is why a lot of the produce on offer at craft markets is made from bits of tin or glass that we as a society would have thrown out as landfill (apart from on the outskirts of townships where the bars are surrounded by piles of bottles that are almost as high as the bars themselves).

Having said all that, I'm not partisan. I love England, and I love that we have so many choices, possibilities, and opportunities. In fact, I think it was my Namibian experience that has made me even more appreciative of my options in all areas of my life here in England.

Another part of my reintegration back into my own UK life, which took a bit of readjusting, was the change in my perceptions of myself and my relationship with Lucy.

Before we headed off on our adventure, I thought I knew myself pretty well.

I also thought I knew Lucy quite well.

But Namibia made me reevaluate. A lot.

Fear?

Boredom?

Hunger?

Exhaustion?

Yep. We did all of them.

Differently!

I had always assumed that friendships are based on sharing common interests and having similar attitudes to the world and its idiosyncrasies. I'm aware of the expression "Opposites attract," but every proverb has its contradiction.

Too many cooks spoil the broth, but many hands make light work. Look before you leap, but he who hesitates is lost. Opposites attract, but birds of a feather flock together.

In the case of my friendship with Lucy, it originated with a mutual interest in psychology and our unique position of being the only forty-year-olds in a room full of twenty-somethings on a master's course at university. Our friendship continued as we progressed through our academic careers. So far, so much for flocking together.

But our travel choices had always been very much at opposite ends of the spectrum. Five stars and cruises for me, physical deprivations and tents for Lucy.

Our African experience caused us both to gravitate away from our polarized positions and venture toward more compromise and tolerance. Lucy learned to appreciate running water when on holiday (!), and I learned to enjoy prolonged contemplation of the night sky due to a lack of electricity and book-reading opportunities in the desert.

Having said that, our responses to situations and emotions remained at odds.

When we were faced with fear (a threat of rolling down a ravine into a crocodile-infested river, or hearing elephants crashing their way loudly toward our tents), we reacted very differently. I would first go quiet and then get extremely shouty and sweary. Lucy would assume (what I now know was fake) bravado and treat the dodgy situation as if it were a massive source of entertainment. This would infuriate me even more, and my blood pressure would go up even further. It's amazing that we didn't kill each other in times of danger—rendering the crocodiles and elephants a superfluous threat.

Boredom also drew different responses. If we were in the truck, I would amuse myself by reciting daft poetry or faffing about with the radio trying to get a signal. Lucy would amuse herself by driving the truck into the deepest sand, up the rockiest ravine, or through the narrowest gap in the trees, just to see if we'd get stuck and need to dig ourselves out, or get punctured and use the last of the spare tires, or get jammed in between trees and need to saw ourselves out with a penknife. This would invoke fear in me. See above. I'm really wondering how we didn't strangle each other now.

Hunger? Surely we all have the same response to hunger?

Well, no. Lucy would get a headache or a stomach-ache if she hadn't eaten for a few minutes, and so would eat the most unpalatable stuff just to stave off the pangs. I remember a ghastly porridge concoction, and those awful dry rusks that went wherever Lucy went. If the rusks rations ran low (or got eaten by porcupines), she would be like an anxious addict—a bit irritable and defensive until we could get her another fix.

I, on the other hand, refuse to waste calories on anything remotely unpalatable, so ended up refusing all of her generous offers of rusks and biltong and just got silently grumpier the hungrier I got. Which must have been infuriating for Lucy. But, as always, she didn't kill me.

A lot of our traveling was pretty exhausting. Driving nine hundred kilometers through bush along straight roads with not a lot to look at apart from the steaming tarmac in front of us or the desiccated dead animals that littered the roadside was absolutely shattering. The effort of driving through sand in the Kalahari also left us staggering with tiredness. My response to exhaustion was to dig out my wine box and neck a couple of glasses until I'd get my second wind, ready for food, lion tracking, dodging hippos during a late-night swim in a river, or whatever other distractions were on offer.

But Lucy would fall instantly and deeply asleep. Under a tree, in a tent, on a rock, she would simply lie down and within minutes would be lost to the world for an indefinite length of time—maybe minutes, maybe hours. Meaning that I couldn't responsibly run with the lions or swim with the hippos, so I would wait impatiently, sedately reading my book until she was awake again. Infuriating, yes? But I didn't kill her.

Having the time and space to evaluate my feelings and attitudes to situations in great detail, I became a lot more aware that I have previously responded to fairly trivial issues with excessive emotion. But now, having pushed myself to the edges of my comfort zone, I am a lot more tolerant of minor irritations.

I undertook an experience that I felt certain would defeat me—and it didn't! So I now feel confident to take on a new challenge.

What's next, then?

Back in Blighty I've adjusted to commuting to work on the slowly moving car park that is the M6 motorway, getting soaked on my motorbike by torrential rain and hearing all about the anxieties of friends who need to queue for the latest fashion item being hyped by advertisers. I think of Teri and me trying to steer Up It Yo up a sheer rock face in Kaokoland, struggling through deep sand in low-ratio four-wheel drive, and sharing a moment with Ndomu, sporting his Manchester United bobble hat at our camp at Enyandi. It puts everyday life in perspective. I think I now see the trivial for what it is.

We wrote this book because, when we got back from our trip with our stories, everyone—yep, literally everyone we know—expressed some wish to do something similar. And they weren't just being polite. We could see it in their eyes, the dream of being able to break away from the bonds of the same old same old, and do something fundamentally different.

A British psychotherapist, Adam Phillips, talks about what boredom means in psychological terms. Boredom is the sticking point when we need to do something different for our own personal development. The child who says "I'm bored" is really saying, "I have developmental needs to pursue, and this is not meeting them!" The same applies to adults. We are all developing, even in our eighties and nineties-plus. We are still going through phases toward some greater personal integrity, higher spirituality, achievement of life in general. For many people, these needs could be invested in children and grandchildren: what they achieve reflects our generativity; a grandchild gets straight As in school—we did that! But perhaps there's still that personal goal or potential that we haven't actualized. I wonder if it is that that we saw in people's eyes when they briefly envisioned doing their own form of achievement when hearing our stories.

I have heard it described as finally getting the chance to perform a long-delayed rite of passage. For me, it might have been a long-desired aim to emulate my stepfather when he went off in his Daimler in his twenties to drive across Southern Africa. His photographs, his stories inspired me to read romantic tales of African exploration, to watch documentaries of African wildlife, and perhaps do some subconscious daydreaming of exploring the world independently for myself. So, this trip was my belated rite of passage to some degree.

I have also wondered what stops people from doing something amazing. Teri and I are perhaps freer to express ourselves through adventure travel. Other people surely do this through creating something incredible at home: running a charity, starting a whole new career, taking up something creative.

I have just heard a sorry tale. I have some older acquaintances who are widowed and live on their own. They were recently talking about whether to get lanyards to wear round their necks with alarm buttons to call for help. They said how vulnerable they feel sometimes at home and worry in case they have a fall. One said she never goes out in the garden without hers in case she has an accident. Now, my mother is eighty-five and said she didn't feel the need for such a thing. OK, she doesn't live alone, actually; she lives with me, but I am never in. So, she is on her own a lot.

So, what's the difference? Confidence, I hear you say, but the question remains, what's the difference? As a psychologist I can see huge links between the way Teri and I approached the challenges of this adventure and having a lanyard round your neck in older age. We could call it positive attitude, self-assurance, perhaps even stupidity. What does civilization do to our sense of risk and safety? Why do I see lots of mature adults cross a quiet road in Britain by using a pelican crossing instead of just walking across (it is not illegal in Britain to cross a road at any point)? Is it the principle that, if someone builds a pelican crossing, we lose our sense of proportion regarding risk? Do we think the road is dangerous, so we use the crossing? Basically, yes. The principle of shared road spaces works in reverse to this principle: If you can't see the delineation between cars and pedestrians, where there are no curbs, lines, or crossing points, everyone takes more care because of the risk perception. Drivers slow down, and pedestrians look where they're going.

Anyway, the reason we wrote this book is because it might inspire other people to do the same as we did, or something completely different, whatever, but something that meets that developmental need, that itch, to go out there and do it!

Rush hour in Namibia.

Postscript

Since our return from Namibia, we have discovered that the Khaudum National Park campsite is being developed by private owners for exclusive, top-of-the-range guests. The Sikereti site is also in line for development. We are not sure how they are going to get guests in there; perhaps by air to avoid all that deep sand. Also, how will they stop the elephants raiding the camp ablution facilities to access the water? Sikereti was beautifully rearranged when we visited. Long may it continue! Also, the Epupa Falls area is being developed. More lodges are planned, and this area is the springboard for accessing Kaokoland. What's next? Tarmac roads into western Kaokoland? Regulated camping? Pink buses? Go to Namibia before it is spoiled and while independent traveling is still just that, where you are on your own and left to your own resources to have an experience of a lifetime.

ABOUT THE AUTHORS

LUCY WEBB BELIEVES IN BUDGETS when it comes to travel, but she certainly doesn't skimp on experiences. In her regular life, Lucy is a doctor of psychology, an associate professor and researcher of mental health at Manchester Metropolitan University. She's contributed to several journals, research reports, industry publications, and textbooks. Lucy lives with her mother and cat in North Staffordshire.

Teri Ford is a foodie who loves luxury accommodations. Like Lucy, she is also a doctor of psychology. She used to work with juvenile and adult offenders in prisons but now spends her time working with rare trees in a specialist arboretum. Teri has also worked in Jamaica. She and her husband live in a renovated farmhouse in Shropshire.

Printed in Great Britain
by Amazon